PRINCETON SERIES ON THE MIDDLE EAST

Bernard Lewis and András Hámori, Editors

THE LEVANT

To Afife

The

LEVANT
A Fractured Mosaic

Second Edition

WILLIAM HARRIS

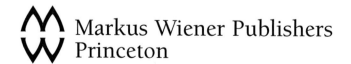 Markus Wiener Publishers
Princeton

Second edition

For information write to: Markus Wiener Publishers
231 Nassau Street, Princeton, NJ 08542
www.markuswiener.com

Library of Congress Cataloging-in-Publication Data

Harris, William W.
  The Levant : a fractured mosaic / William Harris.— 2nd ed., with a new
epilogue including recent changes in the Middle East.
      p. cm. — (Princeton series on the Middle East)
  Includes bibliographical references and index.
  ISBN 1-55876-367-8 — ISBN 1-55876-368-6 (alk. paper)
  1. Middle East—History. I. Title. II. Series.
  DS62.H37 2005
  956—dc22
                                        2005009021

Markus Wiener Publishers books are printed in the
United States of America on acid-free paper,
and meet the guidelines for permanence and durability
of the Committee on Production Guidelines for Book
Longevity of the Council on Library Resources.

CONTENTS

LIST OF MAPS

ABBREVIATIONS

EU	European Union
FBIS	Foreign Broadcasting Information Service (US government monitoring service)
GAP	Güney Doğu Anadolu Projesi (South East Anatolia Project)
GDP	Gross Domestic Product
IMF	International Monetary Fund
NATO	North Atlantic Treaty Organization
PA	Palestinian Authority
PFLP	Popular Front for the Liberation of Palestine
PKK	Partiya Karkeren Kurdistan (Kurdistan Workers Party)
PLO	Palestine Liberation Organization
UK	United Kingdom
UN	United Nations
US	United States

PREFACE TO THE SECOND EDITION

For millennia the Levant has staged world events, and this young millennium is no exception. In 2005, the region projects a kaleidoscopic array of dramas, players, and potential futures. Israeli-Palestinian affairs are in flux as Israel prepares to disengage from the Gaza Strip; Lebanon has jumped in prominence with a shocking assassination and a Syrian retreat compelled by the international community; Syrian and Jordanian militants cause turmoil in Iraq; and the Turkish part of the Levant looks ahead to incorporation into the European Union.

Media prominence, together with repackaging of the region by the entertainment industry, most recently Ridley Scott's refashioning of the Crusader Kingdom of Jerusalem in his film "Kingdom of Heaven," emphasize the need for careful interpretation of the present and past of the Levant. Such interpretation is the task of both the overarching survey attempted here and the detailed scholarly studies that make broad surveys possible. For example, in his excellent book *The Leper King and His Heirs*, Bernard Hamilton presents a Crusader Kingdom of the 1180s substantially different from that of Ridley Scott, with a much more nuanced portrayal of the colorful lord of Transjordan, Reynald of Chatillon.

Through at least the last three thousand years, the Levant has been a pivot of world history. It has seen the emergence and assertion of great religions, the dramatic rise and demise of strange, exceptional little states, and the ebb and flow of mighty empires. World powers repeatedly confronted one another in the region, from Pharaonic Egypt and Assyria to the United States and Soviet Russia. Meanwhile, local populations clung to the mountains, resisting erosion and most innovation: the Maccabees in Judea, the Druze and Maronites in Lebanon, and the Isma'ilis and Alawites in the Nusayriya hills.

From Roman times, transitions from one geopolitical order to another in the Levant occurred only with outside intervention: the Roman arrival; the Islamic conquest; Fatimid, Byzantine, and Turkish intrusions; the First Crusade; the Mamluk assertion; the Ottoman takeover; and the First World War. These involved invasion and occupation of the Levant by outside powers. The context of change in the early twenty-first century, however, is different. The U.S. military intervention in Iraq is part of that context, but in the Levant the U.S. can only pursue democratization and an Arab-Israeli compromise by influence, persuasion, and cooperation with the relatively new "international community."

Today's status-quo forces within the Levant, favoring perpetuated Arab authoritarianism and Arab-Israeli confrontation, remain potent, aside from Muslim and Jewish extremists who aspire to set the region ablaze via assaults on Tel Aviv or the *haram al-sharif*. Whether or not the U.S. nudges the Levant into a new reality—for no other power can do this without the U.S.—also depends on balances and priorities in Washington, which may have little to do with the eastern Mediterranean. In Lebanon a promising opening requires nurturing against sectarian recidivism and Syrian Ba'thist rancor. Setbacks for Lebanon's resuscitation or for Israeli-Palestinian relaxation will elevate the likelihood of upheavals. If the Arab Levant, especially Syria but also Jordan, cannot defuse a looming conjunction of economic, population, and legitimacy crises, it will reap the whirlwind. If Israel does not move toward a modus vivendi with the Palestinian Arabs, it faces a future of severe stress and increasingly tenuous democratic credentials.

The second edition of this book has provided the opportunity to correct errors, entirely my responsibility, and to make adjustments in the main narrative. It has also permitted a fresh look at the highly fluid circumstances of the early twenty-first century, including a new epilogue. I am most grateful to my publisher, Markus Wiener, for his encouragement, to Susie Lorand and Cheryl Fink for their highly professional editorial and formatting work, and to Professors Bernard Lewis and Andras Hamori for their backing as series editors. I would like again to stress my debt to the historians of the various phases of the Levant's past. At the University of Otago, I thank Professors Marian Simms and Rick Garside for their support. Last but not least, my family has continued to be patient, this time with my diversion into recalibration of the book.

Dunedin, May 2005

ACKNOWLEDGEMENTS

I began this project in 2001 at the University of Otago, New Zealand, where I am on the faculty of the Political Studies Department. I would like to thank the department, the School of Liberal Arts, and the University of Otago library staff for their support, and Professors Bob Catley, Alistair Fox, and Gerald Pillay for their encouragement. I am also much indebted to Bill Mooney of the Geography Department for his patient efforts in converting my hand-drawn maps into the highly professional illustrations that buttress the text. Dr. Greg Dawes of the Religious Studies Department helped me to exercise my rudimentary Latin in interpreting sections of William of Tyre's *Chronicon*.

I completed the main text in early 2002 while on leave in the International Relations Department of Middle East Technical University in Ankara, Turkey. I am most grateful to the staff of the International Relations Department, particularly Professors Meliha Altunisik, Fulya Kip-Barnard, and Atila Eralp for providing a congenial environment within which I was able to undertake the difficult task of reviewing the complexities of the modern Levant.

As regards the historical survey in chapters 2 and 3, my attempt to provide a summary and synthesis of geopolitical configurations in the Levant from the Romans to the Ottomans relies on the collective work of historians of the relevant periods. I found the works of the following authors, listed in detail in the notes and in the reference section, particularly helpful for making sense of the course of events:

Roman period—Isaac, Jones, Kaegi, Millar, and Shahid
Umayyad / 'Abbasid period—Bosworth, Hitti, Kennedy, and Salibi
Byzantine resurgence—Edwards, Haldon, Treadgold, and Whittow
Crusader period—Asbridge, Boase, Hamilton, Holt, Lilie, Marshall, Prawer, Richard, Rogers, and Smail
Mamluk period—Amitai-Preiss, Ayalon, Dols, Irwin, and Lewis
Ottoman period—Abu-Husayn, Barbir, Douwes, Issawi, Kayali,

Raymond, and various authors (Faroqhi, Inalcik, McGowan, and Quataert) in the *Economic History of the Ottoman Empire,* edited by Inalcik and Quataert.

I advise any readers who wish to pursue the English-language literature to consult the referenced works by these authors. Most deal with the Levant as part of a broader canvas, or with part of the Levant.

As for my analysis of the modern Levant in chapter 4, I am indebted to the Dayan Center of Tel Aviv University for continuing to send me documentary materials after the close of my involvement with the *Middle East Contemporary Survey.* I would like to salute *al-Hayat* and *Ha'aretz* daily newspapers for their excellence as newspapers of record. I have been an avid reader of both of them for many years, and they have been indispensable data sources for my perspectives on contemporary affairs.

During the revision and correction of the draft manuscript in 2002–2003, I received assistance from Professors Bernard Lewis, Bernard Reich, and Avram Udovitch. I am grateful to them for taking the time to review the text, and for their helpful comments. Professor Lewis made valuable observations for the final editing. I am also grateful to Professor William Hale for introducing me to Turkish affairs in 1999 and 2000.

I would like to thank Susie Lorand, Shelley Frisch, and Cheryl Fink for their splendid efforts in the editorial and design work. Through the final correction process, Susie was a wonderful editorial critic, giving painstaking attention to detail. Susie and Cheryl were very patient with my interminable alterations. I am also indebted to Maria Madonna Davidoff for the eye-catching cover illustration, and to Kristin Gilbert for the indexing. Special thanks are due to my publisher, Markus Wiener, for his close personal interest in all stages of the project, and for reprinting the book after the US invasion of Iraq necessitated the rewriting of the epilogue.

Finally, I could not have written this book without the support of my wife Afife and my sons Chris, Adam, and Hadi. They have been very tolerant of the many hours taken from family time.

University of Otago, Dunedin, New Zealand

INTRODUCTION

The purpose of this book is to interpret the affairs of the eastern Mediterranean littoral between Anatolia and Egypt. The region is today occupied by the states of Israel, Syria, Lebanon, and Jordan, in addition to the Palestinian Arabs of the West Bank and the Gaza Strip, and the Republic of Turkey on the northern margins. I term this region the Levant, as explained in the following chapter.

The Levant is the geographical center of the Middle East and the Arab world, and from the seventh century C.E. onward it became critical for the geographical continuity of Islamic civilization between Asia and Africa. The Levant itself, however, is neither exclusively Arab nor exclusively Islamic, and many local Muslims do not belong to the dominant Sunni "orthodox" branch of Islam. This combination of strategic salience and local complexity has underlain the colorful and violent politics of the region through many centuries—cycles of invasion, imperial imposition, imperial weakening, and fragmentation.

It is important to assess the geopolitics of the Levant from the perspective of the *longue durée*. The history of the region involves a procession of different political dispensations punctuated by abrupt and dramatic changes. The contemporary state system is the shortest-lived of these arrangements and arose out of external intervention and the overthrow of a radically dissimilar imperial order. It is easy to be overly impressed by the power and solidity of modern territorial states. Consideration of their predecessors shows that contemporary affairs are not without precedent and that some paths have been trodden before, albeit under different conditions.

For example, the Levant has been a cruel environment for states or regimes that have lost their internal cohesion or pursued adventurous policies. The Crusader Kingdom of Jerusalem was badly divided in 1186–87, before its defeat by Salah al-Din. Lebanon's Maronites fell apart while challenging Syrian and US schemes to "stabilize" Lebanon in the late 1980s, and these precedents provide a longer-term warning for Israel. The Fatimids paid for miscalculating the strategic balance when provoking the Byzantium of Basil II in 995 and 999—and exactly a thousand years later, Hafiz al-Asad's Syria pulled back at the last moment from making the same error on the same front against the Turkish republic.

The book has three main elements. First, chapter 1 surveys the strategic geography of the Levant and its surrounds. It highlights the region's centrality, openness from all directions, and lack of internal coherence. Such features provide the main markers for understanding the turbulence and transformations of the Levant's long history. The persistence of imperial authority for long periods involved the power and prestige of great civilizations, and masks the fact that maintenance of this authority was often an exhausting struggle.

Second, chapters 2 and 3 review geopolitical developments in the Levant through the two thousand years before the emergence of the contemporary states. This involves a synthesis of the existing literature for the succession of periods from Roman to Ottoman rule. The survey interprets the nature, stability, and demise of each of the major territorial arrangements, as represented in the accompanying series of maps. The glossary explains the sectarian, tribal, and dynastic terminology.

Third, chapter 4 provides an assessment of the modern Levant, in which I consider the affairs of Israel, Syria, Lebanon, Jordan, the Palestinians, and Turkey. Discussion encompasses the rapid population growth, technological advances, and global politics, most recently meaning the global supremacy of the United States, that make the past century different from earlier periods. The modern Levant cannot be divorced from its long history, but the contemporary states also confront circumstances and stresses that have not previously existed.

To the best of my knowledge, the book is the only attempt in recent decades to discuss the whole Levant and the Levant as a whole, presenting the geopolitical evolution of the region from Roman times. As regards contemporary developments, the existing literature concentrates on particular portions of the Levant or on the wider Middle East. There is not much that interprets the Arab-Israeli, Lebanese-Syrian, and Syrian-Turkish arenas together, on the intermediate level of the western part of the "fertile crescent."

CHAPTER ONE

THE STRATEGIC GEOGRAPHY OF THE LEVANT

The Mediterranean littoral between the mountains of Cilicia and the Sinai peninsula represents the crossroads of the Eurasian/African "world island." This modest territorial strip commands the land bridge linking three continents—Europe, Asia, and Africa—and it has been the stage for some of the principal events of human history. The region was the source of two of the great monotheistic religions—Judaism and Christianity. It therefore also supplied the foundations for the third— Islam.

Few other parts of the planet's surface have been so continuously contested for so long by such a variety of states and imperial powers. Domination or possession of the region has conferred strategic advantage and moral prestige throughout the past two thousand years. Since the seventh century C.E. it has been the core of the main body of the Islamic world, between North Africa and Central Asia. If the Byzantines in the tenth century, the Crusaders in the twelfth century, or the Mongols in the thirteenth century had been able to seize the region and sustain such a seizure, the Islamic world would have been split and permanently weakened.

The area between Cilicia and Sinai is the western segment of the "fertile crescent," the relatively well-watered northern margin of Arabia, arcing from the Tigris-Euphrates floodplain to the Mediterranean. In Roman times, it was called "Syria," a word of unknown origin that first appeared as "Suri" on Babylonian hieroglyphs around 4000 B.C.E.[1]

1

The name has no proven connection with "Assyria." "Syria" is the label for the region favored by Western historians for periods up to the First World War.

"Syria," however, was not a name used by local people or rulers after the Islamic conquest, until the Ottomans applied it to the province of Damascus in the late nineteenth century. After the First World War, the term became confused with the modern Syrian state, which, like the Ottoman province, occupies only part of the region. Application of "Syria" to the whole region acquired the connotation of a "greater Syria" ruled from Damascus, and neutralization required the cumbersome expression "geographical Syria."

In Arabic, geographical Syria is called *bilad al-sham*—"the country of the north," meaning north of the Arabian Peninsula. *Bilad al-sham* has been used since pre-Islamic times, but it is not well known in the West beyond specialist circles.

This leaves the term "Levant," an Italian-derived word originating with traders from the medieval Italian city-states. It meant "the point where the sun rises," and referred to the eastern Mediterranean. It implied a source of light, possibly evoking the antiquity of civilization in the eastern Mediterranean, or the presence of the Holy Land.

By the late nineteenth century, the "Levant" became localized to the coastlands of "Syria," Asia Minor, and Egypt, and particularly associated with the cosmopolitan merchant communities of Beirut, Izmir (Smyrna), and Alexandria. These communities, comprising Arab Christians, Armenians, Jews, Greeks, and Muslims who adopted Western ways, produced the "Levantine"—a person straddling Western and Middle Eastern cultures. "Levantine" suggested linguistic and professional versatility, but also insecure identity—belonging everywhere but nowhere.

When modern Turkey and Egypt emerged after the First World War, losing some of their cosmopolitanism in the process of nationalist assertion, the "Levant" finally contracted to "Syria." Between 1920 and 1945 it was frequently used to refer to the French mandatory territories of Syria and Lebanon, but it has since become a recognized term for the western side of the "fertile crescent" in general. I consider that it is the best single word for the region discussed in this book, especially for western audiences.

Three geographical features of the Levant have been of continuous strategic salience since Roman times. First, the openness of the Levant's frontiers in all directions encouraged invasion, made the region a natural bridgehead for pressure on its neighbors, and meant insecurity for any regime in the Levant that did not govern, dominate, or placate these neighbors. Second, the physical centrality of the region between Europe and Africa to the west and Asia to the east attracted great power attention from all directions, particularly after the Islamic conquest. Third, the internal fragmentation of the Levant into coastland, hills, and interior plains—compounded by the human patchwork of rival towns and distinctive sectarian communities—frustrated political coordination in the region, even under great power rule.

On the one hand, from about the eighth century, when Arabic displaced Aramaic as the main regional language, until the early twentieth century, the mass of the population in most of the Levant developed a common Arabic dialect and, to a large extent, common customs and traditions. The only exceptions were Cilicia and the northern Jazira, where Turks and Kurds respectively became the majorities in the late Medieval period. Otherwise, the only interruption was the Latin Crusader ascendancy in the twelfth century.

Against the elements of cultural commonality, however, the Levant has no unifying geographical feature like the Tigris-Euphrates flood plain in the eastern wing of the "fertile crescent." The diversity of local physical environments, the multiplicity of Muslim and Christian sectarian identities, and the wider Middle Eastern commonality of Arabic and Islam limited prospects for distinctive regional identification in *bilad al-sham.*

Anyway, in the first half of the twentieth century the rapid expansion of the Western-oriented, Hebrew-speaking Jewish Yishuv in Palestine, culminating in the establishment of Israel in 1948, terminated linguistic and cultural commonality in the Levant. After 1948, *bilad al-sham* south of the recently finalized border of the Turkish republic was divided between Israel, with its Jewish majority, and the new Arab countries of Syria, Lebanon, and Jordan. There was now an "Arab Levant," a "Jewish Levant," and a "Turkish Levant."

3

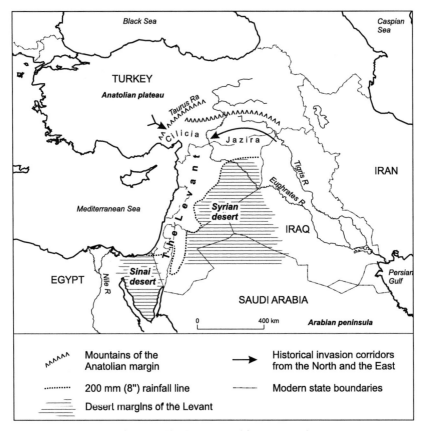

Map 1—The Levant and its surrounds

Vulnerable Frontiers

The Levant, or *bilad al-sham*, has obvious physical limits in all directions (map 1). To the north, there are the margins of the Taurus mountain ranges, historically and climatically a transition zone to the different world of the Anatolian plateau. To the northeast, the Levant grades into the steppe grasslands of the area between the Euphrates and Tigris rivers, known as the Jazira or "island." To the east and south, the Syrian and Arabian deserts mark the Levant off from the lower Tigris-Euphrates river system and the vast arid expanses of the Arabian Peninsula. To the southwest, the largely desolate Sinai peninsula sepa-

4

rates the Levant from Egypt and the lower Nile. Finally, to the west there is the Mediterranean Sea.

These limits enclose an area about the size of Italy, at the end of the twentieth century roughly coincident with the modern states of Syria, Lebanon, Israel, and Jordan. The major discrepancy is in the north, where the present Syrian-Turkish boundary is significantly to the south of the Anatolian margins. Kennedy suggests that the discrepancy derives from the Byzantine reconquest of Cilicia and northern Syria in the tenth century.[2] At that time, three centuries of Muslim Arab settlement and culture were uprooted, being replaced by Greeks, Armenians, and other Christians. When Byzantine rule collapsed in the late eleventh century, Turks and Kurds moved in. The present Syrian-Turkish boundary, which is also the northern limit of the Arab world, is more a legacy of the Byzantine Emperor Nicephorus Phocas than of Atatürk and the French.

On all its frontiers the Levant is exposed to external penetration. Historically, the most frequent military invasions have come from Anatolia in the north, or across the Jazira from the northeast. These were the access routes with water and forage for pre-modern armies. Before the Ottoman period almost all armies approaching the Levant from the east took the route through the Jazira rather than a direct march across the Syrian desert from Iraq—for example, Persian operations against the Romans and Mongol attacks on the Mamluks. Byzantine and Ottoman expansion into the Levant naturally came directly from Anatolia.

Otherwise, access from Egypt to the southern Levant did not involve any unusual difficulty, especially if the advancing forces already had a base at Gaza. There are no notable obstacles on the short Sinai crossing from the Nile delta. Fatimid, Ayyubid, and Mamluk armies regularly made this crossing between the tenth and sixteenth centuries, whether to invade the Levant, to reinforce positions already held in the Levant, or to meet enemies entering the Levant from the north.

Up to the nineteenth century, invasions from either the desert or the Mediterranean Sea by regular armed forces were almost unknown, because of logistical problems in both these environments in premodern conditions. The outstanding exception was the Islamic invasion of Roman Syria in 636, involving a cross-desert transfer of Khalid Ibn al-Walid's force from Iraq. This was the only instance of Arabian Bedouin nomads coordinated as an army of conquest. It depended on the special expertise of desert warriors under skilled strategic guidance—an unusual combination.

As for the Mediterranean approach from the west, the First Crusade avoided it in favor of the land route through Anatolia. Several later Crusades came by sea, but they had bases on the Levantine coast and could combine with local Latin forces. In other words, they were reinforcements rather than invasions. Naval expeditions in medieval times were chancy affairs, at the mercy of winds, currents, and seasonal conditions.[3] Fatimid galleys hugged the coast between Egypt and the Levant ports, while the Ayyubids and Mamluks preferred to fight on land rather than on water. The Latin Levant had the advantages of Italian expertise and, after 1191, possession of Cyprus. Its maritime lifeline to the West was never seriously disrupted. For all sides in the twelfth and thirteenth centuries, amphibious adventures often resulted in disappointment or disaster.

Nonetheless, before and after the Crusades, the sea and desert frontiers were a security problem for Muslim authorities in the Levant, because of vulnerability to raids. Only at the height of Umayyad/ 'Abbasid capability in the eighth century and of Ottoman power in the seventeenth century were the coasts considered tolerably secure. Byzantine naval initiatives accompanied the Byzantine recovery of 850–1050. In 910, Byzantine troops landed at Ladhiqiyya and sacked the town. Later, between the fourteenth and sixteenth centuries, the Mamluks and Ottomans faced challenges from the Franks and Venetians in Cyprus. Only after capturing Rhodes (1522) and Cyprus (1571) did the Ottomans acquire command of the eastern Mediterranean.

To the east, the Levant is open to the Syrian desert (*badiyat al-sham*) from Aleppo in the north to Transjordan in the south. There are no defensible topographic features on the desert margin, which varies from poor steppe east of Aleppo and Homs to rocky wasteland east of the Hauran and the narrow fertile zone of the Transjordan highlands.

Until the advent of modern territorial states and new technologies in the twentieth century, the zone of sedentary agriculture on the interior plains advanced or retreated depending on rainfall trends and the relations between the urban authorities and the Bedouin confederations.

In the tenth century, tribal leaders took over parts of the settled zone. Through the 970s, the Tayy confederation wrested most of Palestine from the Fatimids of Egypt, and in 1023 the Mirdasids, shaykhs of the Banu Kilab Bedouin, inaugurated a 56-year rule of Aleppo. Tayy and Mirdasid advances threatened to transform the strategic situation,[4] perhaps even leading to Byzantine protection of tribal principalities as far south as Gaza. In 1029, a Fatimid army recovered Palestine. The Bedouin never again made such inroads, but Ayyubid, Mamluk, and Ottoman authorities took care to placate the desert tribes.

In the sixteenth century, the Ottomans found military outposts inadequate for stabilization of a long and permeable frontier.[5] After 1574, they recognized the chief of the Mawali Bedouin confederation, successor of the Banu Kilab and Banu Kalb in the northern Syrian desert, as *amir al-badiya,* or "Prince of the Wasteland." For a financial subsidy the Mawali buffered the Ottoman Levant from other tribes. This arrangement broke down in the eighteenth century, when rival tribes encroached on Mawali territory from the south.

Bonaparte's 1798 landing in Egypt marked an historical turning point for the Levant. European technology abolished logistical constraints on approaches from the sea and the desert. Between 1800 and 1918, Britain and France increased their military pressure, commercial penetration, and cultural influence in the eastern Mediterranean. The Ottoman collapse in the First World War opened the way to direct British and French rule in the Levant, and to large-scale Jewish settlement in Palestine under British cover. The new states of Lebanon and Israel were products of this "westernization" of the coastland and parts of its mountain hinterland.

The new accessibility of the Levant across the desert was at first less obvious, because the masters of the new mobility and technology operated from the west. A few hints came with British patronage of the 1916 Arab revolt against the Ottomans, and the unification of most of the Arabian peninsula under the al-Sa'ud family in the 1920s. The

Hashemite family, Britain's allies from the Hijaz, took over Transjordan. The Hashemites then briefly faced military pressure from their al-Sa'ud enemies, resisted with British backing.

The implications became clearer when Saddam Husayn's Iraq loomed as a significant mechanized military force to the east in the 1970s, potentially challenging Syria and Israel. Saddam's diversion into adventures elsewhere—against Iran, Kuwait, and the United States—left the potential unfulfilled in the late twentieth century.

Ironically, after Bonaparte the next challenge to the status quo in *bilad al-sham* based on new military methods came from the Ottoman governor of Egypt, Muhammad 'Ali. In 1831, his son Ibrahim Pasha led a French-trained and -equipped army through Sinai to wrest the Levant from the central government. The Egyptian intervention intensified Anglo-French rivalry, because Britain opposed the weakening of the Ottoman regime.

In 1840, a British-led landing north of Beirut restored Ottoman authority. This was the first time that application of sea power from beyond the Middle East caused a change of regime in the Levant. A further landing at Beirut in 1860 by French troops, backed by a combined European naval force, resulted in the creation of the autonomous province of Mount Lebanon. The long reach of modern Western sea power received additional illustration during the twentieth century, for example the logistical backing for the British army that conquered the Levant in 1917–18, and the intervention of US marines in Beirut in 1958, which saved Lebanon from disintegration.

Strategic Pivot

As the land nexus between Eurasia and Africa, the Levant has always been of great interest to the empires and states of the eastern Mediterranean and southwest Asia. From medieval times, it also attracted growing interest from dynamic new powers reaching out of Western Europe and Central Asia.

For Western Europeans, seizing holy places and profiting from trade routes initially took precedence. For the Mongols, the Levant was the gateway to Egypt and its seizure was crucial to schemes of world conquest. For later Western European imperial powers, Russia, and the United States, the Levant beckoned for a variety of reasons. In the late nineteenth century, command of the southern fringes of Eurasia, commercial and territorial advantage in the event of a collapse of the Ottoman empire, and Christian linkage to Palestine were the chief imperatives. By the mid-twentieth century, the drama of Israel's creation in the heart of the Arab world and the proximity to the oil reservoir of the Persian Gulf, the leading global strategic resource, together took charge.

It is perhaps convenient to consider the pivotal function of the Levant in its eastern Mediterranean neighborhood separately from the region's significance for more distant powers. One can identify an inner circle around the Levant, comprising the Nile valley, Anatolia, the Tigris-Euphrates plain, and the Arabian Peninsula. Historically the first two have regularly been imperial centers, while each of the four regions became a major Middle Eastern state in the twentieth century—Egypt, Turkey, Iraq, and Saudi Arabia respectively. Here the Levant has been the "land between"—a contested space in competition for influence.

Within the inner circle, the strategic role of the Levant has varied through the last two thousand years depending on whether or not the surrounds of the region have been dominated by a single imperial power. In late Roman and Ottoman times, with the eastern Mediterranean ruled from Constantinople/Istanbul, the Levant provided the land link between the imperial center in Asia Minor and Egypt, the preeminent province. Under the Ottomans, the Levant also connected Istanbul to the Islamic holy sites in Arabia—guardianship of these sites was crucial to the prestige of the dynasty.

A different situation prevailed between the seventh and tenth centuries, under the Umayyads and 'Abbasids. For about three hundred years the Levant, together with Egypt, Arabia, and Iraq, was under unchallenged Muslim rule, but with a front facing the Christian Byzantines in Anatolia. In the Umayyad and early 'Abbasid periods, the northern Levant was the base for the "holy war" against the infidel enemy. In the late tenth century, however, Byzantium forcibly moved the frontier south into the central Levant. For almost a hundred years the territorial partition of Syria was the basis for equilibrium between the two great powers of the Middle East—Byzantium and Fatimid Egypt.

Another variant of the Levant's significance for its surrounds applied in the twelfth and twentieth centuries. The Crusader Kingdom of Jerusalem and modern Israel both represented—unusually—states within the Levant capable of challenging neighboring powers. The external reinforcement the two states received and their sensitive location, separating North Africa from southwest Asia, disquieted their neighbors, particularly when added to their respective Christian and Jewish identities in the heart of *dar al-Islam*.

Political fragmentation in the Levant in the Crusader and modern periods encouraged neighboring powers to seek local footholds, both to face the Crusaders or Israel and for advantage in competition among themselves. For example, from his headquarters in Egypt, where he had overthrown the Fatimids, Salah al-Din Yusuf ibn Ayyub (Saladin) secured Damascus in 1174. This enabled him to relieve the Crusader threat to Egypt and to strike north against his Muslim rivals in Aleppo and Mosul. Similarly, efforts by Egypt, Iraq, and Saudi Arabia to assert their influence in the Arab Levant in the 1950s represented attempts to acquire footholds vis-à-vis one another as well as to restrict Israel and Syria.

Strategic interest in the Levant from beyond the Middle East began with Rome. The growth of Rome by the first century B.C.E. to become the world's largest city, and by 100 C.E. to become the world's first city to reach a population of one million, required provisions from far afield. As Egypt and Asia Minor gradually became "breadbaskets" and major revenue sources for the empire, Rome needed a secure hold on the Levant to shield them from any eastern threat. If the Levant fell into hostile hands, Egypt would be separated from Asia Minor and both would be open to invasion.

After Rome surrendered its supremacy in the east to Constantinople in the fourth century, the Levant ceased to be of concern beyond the East Roman/Sassanid Persian sphere. Rome lost its status as a great city, and the disintegrating Western Empire no longer drew on distant trade and supplies. Islamic supremacy in the Middle East from the seventh century on, together with Christian Europe's parlous condition behind the shield of Byzantium, further postponed the reappearance of outsiders from Europe and Asia.

The Turks came first, from Central Asia via Iran, initially as slave soldiers and then as nomadic incursions into Anatolia and the Jazira in the eleventh century. The Turks converted to Islam, became the rulers of Muslim principalities in the Levant and Iraq, and wrested the Anatolian plateau from the Byzantines. Eventually Turkish warriors, as Mamluk and Ottoman sultans, held and defended the Levant against subsequent external threats.

Between 1097 and 1401, new interventions from Western Europe and Central Asia repeatedly shook the established order in the region, beginning with the First Crusade and ending with the capture of Damascus by Timurlane. Although the Mamluks of Egypt successfully ejected the Crusaders and outlasted the Mongols, thereby maintaining Islamic command of the Levant, some degree of external interest in the region from beyond the Middle East was a constant factor from late Medieval times onward.

The First Crusade (1097–1102) aimed at Christian reconquest of Jerusalem and expressed a resurgence of Western European military capability. The impetus was religious ideology—not commerce or grand strategy.[6] It was only in the 1170s, more than half a century after the foundation of the Crusader states, that relocation of the main terminus of the Asian trade routes from Egypt to the Crusader ports aroused serious Western European strategic involvement in the Levant. After the mid-twelfth century, Venice, Genoa, and Pisa experienced a surge in profits from their commercial colonies in Acre, Tyre, and Tripoli. This was probably an important reason for the tenacious Crusader hold on the coast for almost a century after the devastating defeat at Hattin in 1187.

Mongol intervention in the Levant after Hülegü Khan's destruction of Baghdad and overthrow of the 'Abbasid Caliphate in 1258 coincided with the final decades of Crusader occupation of the coastlands. However, despite friendly exchanges, the western and eastern invaders never managed serious coordination. For the Mongols, conquest of Mamluk Syria was crucial to command of the Middle East. The European monarchies had no interest in assisting this scheme. Between the fourteenth and seventeenth centuries, a combination of Mamluk and Ottoman power, religious warfare in Western Europe, and European outflanking of the Middle East with oceanic links to the East Indies meant that the Levant was not bothered from the west.

New circumstances took shape in the seventeenth century. The balance of power between Europe and the Ottomans began to change to the disadvantage of the latter, and France and the Vatican became interested in the Maronites of Mount Lebanon, a Christian peasant population in the core of the Levant. In the eighteenth century the Russians asserted "protection" of Orthodox Christians in Palestine, after defeating the Ottomans in the 1768–74 war, and the British became concerned with the Middle East as the land link between the Mediterranean and British India. Bonaparte's assault on Egypt and the Levant in 1798–1801 was a French bid to command this land link, vigorously countered by the British fleet.

Thereafter the Levant assumed elevated strategic significance in the triangular rivalry of Britain, France, and Russia for pre-eminence in southwest Asia. Britain and France vied for position on the east-west axis through the Mediterranean toward India, while Britain increasingly worried about Russian ambition to cut across this axis from north to south—for Russia the shortest access from the Eurasian interior to the warm seas.

All three powers focused on the eastern Mediterranean, the gateway to southwest Asia. Through the nineteenth century the British sought to deny Russia and France by preserving Ottoman authority. The Russians coveted free passage and even sovereign rights through the Bosphorus to the Mediterranean. For their part, the French patronized the Egyptian seizure of Syria in the 1830s. When Britain displaced France in Cairo in the late nineteenth century, the French intensified their commercial and cultural penetration of the Levant via Beirut and the autonomous province of Mount Lebanon.

Following the Ottoman collapse and the temporary eclipse of Russia in 1917–18, Britain and France divided the Levant between themselves. At this point, new strategic elements of global significance entered the equation.

First, Britain and France respectively promoted the emergence of two new political entities in the region—the Jewish Yishuv in Palestine, and Greater Lebanon. These became the independent states of Israel and Lebanon in the 1940s, the former involving mass immigration of Jews from Europe and the Middle East and the latter representing Maronite Catholic particularity. For Sunni Muslim Arabs, both were Western beachheads. Certainly Israel and Lebanon were extraordinary creations, combining territorial statehood in the Levant with influential populations in the West and making it impossible for the West to detach itself from the Levant's affairs.

Second, Britain's decision before the First World War to change from coal to oil as fuel for the Royal Navy coincided with discoveries of oil fields in Iraq. For Britain, the 1920 League of Nations "mandate" for Palestine, including Transjordan, established a bridge between Egypt and the Mediterranean, on the one hand, and the increasingly significant energy resources of Iraq and the Persian Gulf, on the other hand. Like Egypt and Palestine, Iraq and the Gulf shaykhdoms were under British oversight after the Ottoman collapse.

British and French domination lasted less than thirty years, but the global salience of the Levant persisted. From the 1950s to the 1980s, the Levant was a contested zone in the Cold War competition of the United States and Soviet Russia. It lay between Turkey, the eastern bulwark of the US-led NATO alliance, and the Persian Gulf, by this stage an oil reservoir vital to the Western economies. It was also a weak link in the US effort to coordinate the countries of southern Eurasia with the West, thereby containing Russia in the continental core.

Western association with Israel, particularly the 1956 Anglo-French-Israeli attack on Egypt, helped the Soviet Union to present itself as an ally of Arab nationalism, which in the Levant translated into Soviet patronage of the new Syrian state that became Israel's bitter enemy. By the early 1980s, Syria hosted thousands of Soviet military advisers and provided naval facilities for Russia, which thereby leapfrogged Turkey and positioned itself in the heart of the Middle East. Soviet influence in Syria helped to propel the US into a de facto alliance with Israel from the 1970s on.

In the late 1980s, the second Russian eclipse of the twentieth century, with the demise of Soviet communism and the end of the Cold War,

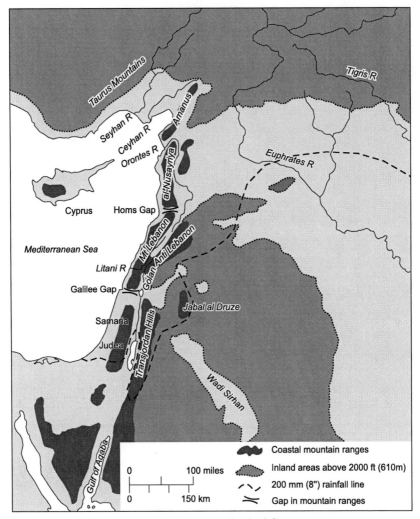

Map 2—The Levant: physical features

again sharply reduced influences on the Levant from the Eurasian interior. Through the 1990s, however, the political fragmentation and religious salience of the Levant, combined with the Arab-Israeli dispute and the proximity to Persian Gulf oil, guaranteed undiminished global prominence for the region.

Internal Fragmentation

One reason that *bilad al-sham* never coalesced into a political unit was its compartmentalization between coastlands, uplands, and interior plains, with no natural center of gravity (map 2). In physical terms, the Levant comprises three north-south axes of coast, coastal mountains, and an interior zone of plains and plateaux grading into the Syrian Desert. The coast and interior plains are open to both north and south and became invasion axes, whether from Egypt, Anatolia, or the Jazira. The mountains hindered communications between the coast and the interior and thereby facilitated cultural differentiation between the Mediterranean ports and the inland cities.

The coast was open to influences from Europe to the west, whereas the interior had a strong continental orientation reinforced after the middle of the seventh century by the common Islamic civilization of southwest Asia. From Roman times on, it was difficult to bind coast and interior under a single authority. In the late 'Abbasid, Crusader, and modern periods, separate states arose in these two zones. In the Ottoman period overall imperial authority persisted, but rival provincial governors, for example in Damascus and the ports of Acre and Tripoli, sometimes behaved like sovereign powers.

The uplands separating the coast from the interior are the principal physical feature of the Levant. A line of hills and mountains immediately inland from the Mediterranean parallels the shore from the Amanus range (Nur Dağları) of Cilicia in the north to the Palestinian uplands in the south, with Mount Lebanon as its center and climax. In this book, Mount Lebanon refers to the Lebanese coastal range from the Homs gap to the Litani River. The hills have served as a defensive barrier, whether for coastal states vis-à-vis the interior, or vice versa. In the former case, the Crusaders fortified various locations in the uplands, whether to command the surrounds, shield the coast, or guard gaps through the ranges. In the latter case, the Mamluks and Ottomans watched the mountain populations for any sign of subversion by foreign powers, primarily from Europe, that might compromise their authority in the interior.

Throughout the past two thousand years, the hills have also been home to tribes and religious minorities at odds with their rulers. For Rome, the Jews of Judea and the Ituraean tribespeople of Mount Lebanon represented security problems. Under Orthodox Christian East Roman rule, Monophysite Christians favored the hill country around the Orontes valley, where the imperial hand was lighter than on the coast and in the towns. In the early Islamic period, Shi'ism took root in Mount Lebanon.

Major developments occurred in the hills in the early eleventh century. Many Maronite Christians, finding renewed Byzantine rule in northern Syria inhospitable, headed south to join co-religionists in the mountains east of Tripoli. Almost simultaneously, believers in the divinity of the Fatimid Caliph al-Hakim began converting Shi'ite Muslims in Mount Lebanon. After the demise of al-Hakim, more of these Druze came into the area to avoid persecution. In this way the Maronite-Druze cohabitation of Mount Lebanon, a major element in the subsequent history of the Levant, emerged out of the eleventh century Byzantine-Fatimid stalemate.

The twelfth-century Crusader states coexisted with a complicated sectarian geography on their inland margins.[7] To the north, the hill populations comprised Armenian Christians in Cilicia, and dissident Twelver Shi'ites, the Alawites, inland from Ladhiqiyya. Alongside the Alawites, Isma'ili Shi'ites took advantage of the Crusader-Muslim frontier to consolidate a small mountain domain around the fortress of Masyaf. These were the Assassins, an offshoot of a similar principality in the Elburz mountains of Iran, who rejected Sunni Muslim authority. Between Masyaf (map 7) and the Homs gap, the hills hosted a mixture of Alawites, Maronites, Orthodox Christians, and Crusader settlers around the great redoubt of Crac des Chevaliers (Qila'at al-Husn), which commanded the gap.

Maronites, Twelver Shi'ites, and Druze dominated Mount Lebanon from the Homs gap to northern Palestine, a situation that continues eight centuries later. However, the local distribution of these communities was different in the Crusader period, with Shi'ites being the majority in the heart of the mountains and Maronites largely restricted to the far north.

Southward, the Palestinian hills of the Galilee, Samaria, Judea, and

Transjordan contained a jumble of Sunni Muslim peasants, Twelver Shi'ites, Orthodox and Jacobite Christians, Bedouin tribes, and Jewish communities. In the southern Levant, the uplands intersect directly with the desert, without the eastern margin of agriculture and steppe that exists north from the Hawran and Damascus. Only in Palestine did the hills have a Sunni Muslim majority, probably reinforced by Bedouin infusion, by Crusader times.

The Crusaders established a modus vivendi with the mountain communities. Apart from some taxes and tribute, the Crusaders governed with a light hand. This was more the result of lack of resources than of any special wisdom on the part of Frankish leaders, but it did ensure quiescence in the hills.[8]

Away from the coast, Franks settled only in the environs of Jerusalem, southern Transjordan, Antioch, and Edessa, with a scattering of castles over the 300 miles of uplands between the Galilee and Antioch. If the mountain communities had turned against the Franks, the lucrative land trade into the coastal ports would have been compromised. As it was, even the Muslims rarely caused problems, to the disquiet of Muslim visitors from elsewhere.[9] Through almost two centuries of Crusader activity in the Levant, the Druze featured only intermittently in the historical record, and the Shi'ites and Alawites hardly at all. They collaborated, wavered between Christian and Muslim powers, or stood aloof. Some Maronites, but not all, encouraged links with the Latin Christians.

Subsequent Muslim rulers did not forget the suspect allegiances of the mountain communities in Crusader times. Both the Mamluks and the Ottomans knew that disaffection in the hills could menace their command of the coasts and the interior. Between 1266 and 1273, the Mamluk Sultan Baybars wore down Isma'ili independence in the north Syrian hills.[10] Between 1264 and 1375, the Mamluks launched a succession of attacks on the Armenian state in Cilicia, a Mongol ally. Mount Lebanon experienced similar treatment in 1300 and 1305. The Mamluks feared that the Druze, Shi'ites, and Maronites might provide opportunities for Frankish subversion from Cyprus, and were determined to impose Sunni Muslim authority. Punitive expeditions particularly affected the Twelver Shi'ites of the Kisrawan district, paving the way for their displacement by Maronites in the sixteenth and seventeenth centuries.

The Ottomans inherited Mamluk concerns when they seized the Levant in 1516. Ottoman attention concentrated on Mount Lebanon, where the Druze rebelled, the Maronites forged links with Europe, and the Shi'ites had affinities with Safavid Iran, the enemy to the east. This was the most sensitive location in the Levant: halfway between Anatolia and Egypt, flanking Damascus, and with an open Mediterranean shore. Until the nineteenth century the Ottomans managed the situation with a judicious mixture of indirect control through local lords, divide-and-rule tactics between local factions, and military expeditions when necessary.

From about the mid-nineteenth century, the mountain communities began decisively to assert themselves. The Maronites led the way. By the 1850s, Maronite population growth and aspirations for autonomy threatened Ottoman territorial integrity in the Levant. The Maronite demographic and economic ascent also destabilized the Maronite-Druze balance on Mount Lebanon, precipitating sectarian violence in 1860. Only the creation of the autonomous province of Mount Lebanon under joint European and Ottoman oversight contained the situation until the Ottoman collapse in the First World War.

Most significantly, the Maronites inaugurated the phenomenon of "the mountain coming to town"—large-scale migration of mountain peasants to the cities of the coast and the interior. From the 1830s, Beirut's Sunni Muslim and Orthodox Christian bourgeoisie faced increasing competition from Maronites moving out of the hinterland.[11]

Then, from the 1920s, French rule in Syria awakened the previously marginal Alawites of the Nusayriya hills. France sponsored an autonomous Alawite province between 1920 and 1936, introduced modern education, and encouraged Alawite participation in the colonial armed forces. Members of a new Alawite lower middle class eventually took command of the Syrian state in the 1960s, via the army and the pan-Arab Ba'th party. Thereafter Alawites increasingly migrated out of the hills to Syria's main cities, especially to the port of Ladhiqiyya and to Damascus.[12] From being almost non-existent in Damascus before the 1950s, they became a large part of the ruling class and the public-sector bourgeoisie.

Finally, in the 1960s, Twelver Shi'ites from Lebanon's southern hill country began a massive relocation to Beirut.[13] The Shi'ites thereby returned to central Lebanon, but this time to the expanding coastal metropolis, where they challenged Sunnis and Christians alike.

Overall, the mountain sects—Maronites, Shi'ites, Alawites, and Druze—comprised about 25% of the combined population of Syria and Lebanon in the late twentieth century, as against a Sunni majority of 65%, primarily in the Syrian interior. Yet Syria and Lebanon became the only Arab countries with non-Sunni heads of state—an Alawite in Damascus and a Maronite in Beirut. This indicates the salience of the "mountain" in modern times.

The assertion of the mountain communities fractured the Arab Levant in the twentieth century, at the same time as the Arabs faced the Turks in the north and retreated before the Jews in the south. The Homs and Galilee gaps (map 2) divide the hill zone into northern, central, and southern segments, each of which became a distinctive political arena after France and Britain took charge of Syria and Palestine respectively in 1918–20.

In the north, the hills were split between the Turkish republic and the new state of Syria when France approved Turkey's incorporation of the province of Alexandretta in 1939. Alexandretta (Hatay) was part of French mandatory Syria between 1920 and 1939, and the Syrians angrily rejected the Turkish annexation. The issue poisoned Syrian-Turkish relations for the rest of the century. The northern hills also provided Syria's political leadership from the 1960s on, overturning the natural order for the Sunnis of Damascus and Aleppo.

Meanwhile, the central ranges became the new state of Greater Lebanon, established by the French at Maronite insistence by cobbling together Mount Lebanon with portions of the Ottoman provinces of Beirut and Damascus. This created a multisectarian country with no majority population and no common understanding of "national identity" among Christians, Shi'ites, Sunnis, and Druze. Again, the Syrian Arab nationalists in Damascus viewed the territorial dispensation as unjust, which made for a problematic Lebanese-Syrian relationship when the two entities achieved independence from France in 1945. The fact that "the mountain came to town" in both Lebanon and Syria did not make for any commonality, because different "mountains" with different outlooks came to Beirut and Damascus respectively.

To the south, Jewish immigration increased the Jewish proportion of the population of Palestine west of the Jordan River from about 8% in the late nineteenth century to nearly 40% by 1948, when the British departed. In the first Arab-Israeli war of 1948–49, the Jewish community of Palestine declared its independence as the state of Israel in May 1948, confronted Palestinian Arab fighters and regular Arab armies, and conquered the coastlands, the Galilee, and the southern desert. Apart from Gaza, the Arabs retained the uplands of Samaria, Judea, and Transjordan. The latter territories came under the British-backed Jordanian monarchy, originally established in 1921 under British protection to the east of the Jordan River as a principality for the Hashemite emir 'Abdullah.

With Palestinian Arabs driven inland, Jerusalem divided, and a new Jewish-Arab front line on the margins of the hills, the highlands of Samaria and Judea, or the "West Bank," took center stage in the continuing conflict. In 1948–49, 500,000 Palestinian Arabs, mainly from the coastal plain, fled into the West Bank, Gaza, and Transjordan, while 150,000 fled the Galilee into Lebanon. They squatted in squalid refugee camps, and demanded the right to return, refused by Israel. For their part, the Israelis felt at a topographical disadvantage vis-à-vis the West Bank and the Syrian Golan Heights.

A crisis between Israel and the surrounding Arab states in May–June 1967 led to a stunning Arab military defeat. Israel occupied Arab East Jerusalem and the West Bank, as well as the Syrian Golan, Gaza, and the Sinai Peninsula. By the late 1970s, an increasingly bitter struggle developed between the Israeli conquerors and the Palestinian Arab inhabitants for control of the land and resources of the West Bank highlands, with the Palestinian Arabs determined to preserve their major remaining foothold west of the Jordan River.

As for the Jordanian monarchy, thrown back across the river and facing greatly superior Israeli power, the only imperative was survival, with determination not to be burned away on the altar of Arab resistance to Israel. In 1970–71, King Husayn expelled Palestinian guerrillas who were both attacking Israel and challenging his rule. These guerrillas, including the command of the Palestine Liberation Organization (PLO), moved to Lebanon, where they assisted the disintegration of the Lebanese state.

In sum, the clash of Arab, Jewish, and Turkish nationalism almost guaranteed the physical reduction of the Arab Levant after the Ottoman collapse. The fact that the Arab Levant was also divided between the mountain sects and the Sunni majority of the interior, as well as among sects and localities, made the emergence of several modern Arab territorial states, all potentially unstable, unsurprising. The specific configurations of Syria, Lebanon, Jordan, and the Palestinian Arab entity of course owe a great deal to British and French manipulations and the new Jewish state. This should not be taken, however, to mean that the most likely alternative, without Britain, France, and Israel, would have been an easy coalescence into a Greater Syrian Arab state.

Population Growth, Limited Resources, Compressed Space

The twentieth-century division of the Levant into four independent countries, with a fifth emerging and with the far north in the hands of a sixth, coincided with population growth and technological advances that exacerbated tensions within and among these countries. The interesting parallels between the politically splintered medieval Levant and its modern counterpart can only be limited comparisons because of the demographic and technological transformation of the region after about 1800.

For example, the Crusader Kingdom of Jerusalem contained about 150,000 European settlers and half a million "native" Christians and Muslims after 1150.[14] The modern states of Israel and Lebanon have 6.6 and 4 million people respectively, in roughly the same space. Through the early modern period, from the sixteenth century to 1800, the population of the Levant was probably stable at about 2 million. This number began increasing in the nineteenth century to stand at 2.5 million in 1878 and 4.5 million in 1913/14.[15] Between 1914 and 2000, the population south of the Turkish border exploded to about 35 million.

21

Particularly dramatic increases were registered by the Jews of Palestine (Israel after 1948), up from less than 100,000 to 5.4 million, and by the population of the modern Syrian state, up from two million to 17 million. The Christian proportion in the region declined from about 25% to around 10%, although the Maronites, with their compact position on Mount Lebanon, held their own better than other Christians. In the Arab Levant in 2000, Christian proportions varied from about 35% in Lebanon to 10% in Syria and 4% in Jordan and among the Palestinians. Away from Lebanon (70% Christian and Shi'ite), mainly Alawite coastal Syria, and the Druze mountain southeast of Damascus, Sunni Muslims were the overwhelming majority.

People also became more concentrated in a few large, sprawling cities. In 1914, Damascus, Aleppo, Beirut, Tel Aviv–Jaffa, and 'Amman had populations of 220,000, 200,000, 150,000, 40,000, and 5,000 respectively.[16] In the late 1990s, the inhabitants of the corresponding metropolitan areas numbered 2.6 million, 2.3 million, 2.1 million, 2.8 million, and 2.7 million.[17] The proportion of the Levant's population in these five cities increased from about 14% to more than one-third through the twentieth century.

The demographic explosion, together with technological innovations, had far-reaching consequences. Population growth, rising living standards, and the demands of modern industry and agriculture brought pressures on resources inconceivable before the mid-twentieth century.

For example, only in the 1980s did it become apparent that the Euphrates River might not fully satisfy the needs of both Turkey and Syria. Turkey commands the headwaters, asserts that it has primary rights to water originating on its territory, and has constructed a series of dams for irrigation and hydroelectricity production. Syria depends on the Euphrates for 80% of its water supply, and has asserted the right of downstream states to equal shares, rejected by Turkey. Syria and Turkey agreed in 1987 on a through-flow adequate for Syrian consumption into the twenty-first century, but Turkey reserved the option of reducing the flow in case of prolonged drought or expansion of Turkish requirements. Through the 1990s, the water dispute was intertwined with Syrian support for the Kurdish insurrection in eastern Anatolia and Syria's claim on Alexandretta.

Concern about water resources in the southern Levant—Israel/ Palestine and Transjordan—emerged earlier, in the late 1940s. This was because of the Arab-Israeli confrontation, the semiarid climate, and the division of the small Jordan River basin among all four states of the region. Nonetheless, even here permanent tightness of supply was a twentieth-century phenomenon. Only in contemporary times have aquifers, rivers, and watersheds become prominent dimensions of the geopolitics of the Levant.

That said, the outlook into the twenty-first century is grim. The intersection of political fragmentation, population increases, and global warming is potentially catastrophic. With the exception of Israel and Lebanon, already among the world's most densely populated countries by the late twentieth century, the Levant continues to exhibit natural increase rates above 2.2% per annum. Even with expected further declines in these rates, the population of the Levant will probably pass 50 million by 2015. Jordan has a recurrent water deficit, Israel requires continued access to West Bank aquifers, and Syria looks ahead to a shortfall.

The climatic forecast for the Levant through the twenty-first century is for a temperature rise of 8 degrees Fahrenheit (4.5 degrees Celsius) by 2100,[18] and for a drop in wet season precipitation of 1–2 inches (18–50 millimeters) by 2070–2100.[19] The worst precipitation losses would be in northern Syria and the Jazira. The forecasts indicate severe summer heat stress on the coast and in the interior plains, and a fall of perhaps 10% in the already modest annual rainfall. In the best scenario of economic rationalization, inter-state collaboration, and less than anticipated climatic deterioration the challenge is formidable. In worse-case scenarios of failure to settle Arab-Israeli affairs and regime incompetence in Syria and Lebanon, disaster looms.

Increasingly mobile and destructive military capabilities after 1900 also emphasized the short distances and limited spaces of the Levant. Concentration of population in metropolitan centers led to strategic vulnerability in the context of Arab-Israeli hostility and poor relations between Syria and Turkey. By the late twentieth century, Israel and Syria had ballistic missiles and non-conventional weapons—in the Syrian case, chemical warheads and biological agents, and in the

Israeli case, a nuclear arsenal. Post-Ottoman political fragmentation meant that no capital or major city was further than 70 miles from an international boundary, and in the 1990s all local states feared attack or subversion from their neighbors.

From the 1950s on, air strikes could be made into state heartlands within minutes. Paradoxically, large fast-moving land forces considerably raised the value of topographical obstacles and higher ground, to buy time for reaction and mobilization, while missiles, air power, and satellite observation seemed to make territorial buffering irrelevant. In any event, Israel and Syria were not prepared to take chances, which gave strategic salience greater even than in the Crusader period to intervening uplands such as the Golan plateau and the Lebanese hills.

Population growth and urban development have heightened the claustrophobia of small territorial states. Ironically, in view of the later relative decline of the Christians of *bilad al-sham,* the Maronites led the population boom. In the late nineteenth century, the autonomous province of Mount Lebanon could not support its expanding population, and thousands left for the Americas and Australia.

In the late twentieth century, fierce Jewish-Arab competition for land in the southern Levant was exacerbated by relentless demographic pressure. In 2003, Israel, the West Bank, and Gaza approached the population density of New Jersey in a space that is more than half desert, with three million Palestinian refugees and their descendants asserting their right of return from neighboring countries. On the West Bank, a Palestinian Arab state would, at most, control an area a little bigger than Rhode Island. Here, 2.2 million Palestinian Arabs occupied several tiny territorial compartments, intersected by lands Israel has allocated since 1967 to 400,000 Jewish settlers (including the East Jerusalem housing estates).

In the interior of the Levant, the regimes in Syria and Jordan have struggled against the odds to satisfy the minimal material aspirations of their youthful populations, of which more than half are under the age of 21. In the 1990s, Syria, the Arab regional power of the Levant, stagnated under an authoritarian regime terrified of allowing serious initiative by its citizenry. The Arab Levant is overcrowded, polluted, and probably incapable of absorbing the menacing demographic bulge inflating the working-age population. The ramshackle Syrian economy remains dominated by a corrupt and inefficient public sector. Syria entered the twenty-first century isolated from the global electronic revolution and dependent for its viability on the Beirut banks and on siphoning off money from Lebanon. Syria's political command of the Lebanese coexisted uneasily with Lebanon's commercial superiority.

Modern states in the Levant exist within rigid boundaries, as opposed to the vague frontiers of earlier periods. In medieval and early modern times, princes and warlords were interested in clarity about who received taxes from whom and who commanded strategic topography, but not in drawing lines. Up to the late Ottoman period there was often no precise point at which a traveler passed from one jurisdiction to another—in the twelfth century, a zone of shared revenues lay between the Kingdom of Jerusalem and the Emirate of Damascus (map 7).

The shift from frontiers to boundaries began in the mid-nineteenth century, with the demarcation of autonomous Mount Lebanon and sharper definition of Ottoman districts. The Anglo-French-Turkish carve-up of the Levant after 1918 brought modern boundary lines. These deserve more academic attention than they have received. They vary from the straightforward Jordan River/Wadi Araba boundary between British mandatory Palestine and Transjordan to the tortuous French division of Lebanon from Syria in the anti-Lebanon mountains. The delineation of the Sanjak of Alexandretta, comprising four districts of the Ottoman province of Aleppo, represented the only use of preceding administrative boundaries. In the north, the Aleppo-Mosul railway became the Syrian-Turkish border across the Jazira plain.

Fences, barbed wire, and guard towers separated the Jewish, Arab, and Turkish Levants after the British and French departed. Israel's fences enclose the Palestinian Arabs of the West Bank and Gaza, and the Syrian-Turkish border cuts through Arab and Kurdish populations. Within the Arab Levant, modern boundaries produce friction. Syria resents Lebanon's statehood and rejects reciprocal establishment of embassies. In 1995, an official in the Syrian embassy in Washington told me that Lebanon should not exist. Boundaries along the Yarmouk River between Jordan and Syria and al-Kabir River between Lebanon and Syria also involve water rights. As regards a 2002 Syrian-Lebanese project to share the Nahr al-Kabir, a Lebanese journalist observed that each state would contribute $50 million for dams and other works "while the benefits will be distributed 60% to the sister [Syria] and 40% to helpless Lebanon [*lubnan al-maghlub ala amrihi*]" (Henri Lahhud in *al-Nahar,* 30 April 2002).

The Levant in the early twenty-first century is a geopolitical pressure cooker. Never before in the region's history have so many people lived split by such fixed political boundaries in such a precarious balance with an overtaxed physical environment. It is easy for extremism and bigotry to flourish where Palestinian Arabs feel so aggrieved by territorial losses and physical displacement, Israelis and Arabs feel so threatened by each other, and most Arabs feel so alienated from their regimes. In the Arab-Israeli case, however, extremism and intransigence point only to a "black hole" of mounting violence, perhaps even to a human and environmental catastrophe.

Whatever the defects of the Ottoman Empire, people in the Levant at least had a single government and freedom of movement within their region. For example, to travel by land from Jerusalem to Beirut, less than two hundred miles apart along the coast, they did not have to use an indirect route through 'Amman and Damascus, crossing three international boundaries—the situation after 1948. Despite sectarian tensions, the relative relaxation of the late-nineteenth-century Levant was a clear contrast to the pressures and claustrophobia of the fractured Levant of the so-called "Age of Globalization," at the outset of the twenty-first century.

PANORAMA: FROM THE ROMANS TO THE OTTOMANS

The usual political status of the Levant through the past two millennia has been subjection to larger empires. Indeed, such subjection has characterized sixteen of these twenty centuries, broken only by two periods of political fragmentation—three centuries in medieval times and the half-century of the contemporary state system.

Between the arrival of Pompey's army in Cilicia in 63 B.C.E., inaugurating Roman domination, and the collapse of Ottoman rule with the British advance from Egypt in 1917–18, the history of the Levant exhibited a measure of symmetry. It was bounded at the beginning and end, respectively, by centuries of Roman and Ottoman overlordship from the distant capitals of Rome and Constantinople/Istanbul. The Romans and Ottomans both had wider concerns in Europe and the Mediterranean. In contrast, through the middle centuries between the Arab-Islamic conquest from the south in 636–38 and the swift Ottoman thrust from the north in 1517, the Levant was mainly ruled from within or from its Middle Eastern neighborhood.

For about a century after the Islamic conquest, the Umayyad Caliphate, based in Damascus, commanded a domain stretching from the Atlantic to Central Asia, the only time the Levant has itself been an imperial center. After the Umayyads gave way to the 'Abbasids in 750, the capital shifted to Baghdad, and the Levant reverted to provincial status. In the tenth century, 'Abbasid control weakened, the Islamic empire disaggregated into regional states, and the Byzantines reconquered northern Syria.

Through the following three centuries the Levant was fragmented, most prominently in the twelfth and thirteenth centuries, when the Western European Crusaders established several states on the eastern

Mediterranean littoral. The interplay among the Crusaders, local Muslim principalities, the Byzantines, and the Armenians provides the closest historical parallel to modern geopolitics.

In the late thirteenth century, with the rise of the Egyptian Mamluks and their blockage of the Mongols, the Levant again came under a single imperial authority, this time based in Cairo. Egyptian Mamluk concerns in the Levant make an interesting comparison with those of the Iraq-based 'Abbasids. More generally, the two centuries of Mamluk rule exhibit parallels with the earlier Umayyad-'Abbasid hegemony.

In both periods, a single Islamic authority commanded the territory between Cilicia and Sinai, but with hostilities on the Anatolian margins, fear of seaborne raids, and episodes of internal conflict. For the Umayyads and 'Abbasids, the Byzantines were the main enemy, by land and sea. The Mamluks confronted the Mongols and, after the 1450s, the Ottoman Turks to the north. In the late thirteenth century, after expelling the Crusaders, they razed coastal fortifications to deter any Western European return.

Otherwise, however, the strategic emphasis differed. The Umayyads and 'Abbasids concentrated their military attention on the Cilician frontier with Byzantium, where they usually had the initiative up to the ninth century. Away from the Byzantines, local factionalism was the main preoccupation in the Levant. The region was not critical to the 'Abbasid power base in Iraq, which was buffered by the Syrian steppe to the west but vulnerable to threats from the Iranian plateau.

In contrast, after 1250 the Levant covered the eastern approaches to Mamluk Egypt, and Mamluk control of Palestine and Transjordan was critical for the security of Cairo. For the Mamluks, every part of the Levant had military salience. Aleppo and the north were the first line of defense and the base for attacks against the Mongols and their Armenian allies. Damascus and the Lebanese mountains were crucial for holding the region together under Mamluk rule. Palestine guarded Egypt, and its Mamluk administration centered on Gaza and the old Crusader fortresses of Safed and Karak—obvious strategic locations.

The Ottoman capture of the Levant and Egypt in 1517 marked a return to the environment of the Roman period. First, with the whole eastern Mediterranean dominated by one power, the Anatolian margins and the approaches to Egypt no longer had strategic significance. Second, the main security problems in the region from 1517 until Bonaparte's invasion of Egypt in 1798 were, as during the first three centuries of Roman rule, suppressing local dissidence and policing the desert frontier. Jewish, Samaritan, and Palmyrene challenges to Roman rule might be compared to Ottoman difficulties with Mount Lebanon and over-mighty provincial governors.

In both the Ottoman and Roman cases, hostile forces almost never threatened the Levant until the last century of control by these empires. Before the late eighteenth century, the only hint of invasion of the Ottoman Levant was a plan by Shah 'Abbas to follow up his capture of Baghdad in 1624 by proceeding to Aleppo. However, this scheme came to nothing. Similarly, the penetrations of northern Syria by the Sassanid Persian monarch Shapur I in the 250s were the only time a foreign army appeared in the Roman Levant between the establishment of Roman authority in the first century B.C.E. and the Sassanid sack of Antioch in 540.

Ottoman and Roman circumstances differed in that the Romans maintained a more elaborate military presence within the Levant and had to cope with a more troublesome land front after the conquest of the Jazira by Septimius Severus in 197–98. Within the Levant, the Ottomans had problems with the mountain peasants and the steppe nomads, but did not face any local military challenge as serious as that presented to the Romans by the bitterly alienated Jews of Judea.

To the east, although both the Romans and the Ottomans confronted the power occupying the Iranian plateau, for Rome the Jazira represented the frontier with the main enemy. Here the command of the Tigris-Euphrates flood plain (modern Iraq) was crucial. Sassanid Persia, with its capital at Ctesiphon, near Baghdad, ruled the eastern part of the "fertile crescent" as well as the Iranian plateau. The Sassanids therefore impinged on the Roman Levant. In contrast, after the conquest of Baghdad by Süleyman the Magnificent in 1534, the Ottomans commanded Iraq until 1917, with the exception of an Iranian reappearance in 1624–38. The "front" between the Ottomans and Safavid Iran was thus more removed from the Levant than the Roman-Sassanid battle arena. Consequently, whereas the Levant was always a

Roman military preoccupation, whether for internal or external reasons, it was a military backwater for the Ottomans, at least until Bonaparte's intervention in Egypt.

Roman and Ottoman rule in the Levant both collapsed within about a century of the onset of major crises, in the 540s and the early nineteenth century respectively. In the 540s, a Persian invasion was followed by the first bubonic plague epidemic in the Mediterranean. Antioch, the major city of Syria, never recovered from the double blow, made worse by earthquakes in 526 and 588. The plague altered the balance of power in the Middle East, because it affected the port cities of the East Roman Empire more severely than the less urbanized lands of Arabia and Sassanid Persia. The erosion of Roman resources made the Levant more vulnerable, and this was reflected in the Persian occupation of the region between 603 and 628. The Romans were only beginning to restore their presence when they had to face the Muslim invasion in the 630s.

As for the Ottomans, the loss of Egypt after 1798, with the French seizure followed by the autonomous rule of Muhammad 'Ali, coincided with the Wahhabi rebellion in Arabia. Further, the de facto independence of Egypt meant that the Levant was a military frontier for the first time since 1517—in 1831 the Egyptian army temporarily seized the whole area up to Cilicia. The Ottomans, unlike the Romans, managed an impressive reassertion of their authority in their last decades. Nonetheless, the Maronite Catholics effectively detached Mount Lebanon, while Palestine remained exposed to the south with the British takeover of Egypt in 1882. When the Ottomans joined Germany in the First World War the Levant became a front line, with a British thrust across Sinai and Bedouin raids from Arabia. The final British breakthrough at Megiddo in September 1918 was as dramatic as the Muslim victory over the Romans in 636, with the Turks falling back 400 miles to the Anatolian margins within a few weeks.

CHAPTER TWO

ROME, ISLAM, AND BYZANTIUM

The Roman Levant

Roman forces reached the northern Levant in the 60s B.C.E. as part of an effort by the Roman republican regime to consolidate its command of the Mediterranean, after expansion across Greece into Asia Minor. In 63 B.C.E. Pompey executed commissions to rid the Mediterranean of pirates and to defeat Mithridates, the king of Pontus in northeast Asia Minor. The war against the pirates brought Pompey's fleet to Cilicia, where "the most formidable of the pirates" retreated to "castles and fortresses near the Taurus mountains."[20] Following their surrender, Cilicia became Roman territory. The war against Mithridates brought Pompey's army to the Euphrates, where he found that the collapse of Seleucid authority had left a power vacuum in Syria.

According to Plutarch, writing in the time of Trajan, Pompey had a "consuming passion" to reach the Red Sea "so that he might extend his conquests to the ocean that surrounds the world on all sides."[21] Pompey led his army into Syria and declared it a Roman province "since this country had no legitimate kings of its own."[22] He then subjugated the Jewish Hasmonean Kingdom in Judea and extracted the submission of "the King of the Arabs round Petra." Pompey also received an embassy from the Parthian monarch of Persia, who "suggested that the Euphrates be considered the boundary between his empire and that of the Romans."[23] This became a consistent Persian demand through the following six centuries, and Roman dismissal of it brought much grief.

The Roman annexation of Egypt with the defeat of Antony and Cleopatra by Octavian (Augustus) in 30 B.C.E. increased the significance of the Levant as the land bridge between Asia Minor and North Africa. The Romans preferred to move their legions from Europe to the east, and within the eastern Mediterranean, by land rather than sea because of the risks of sea transport, especially in winter. From this point on, the Romans could not tolerate any challenge in Syria and Judea, though they allowed the existing local authorities to continue to exist as tributaries. Until the late first century C.E. the Roman presence in the Levant consisted almost entirely of military personnel, and in much of the region it was convenient to administer the population through local rulers.

From the geopolitical perspective, Roman rule in the Levant may be divided into two periods. Up to the extensions of Roman territory across the Euphrates in 165 and 197–98, the main security preoccupation was what Millar terms the "inner frontier"[24]—the truculent populations of the uplands separating the coast from the interior, above all the Jews of Judea. Rome and the Parthians of Persia competed for hegemony over the Armenians in the difficult terrain of eastern Anatolia, but further south a status quo satisfactory to both sides was generally maintained on the Euphrates.

A temporary Roman occupation of Iraq by Trajan in 114 illustrated Rome's impetus to emulate Alexander, but in 117 Hadrian abandoned the expansion as unsustainable. The Parthians themselves never penetrated the Levant in the first two centuries C.E. The establishment of Roman provinces in the Jazira, a little before the Sassanids displaced the Parthians as rulers of Persia in 220, altered the strategic environment. From about 200 on, the Roman emphasis, with the "inner frontier" subdued, was on the "outer frontier" facing Sassanid Persia in the north and the Arab nomads along the desert margins.

Map 3 depicts the organization of the Roman Levant between the time of Augustus and that of Nero. The Romans permanently stationed three legions in the north, in the military province of Syria, but until the 60s C.E., administration of the southern Levant mixed Roman rule with management by local agents, varying from time to time and from place to place. The Romans asserted sovereignty and sometimes collected taxes, but tried to operate without maintaining a large military presence south of Mount Lebanon.

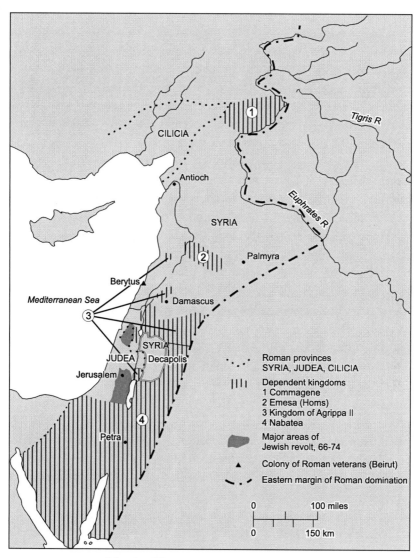

Map 3—The Roman Levant, ca. 70 C.E.

Data sources: Isaac, 1992; Millar, 1993; Talbert, 1985; Talbert, 2000.

The mountain ranges of modern Lebanon, controlled in the early decades of Roman penetration by unruly tribes known as Ituraeans, presented the Romans with a security problem. The Ituraeans practiced banditry against the settled population of the coast and threatened the coastal route linking Asia Minor with Egypt. Then, as now, Mount Lebanon was the pivot of the Levant, separating Syria from Palestine, and Roman command of the region would be vulnerable until the Ituraeans were neutralized. In 14 B.C.E. Rome established a colony of army veterans at Beirut, the only significant Latin settlement ever planted in the Roman Levant. According to Issac, this was to provide a friendly base for military operations in the mountains by the regular army—the veterans themselves could not be expected to take such initiatives.[25] Veteran settlement extended to the Biqa', where Ba'albak (Heliopolis) also served as a military base. Subjugation of Mount Lebanon took some time. Roman forces conducted expeditions against Ituraean strongholds at least into the first century C.E.[26]

To the south, the Jews of the Judean uplands resented Roman liquidation of their hard-won independence from the Seleucids. Judea remained a subject kingdom until 6 C.E., when it was made a Roman province. Claudius transferred it to Agrippa in 41, as a reward for backing his accession, but it reverted to direct Roman control with Agrippa's death in 44. The combination of popular hostility against Rome and the absence of Roman armed force led to full-scale insurrection in Judea, Samaria, and the Galilee in 66. The mountainous terrain, the size of the Jewish population, which may have numbered more than one million,[27] and the unique "national" character of the rebellion made the Jewish war of 66–74 the most severe test of Rome's command of a province. The Roman historian Tacitus indicates that Rome assembled almost its entire eastern Mediterranean military capability for the siege of Jerusalem in 70.[28]

The Jewish war demonstrated two enduring features of the geopolitics of the Levant: the salience of the mountains and the fractiousness of the population. The desperate sieges of hilltop redoubts and cities leave no doubt of Roman realization of the dire consequences of not re-establishing Roman supremacy in Judea. The hills of Judea and Samaria dominate the coastal plain and the main land route from Syria to Egypt. Jewish success would have crippled Roman prestige and probably allowed Parthian Persia a bridgehead threatening Egypt, through an alliance with the Jews.

As for the population, the war illustrated both the cleavage between the Jews and the rest of the inhabitants of the Roman Levant and the lack of cohesion among the Jews themselves. Tacitus notes Roman mobilization of "strong levies of Arabs, who felt for the Jews the hatred common between neighbours."[29] Josephus, author of the best contemporary account of developments in the first-century Levant, refers to the eagerness of "the people of Damascus . . . to exterminate the Jews in their midst."[30]

Josephus also comments repeatedly on destructive factionalism among the Jews. In the early stages of the war "every town was seething with turmoil . . . As soon as the Romans gave them a breathing-space they turned their hands against each other."[31] During the Roman siege of Jerusalem "internal strife continued to rage . . . between [the factions] the people were being torn to pieces like a great carcase."[32] These descriptions of the Jewish situation almost 2,000 years ago could be translated without modifying a word to the internecine warfare within the Shi'ite and Maronite communities of Lebanon in 1988–90.

For the Romans, the lesson taken from the Jewish revolt was the necessity of direct Roman rule throughout the Levant. Rome was lucky not to have problems with the Parthians and Armenians when it stripped its forces in Syria and Asia Minor to deal with Judea. In the early 70s, the Roman governor of Syria invaded Commagene and converted it into a Roman province. Josephus describes the capital of this tributary kingdom, Samosata, as "lying on the Euphrates, making it very easy for the Parthians, if they had a mind to it, to get across."[33] At the same time, the Romans also terminated the autonomy of Emesa (Homs), which covered an important segment of the desert fringe in the northern Levant. Similarly, when Agrippa II died in the 90s his various domains were absorbed into the provinces of Syria and Judea. Finally, in 114, a Roman detachment marched into the tributary kingdom of Nabatea, which Rome combined with the Transjordan cities of the "Decapolis" to form the new province of "Arabia."

> While traveling in the Jazira, I have found that inspecting the landscape between the Euphrates and Tigris rivers helps to clarify why the Romans found the Euphrates an unsatisfactory frontier, and why they extended their territory so far beyond it. First, at Zeugma and al-Bira (Birecek), the main river crossing from the east, higher ground dominates the Euphrates on the eastern bank and the river does not present a difficult obstacle, especially during low flow in late summer and fall. It was therefore not an impressive natural defense for the Romans. Second, the fertile grassland of the Jazira, both the elevated portions north of Şanlıurfa (Edessa) and the lower plain, is a tempting prospect for conquest. Third, once across the Euphrates there is no good stopping point short of the hills around Mardin, about 150 miles to the east. Unlike the Romans, the Mamluks had to make do with the Euphrates when facing the Mongols in the thirteenth century, but they took care to secure a fortified rock outcrop at al-Bira as a foothold on the eastern bank.

In Judea itself, the Romans razed the walls of Jerusalem after the siege, except for fortifications for the Roman garrison. From 70 until the third century, Judea (Syria Palaestina after 139: map 4) hosted the largest military occupation force of any Roman province not on the imperial frontiers. This presence, however, did not prevent a second Jewish uprising in 132–35. Again Rome lost control of parts of Judea for several years. Again the Romans considered the revolt a challenge to the integrity of the empire; the Emperor Hadrian came in person and suppression of the Bar Kokhba rebels required four legions.

Thereafter Jerusalem was rebuilt as the Roman colony of Aelia Capitolina, at first pagan but increasingly Christian by the fourth century, and Jews were excluded from the city and the surrounding Judean highlands. From this time on, the main Jewish population was in the Galilee and the Golan, and the majority of the inhabitants of central Palestine were non-Jewish—Samaritans, Semites of Greek culture ("Syrians"), Arabs, and Romans.

Pax Romana?

In the late second century, the strategic emphasis shifted north and east (map 4). In 165, Lucius Verus led a campaign across the Euphrates

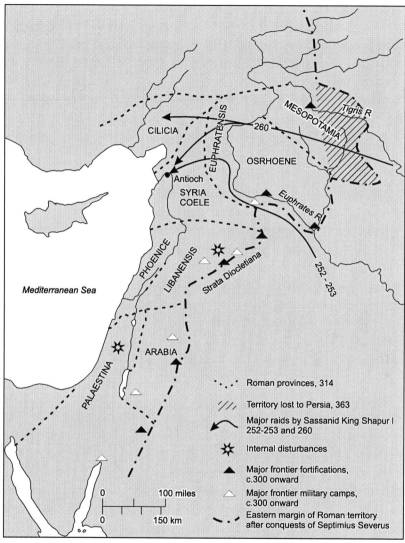

Map 4—The Late Roman Levant, ca. 200–600

Data sources: Isaac, 1992: Jones, 1964; Millar, 1993;
Talbert, 1985; Talbert, 2000; Treadgold, 1997.

into the Jazira and Iraq. Rome thereby acquired a solid foothold in the Jazira for the first time—the small vassal kingdom of Osrhoene on the east bank of the Euphrates, which included the town of Edessa (modern Şanlıurfa). In 197–98, Septimius Severus, who had contemplated the grasslands across the Euphrates as commander of the legion based at the river frontier post of Zeugma in the 180s,[34] extended Roman territory eastward. After a successful war against Persia, he pushed the frontier across the Khabur River, most of the way to the upper Tigris. He based two legions in the new province of Mesopotamia.

Severus claimed that he was establishing a buffer for Syria,[35] but in fact he stripped away Persia's cover for lower Iraq, including the Persian capital at Ctesiphon. This guaranteed perpetual hostilities between the two empires when the Parthians gave way to the more energetic Sassanid dynasty in Persia in 220. The Sassanids were determined to drive the Romans back to the Euphrates, and through the following four centuries border warfare gradually became more intensive. The Sassanids could invade the Roman Jazira or probe around its flanks to the north, exploiting difficulties between Rome and the Armenians of eastern Anatolia, and the south, encouraging desert nomads to raid the central Levant.

In the early third century, Rome maintained about eleven legions on its eastern frontier: two in eastern Anatolia (Cappadocia), six in the Jazira and Syria, and three in the southern Levant (Palestine and Transjordan).[36] This was at least one-third of the regular forces of the empire and equal to the commitment along the Rhine and Danube. The deployment reflected the shift in priorities from Palestine toward the Jazira front and its flanks.

At the same time, Severus reformed provincial administration in the Levant, cutting the large province of Syria into two units because his rival for control of the empire, Pescennius Niger, had used the three Syrian legions as a power base. Henceforth no provincial governor would have more than two legions. The expansion into the Jazira and the frequent presence of the emperor on the Persian front also elevated the status of Antioch as the chief city of the Levant, despite its peripheral location. Antioch was located at the intersection of the land route from Europe through Anatolia to the Jazira with the sea route through its port of Seleucia; the Persian wars made it a second imperial capital after Rome and, later, Constantinople.

Between 235 and 285, the Levant shared in the general turmoil of the empire as central government faltered amid a bewildering succession of rulers and revolts. Anarchy, currency debasement, and ruthless tax exactions caused inflation, famine, and population decline.[37] The Palestinian Jews, however, did not again challenge the Roman state. Although they were still the largest community in the southern Levant, they were no longer a majority and had lost their former strategic position in the Judean highlands. The Jewish patriarchate, which led the community after the Bar Kokhba defeat, maintained an accommodation with the Roman authorities, and through the third century economic distress demoralized the ordinary people, both Jews and non-Jews. Civil wars and rural insecurity also compelled towns in Syria and Palestine to begin building walls.[38]

The Sassanids of Persia took advantage of the Roman crisis. In the 250s, Shapur I twice raided into northern Syria and briefly seized Antioch. Shapur used routes along the south bank of the Euphrates—the desert fringe—and through the heart of the Jazira (map 4). In 260, he captured the Emperor Valerian. For twelve years thereafter no Roman emperor appeared in the Levant.

Fortunately for Rome, Odenathus, a leading citizen of the oasis town of Palmyra, salvaged the situation on the Persian front. Immediately after Valerian's loss, Odenathus organized a force that defeated Shapur's army while the latter was withdrawing across the Euphrates. Palmyra, part of Roman Syria since Pompey's time, guarded the desert fringe and the western end of the caravan route from Iraq. Odenathus was a member of a distinguished Palmyrene family and a Roman senator. In the early 260s, he helped clear the Persians from Roman Mesopotamia, raided as far as Ctesiphon, and commanded Roman forces in Syria. After his murder in 267, his wife Zenobia and son Vabalathus took charge in Palmyra. Vabalathus claimed imperial rank, invaded Egypt, and occupied northern Syria, including Antioch.

Unlike the Jewish rebellion, the Palmyrene assertion was not an attempt to secede from the empire—it was a bid for precedence within the Roman state facilitated by the allegiance of Roman forces to the

Palmyrene pretenders. In 272, the Emperor Aurelian marched through Anatolia and restored imperial authority in the Levant. He captured Zenobia and left a garrison in Palmyra. The brief rise of a frontier settlement, with the status of a Roman colony, to become the center of a substantial part of the empire in opposition to Rome is unique in Roman history. It involved a chance combination of Palmyra's wealth from the caravan trade with local initiative in the midst of the dislocation caused by Shapur's invasion.[39]

Map 4 shows the main features of the Roman Levant after the mid-third century. The Emperor Diocletian stabilized the empire's internal affairs after his accession in 285, and in the 290s he established the military distribution along the eastern frontier that was to prevail with limited adjustments until the seventh century.[40] In the Jazira, Diocletian and his successors emphasized fortified towns that would hold out to the rear of any Persian advance. Roman strategy after the third century was to tolerate Persian penetration while withdrawing the peasant population into urban redoubts and torching the grasslands to deny sustenance to the enemy.[41] The Persians would thus encounter major Roman field forces only when their logistics were extended, their supplies limited, and their rear endangered by unconquered Roman strongholds.

Border warfare in the mid-fourth century was regular and destructive, with both sides making thrusts in eastern Mesopotamia. It culminated in an abortive Roman invasion of Iraq in 363 during which the Emperor Julian was killed and Persia's own "scorched earth" policy caused a supply crisis for the Roman army.[42] To extricate the army, Julian's successor Jovian ceded Nisibis and a wide tract of eastern Mesopotamia to Persia. This proved a permanent loss, but the shortening of the frontier and the establishment of a more convenient division of the Armenians between Rome and Persia in 386 contributed to long truces up to the sixth century.

South of the Euphrates, Diocletian and his successors made an impressive military investment along the desert frontier to Eilat on the Gulf of Aqaba. This began with the "Strata Diocletiana," forts and garrison camps along the road from the Euphrates through Palmyra to Damascus (map 4). It continued with an upgrading of facilities on the eastern margin of the province of Arabia. By the early fourth century it seems that elements or the whole of eight legions were stationed on the desert margins—four on the "Strata Diocletiana" and four in Transjordan.[43] Even given the smaller size of Roman legions by this period,[44] the deployment reflected a new emphasis on the desert margins vis-à-vis the main Persian front in the Jazira. As for Eilat, Stemberger notes that increasing disruption of the land trade through Persian Iraq to South Asia made it important to safeguard the Red Sea passage to the Indian Ocean.[45]

Inauguration of these arrangements coincided with the first Roman campaign against Arabian desert nomads ("Saraceni") in about 290, but it is difficult to believe that problems with these nomads were sufficient to explain the frontier investment. It would seem more plausible to cite a combination of factors. First, the Persians themselves had already marched up the south bank of the Euphrates to threaten Syria in 253, and by the fourth century were encouraging nomad raids as an adjunct to warfare in the Jazira. The steppe and desert were thus becoming part of a wider war zone. Second, the area of settled farming was expanding eastward into the steppe both north and south of Damascus. Indeed, by the late Roman period the settlement zone on the Levant's interior plains was probably broader than at any subsequent time up to the late nineteenth century. In consequence, nomads had closer and more attractive targets for their depredations. Third, the "Strata Diocletiana" was a critical communications axis between the southern Levant and Mesopotamia, for both military movement and trade. Certainly it is easy to understand Isaac's perspective that it was more a fortified transport route than a defense line.[46]

Through the fourth and fifth centuries Christianity, the state religion of the empire after the conversion of the Emperor Constantine in 312, gradually became the dominant faith of the people of the Levant. This had security implications in Palestine, where official attitudes hardened toward the Jews of the Galilee and the Samaritans of the highlands north of Jerusalem.[47] In the early 350s, a Roman column crushed the last significant Jewish uprising. The last pagan emperor, Julian, caused a brief sensation when he authorized the rebuilding of the Jewish Temple in Jerusalem in 362, but he died the next year and the

Christians swiftly reasserted their primacy in Judea. Thereafter, Arab nomadic incursions and the situation of the Samaritans were the main security preoccupations in the southern Levant. In the north, perturbations between Christians and pagans in Antioch, and banditry by the Isaurian mountain tribes of western Cilicia, occasionally disturbed local affairs.

Otherwise, the Roman Levant enjoyed exceptional peace and stability, during which population growth made up for the losses caused by the third-century crisis. The Persians were diverted by the Huns and other threats from Central Asia, and in 442 made a treaty with the Romans that lasted for sixty years. With relaxation between the Romans and Persians, raids by desert nomads were more a policing problem than a military threat. The Romans relied on arrangements with Christianized Arab tribes to protect the settled interior from other tribes. In 502, the Emperor Anastasius concluded a treaty with the Ghassanid and Kinda Arabs, resident within the Roman provinces of Arabia and Palestine as well as in the northern Arabian Peninsula, for provision of auxiliary forces for the Roman army.[48]

Overstretched and Overwhelmed

The sixth century opened badly, warfare with Persia being renewed in Mesopotamia in 502–506, but the real deterioration came with the long reign of Justinian (527–65). It is ironic that the dynamism of the greatest late Roman emperor facilitated disasters in the Levant, for more than a century an oasis of calm while barbarian invasions transformed the Mediterranean world. First, Justinian's campaigns in the western Mediterranean removed troops from the east and exposed the Levant to the Persians and nomads. Second, his ambitions overstretched resources at the same time as the bubonic plague curtailed the empire's tax base.

The diversion of troops to Italy in the late 530s allowed the Persian ruler Khusrau to invade Mesopotamia and Syria in 540, and to pillage Antioch. Justinian's able military commander Belisarius restored the territorial situation, but in the early 540s the plague decimated the urban population, while Roman-Persian hostilities ravaged the Jazira.

After 545, the region had a breathing space from the Persians, during which the energetic Bishop of Edessa, Jacob Baradaeus, succeeded in drawing much of the population of Syria and Palestine away from Orthodox Christianity toward the Monophysite version of the faith.[49]

Hostilities with the Persians resumed after Justinian's death. In 572, the Romans patronized an Armenian rebellion against Persia. In the subsequent fighting the Persians captured the border fortress of Dara, the first city in the Roman Jazira to fall to the enemy in two centuries, and raided into Syria.

In 580, the Romans marched into Iraq, but the campaign was aborted when the Roman commander accused his Ghassanid Arab allies of assisting the Persians. This had serious consequences, because the Ghassanids had guarded the frontier of the Levant south of the Euphrates during Justinian's reign, enabling the Romans to transfer forces elsewhere. The Ghassanids held the Lakhmids, Arab allies of the Persians, at bay, and in 575 the Ghassanid leader Mundir even raided the Lakhmid stronghold of Hira,[50] only 100 miles from the Persian capital.

The Roman overthrow of Mundir in 580 provoked the Ghassanids into raiding the provinces of Arabia and Phoenice Libanensis, which they had hitherto protected. They even defeated a Roman regular force at Bostra.[51] The Romans suppressed the rebellion and later restored relations with the Ghassanids, but these developments weakened their Arab friends and left the Levant open to the desert.

The first half of the seventh century witnessed the collapse of the Roman Levant in the midst of almost thirty years of warfare, with the climactic struggle between the Roman and Persian empires followed by the Islamic conquest.

This time the Persians took advantage of a Roman civil war against the usurper Phocas, who overthrew the Emperor Maurice in 603. In 610, a Persian army overran Mesopotamia and inland parts of northern Syria without serious opposition, while Roman rebels held the rest of the Levant. In the same year Heraclius, son of the governor of Africa, sailed from Carthage to Constantinople and deposed Phocas. In 611, the Persians seized northern Syria, including Antioch and Homs, cutting off Anatolia from the southern Levant. Heraclius had no time for a proper response, and in 613 the Romans were driven out of Cilicia, after which the Persians took Damascus and Jerusalem.

For the next fifteen years the Levant was under Persian occupation, a base from which the Persians invaded Egypt and Anatolia, in the latter case aligning with Avars and Slavs surging through the Balkans. The occupation disrupted the economy of the Levant,[52] which was severed from what remained of the Roman Mediterranean. The demographic decline inaugurated by the sixth–century plagues continued. The population of the Levant in the second and fifth centuries, before and after the third–century anarchy, may have exceeded 5 million[53]— neither this population nor the spread of settled farming into the steppe[54] was to be recovered until the twentieth century. Kaegi suggests that the region's population fell by about 40% through the sixth and early seventh centuries.[55]

The Persians punished Christian resistance in Jerusalem by removing part of the population to Persia, and they briefly permitted Jews to resettle in the city. Nonetheless, their main concern was to court the Christian majority. The Persians favored Monophysites at the expense of Orthodox clergy in the church hierarchy, though there is little evidence that the Monophysite population responded positively. In 628, Heraclius mounted a counteroffensive into Iraq via eastern Anatolia, the shattered Persians asked for peace, and the Romans restored their rule in the Levant.

In the early 630s, the Roman Levant could not have been more vulnerable. It no longer had defenses south of the Euphrates, it had no shield of allies or intelligence sources in the Arabian Desert, and the regular forces were deployed in the Jazira facing Persia. Strategic thinking, as so often in history, faced the future with the mentality of the past. No one believed that a fundamental threat to the empire could come out of the south. The first probes of the new Muslim community of Mecca and Medina reached into Transjordan just as the first Roman patrols returned to the old frontier road.

The initial Roman-Muslim clash occurred south of Amman in late 633, when the Muslims apparently interpreted Roman re-entry to the area as preparation to strike at them.[56] Muslim success in taking southern Transjordan stripped away the flank of Roman Palestine. In 634, aided by disgruntlement among Arab tribal allies of the Romans about payment arrears, the Muslims penetrated to Gaza and defeated a small Roman force, killing the Roman commander of Palestine. The Muslims then routed Roman reinforcements headed by the emperor's brother. This opened the Palestinian countryside to Muslim raiding, with Roman troops isolated in the walled towns. In early 636, the Muslims raided north, briefly seizing Damascus and Homs.

Heraclius was now forced to bring the Muslims to battle. An imperial army including Armenian and Arab contingents met a roughly equal Muslim army south of Damascus in mid-636. The site, above the Yarmouk River, commanded fertile plains on the main interior axis between Palestine and Syria. The Muslim commander Khalid Ibn al-Walid, in an unprecedented maneuver, had already brought his cavalry across the desert from Iraq. The Muslims demonstrated that they could combine their desert mobility and cavalry skills with coordination of massed troops in their August 636 defeat of the Romans.

The disaster left Heraclius, probably based in Antioch, no choice but to trade space for time by retreating northward. For the second time in thirty years the East Roman Empire had lost its continuity between Anatolia and Egypt. The victory of the Arab Muslims at Yarmouk gave them the central Levant.

The Muslims encountered a largely unarmed population. The Jews welcomed the end of Christian Roman authority, but by the early seventh century they were only 10–15% of the people of Palestine,[57] and less in Syria. They could look forward to being allowed back into Jerusalem, but not to much else, and certainly not to any political resurgence. There was thus little reason for them to be overjoyed about swapping Christian for Islamic overlordship. Similarly, despite estrangement between Monophysites and the Orthodox Church, Monophysite Christians exhibited various responses to Arab Muslim rule, strongly negative as well as positive. Damascus, for example, resisted the Muslims.[58] The coastal towns of Caesarea, Beirut, Jubayl, and Ladhiqiyya held out until 640, but they were isolated and untenable. As with the Persians in 613, possession of the Levant cleared the way for the Muslims to invade Egypt, where Roman forces were also weak and dispersed after the Persian occupation.

Umayyads and 'Abbasids

The Arab Muslim victories of the late 630s, with Roman Syria and Egypt and the whole of the Persian Empire added to Muslim Arabia to form a new empire, transformed the geopolitics of the Levant. The only opposition came from a rump East Roman state reduced by the end of the seventh century to Anatolia and footholds in the Balkans and southern Italy. Although some historians use the label "Byzantine" to refer to the East Roman Empire after Constantine's transfer of the capital from Rome to Byzantium (Constantinople) in 324, I concur with Whittow in making the shift in terminology coincident with the Muslim conquests. In any case, "Byzantine" is a modern scholarly usage. The people of the empire continued to call themselves "Romans," though in Greek rather than Latin.

Heraclius pulled back in stages to the Taurus Mountains of Cilicia, the barrier behind which East Rome metamorphosed into the medieval Byzantine state.[59] A brief truce in 637, when the Muslims paused for breath in the central and southern Levant, enabled Roman soldiers to retain the Jazira for a couple of years. This provided a pathway through which Christian Arabs escaped into Anatolia. Heraclius perhaps also hoped that it might buffer his Armenian homeland. However, there was no natural line on which to hold the Jazira against superior forces moving up from the south, and the Muslims could not tolerate a wedge across the route between Iraq and the Levant.[60] In 638–39, the Muslim advance resumed with the capture of Antioch and the Jazira towns. Heraclius razed the lowland settlements of Cilicia to create a no-man's land in front of the Taurus as he and his successors concentrated on fortifying the mountain passes.[61]

Umayyad and 'Abbasid history proceeded like Roman history read backward. From the Arab conquest until the 'Abbasids lost their authority in the Levant during the "anarchy" in Iraq in the 860s, the region was united as provinces of the Caliphate, like the Roman situation after the early second century. From the late ninth century, the Levant disintegrated into separate jurisdictions, with diminishing acknowledgement of 'Abbasid authority. This resembled the complexity of the early Roman period, but with a trend away from rather than toward imperial imposition.

As for geography, the main orientation was to the northwest against Byzantium, compared with the Roman orientation to the northeast against Persia. This was a radical change from the Roman military frontiers facing the east and the desert. Further, with the capitals of the Arab-Islamic empire in either Syria or Iraq and the main territorial spread eastward across southwest Asia, the Levant ports declined. The Mediterranean, previously the link west to imperial capitals in Rome and Constantinople, was now the maritime extension of the Muslim/Byzantine war zone.

Map 5 shows the Levant under the Umayyads and 'Abbasids. Internally, the provincial divisions were simpler than in the late Roman period, reflecting population decline and the initial irrelevance of the desert margin. In the 640s, Mu'awiya, the Caliphate's representative in Syria, who in 661 inaugurated Umayyad imperial rule from Damascus, organized the Levant into four military districts (*ajnad,* sing. *jund*). One, based on Homs, served as a command for warfare against the Byzantines. One, based on Damascus, covered the central Levant. Two supervised Palestine, which had elevated significance for communications among Iraq, Syria, and Egypt. All stretched from the coast to the desert. The Jazira had its own governor.

Homs proved too far south of the Taurus to be a good command point. The Homs *jund* was also unwieldy, considering that its governor would not want to be diverted by its local affairs. After 680, the Caliph Yazid founded the new *jund* of Qinnasrin, within which Aleppo became the principal stronghold. Except for Ramla on the Palestinian coastal plain, all the administrative centers were in the interior, on a north-south route connecting Aleppo and Homs to the Umayyad capital at Damascus, and then passing through Tiberias to the Palestinian coast on the easiest route to Egypt. Aleppo provided access to the war zone, which extended from Cilicia to Armenian eastern Anatolia. Aleppo was also the rallying point for troops coming both across the Jazira from Iraq and north from Damascus. In this arena Antioch was less relevant; the chief Roman city of the Levant became a secondary town.

Although the Caliphate generally had the advantage in the struggle

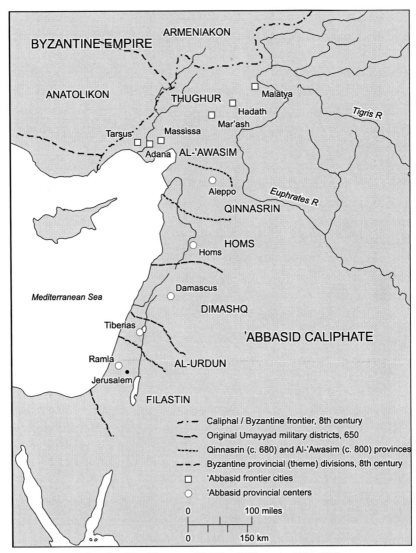

Map 5—The Umayyad/'Abbasid Levant, 700–800

Data sources: Haldon, 1999; Hitti, 1968; Kennedy, 1986; Salibi, 1977; Treadgold, 1997.

with the Byzantines until the defeat of the Arab siege of Constantinople in 718, the frontier on the Taurus stabilized into a marchland of local warlords and mutual raiding expeditions. During the Muslim civil war of 656–61, between the Caliph 'Ali and Mu'awiya, the Emperor Constans II established a defensive system on the Anatolian plateau, with soldiers established on the land up to the frontier and organized into several provincial armies. Decentralized defense, strategic depth, and holding strong points to the rear of invading Muslims helped the Byzantines to secure Anatolia through the late seventh century.[62]

In the 680s, after a reverse inflicted in 677 on Muslim armies that had penetrated to the Sea of Marmara, the Emperor Constantine IV briefly took the offensive against a Caliphate again wracked by civil war. Assisted by the Mardaites, rebellious Christian tribes behind Muslim lines in the Amanus and Lebanon mountains, who harassed Muslim forces in the Syrian interior, Constantine's navy raided along the Levant coast in 685 as far as Ascalon (Ashqelon). In 689, Justinian II recovered much of Cilicia and made a land incursion as far south as Mount Lebanon, again with the aid of the Mardaites and Arabs disaffected from the Caliph 'Abd al-Malik. The Caliphate got rid of its Mardaite problem through an arrangement with the Byzantines by which up to 20,000 Mardaites shifted to Byzantine territory through the late 680s.[63] In the early eighth century, the Umayyads recovered the initiative, with the Byzantines forced out of the Cilician lowlands in 710–12. Thereafter, there were no further significant territorial changes on the northern frontier of the Levant for more than two centuries.

From the 640s to 750, the Levant was an imperial center for the first and only time in its history. Umayyad Syria shone like a bright star, as Damascus became the capital of a new civilization extending east toward India and west toward the Atlantic. Syria, however, paid a terrible price for this brief primacy. The decentralized nature of Umayyad rule meant that the Levant had to carry the main burden of financing the imperial government and armies, with only limited transfers of resources from other parts of the empire. Umayyad caliphs relied heavily on Syrian Arab forces to suppress rebellions in Syria, Arabia, and

Iraq, to confront the Byzantines, and to extend Muslim conquests.

On the one hand, the expenditure of the caliphs and the consumption of the Arab elite had positive effects for inland towns like Jerusalem and Damascus. In 691, 'Abd al-Malik built the first great Islamic shrine, the Dome of the Rock, on the Jewish Temple Mount in Jerusalem, to mark the point where Muslims believe that the Prophet Muhammad ascended to heaven, and to overshadow the Church of the Holy Sepulchre. This emphasized Jerusalem as Islam's third holy city after Mecca and Medina. It also intensified the clustering of holy sites on and around the Herodian Temple platform, now for all three monotheistic religions. 'Abd al-Malik's son, the Caliph al-Walid, added Jerusalem's al-Aqsa mosque, the Umayyad mosque in Damascus, and non-religious buildings. Several caliphs constructed palaces on the steppe margins.

On the other hand, despite such investment, agricultural recovery with improved security, and caravan trade from the east, the Levant remained in decline from its late Roman peak. Even the most able Umayyads could not reverse the effects of the plagues, wars, and collapse of Mediterranean commerce that preceded the Islamic conquest.

In this context, divisions among the Syrian Arabs proved injurious. The Muslims moving out of Arabia into the Levant brought not just their religion and language, but also their tribal feuding, expressed in the old northern-southern split of "Qaysi" and "Yamani."[64] The Arabs who accompanied Mu'awiya into the northern Levant, who settled near Aleppo and in the Jazira, were largely Qaysis. Those entering the central and southern Levant were Yamanis, with links with the Ghassanid Christians. The Caliph Marwan came to power in 683 with Yamani backing, taking Damascus after defeating the Qaysis at Marj Rahit. In the 690s, 'Abd al-Malik balanced between the élite factions while he used Syrian forces to defeat Arab opponents in Iraq. A brother held the Jazira, linking with the Qaysis, while 'Abd al-Malik's son Sulayman held Palestine, linking with the Yamanis.[65] The Umayyads themselves thus became factionalized.

Energetic rulers like al-Walid, 'Umar II, and Hisham enlarged the empire while keeping factionalism at bay through the early eighth century, but the Levant was a weakening base vis-à-vis the population and resources of Iraq. After Hisham's death in 743 the Syrian army, sapped by losses against the Byzantines (740) and the North African Berbers (740–42), disintegrated into Qaysi and Yamani segments. In the late 740s, much of the Levant fell to Yamani rebels, with Marwan II moving his capital to Harran in the Jazira. This coincided with an uprising in eastern Iran in favor of the 'Abbasid branch of the Prophet Muhammad's family, backed by Arabs who wanted renewed Muslim unity and Iraqi and Persian converts who felt sidelined by the Syrian Arabs.

In 749 the 'Abbasid party installed al-Saffah as the first 'Abbasid caliph at Kufa in Iraq. Thereafter the 'Abbasid army defeated Marwan II in northern Iraq and marched across the Jazira to a welcome by the Yamani Arabs in Damascus. Marwan was pursued into Egypt, where he was killed.

Between Iraq and Egypt

The core of the Caliphate now shifted to Iraq, reflecting the increasing weight of the eastern Islamic lands. The Levant returned to provincial status, and the loss of the caliphal court meant a downgrading of Damascus and the other inland towns. In 762, the Caliph Mansur founded Baghdad as the 'Abbasid capital. Egypt, with a similarly large population and taxable wealth, provided the only serious competition to Iraq. Egypt, however, still had only a relatively small Arab and Muslim élite among a Coptic Christian majority and was peripheral in the 'Abbasid Caliphate, especially with the independence of Spain and the Maghrib. Nonetheless, the existence of two power bases within the central Islamic lands—Iraq and Egypt—indicated renewed salience for the Levant, though as an arena between Islamic powers, not a center in its own right.

Under the 'Abbasids, the war-zone with Byzantium was the most prosperous part of the Levant. The Umayyad Caliph Hisham founded garrison cities along the Taurus margins[66]—Tarsus, Adana, Massisa, Mar'ash, Hadath, and Malatya (map 5). These were reinforced by the 'Abbasid Caliphs al-Mahdi (775–85) and Harun al-Rashid (786–809), who encouraged warrior settlers to come from as far as eastern Iran (Khurasan) and the Yemen. Harun al-Rashid organized the settlers into the new province of Al-'Awasim (literally the "guardian fortresses") north of Aleppo (map 5). Settlers got tax breaks and Harun dedicated the revenues of Al-'Awasim—most of northern Syria and the Jazira—to the war against Byzantium, supplemented with caliphal subsidies.[67]

Districts adjacent to the Taurus range, in both Cilicia and the Jazira, were termed Thughur (literally "break-in points"), in which warriors engaged in the holy war would gather in *ribat*s or frontier forts. Raiders (*ghazis*) would assemble every summer for attacks through the mountain passes, with less regular expeditions under the caliph or a senior Muslim commander. The Byzantines organized similar military districts (*kleisourai*), fortresses, and warrior raiders (*akritai*) on their side of the mountains.[68]

Harun al-Rashid took his "holy war" duties seriously, and spent much of his reign in the Jazira. In 781–82 and 806 he led the Caliphate's main forces into Anatolia, with no conclusive result. Indeed, about 810 the Byzantines recaptured Tarsus, which they then held for twenty years, compromising the 'Abbasid defenses. The Caliph al-Ma'mun recovered Tarsus in about 830, and he and his successor al-Mu'tasim used it as their base for expeditions through the Cilician Gates during the 830s, culminating in al-Mu'tasim's sack of the central Anatolian town of Amorion in 838. In the late ninth century Tarsus was an impressive walled city with a permanent population of up to 40,000 and more than 20,000 houses for Muslim warriors from throughout the Caliphate and beyond.[69] Pious endowments provided finances, lodgings, food, and facilities for these warriors. For more than three centuries, from the 640s until the Byzantine resurgence in the mid-tenth century, the northern Levant was the premier external front of the Muslim World.

Behind the front, in the central and southern Levant, urban decay meant autonomy for mountain peasants and increasing prominence for nomadic tribesmen through the 'Abbasid period. Arabic displaced Aramaic as the leading language by late Umayyad times, though the latter persisted for centuries in pockets and as its Syriac written form among Christians, particularly in Lebanon and the Jazira.

Conversion to Islam was slow and uneven. The Umayyads ran a tolerant regime, dependent on revenue from Christians, in 700 still about

80% of the population. Incentives to change religion increased under the 'Abbasids, as disabilities and second-class status for Christians and Jews became more marked, and more Christians moved to Byzantine territory. Nomadic Arabs converted first, sometimes at government insistence, and by 850 the majority in the main towns was probably Muslim.[70] However, it may have been another century before Christians were a minority in the largely rural Levant.

North of Palestine, dissident Islamic beliefs penetrated the mountains from the ninth century on. In parts of the Upper Galilee (Jabal 'Aamil), Mount Lebanon, and the Nusayriya hills, incoming tribes and local converts gave their loyalty to the party of the Caliph 'Ali, in opposition to the official Islam of the 'Abbasids. This divergence paralleled the popularity of heterodox Christianity in the same hills and mountains.

Before 'Alid sympathies took hold in the Syrian hills, a new Christian sect emerged in the Orontes Valley. Followers of the monks of the monastery of Marun espoused the compromise view of human and divine elements in Christ adopted by the Emperor Heraclius in the 630s to reconcile orthodox "double nature" doctrine with the "single nature" (Monophysite) perspective of most Christians in Syria and Egypt.[71] In the event, these "Maronites" became the only upholders of the compromise (two natures in Christ, but a single will), which the main Christian parties rejected. Maronites multiplied under Umayyad rule, and established themselves in northern Mount Lebanon.

The 'Abbasids, who commanded the Levant from Damascus when they commanded the Levant at all, could not afford to leave Mount Lebanon, which flanked Damascus, open to Byzantine subversion. A Maronite uprising in 759–60 indicated the danger.[72] The 'Abbasids maintained garrisons in Beirut and Ba'albak, in addition to the governor's retinue in Damascus.

In such circumstances, the 'Alid Muslims of Jabal 'Aamil and other parts of the Lebanese ranges had regular contact with developments in the wider Islamic world. They aligned themselves with Iraqi Shi'ite beliefs that crystallized with the succession of 'Alid Imams from the martyrdom of 'Ali's son Husayn in 680 to the death of the last revealed Imam in 874. The full Twelver Shi'ite doctrine, including the concept of the twelfth "hidden" Imam, emerged in Baghdad in the 940s. There-after, it is appropriate to refer to a Twelver Shi'ite community in the Lebanese hills.

The Maronites and Shi'ites of the mountains generally lived beyond government control, but they almost never challenged the political order of the Levant under the 'Abbasids or the subsequent Muslim principalities. They lay low and survived to become significant later.

The unravelling of 'Abbasid rule in the Levant during the ninth century reflected chaotic succession struggles in the Iraqi core of the Caliphate, beginning with the contest between al-Amin and al-Ma'mun after the death of their father Harun al-Rashid in 811. At first the challenges in the Levant were from Umayyad pretenders with Yamani Arab tribal support, in Damascus in 811 and in Palestine in 842. At this stage, Qaysi Arabs in northern Syria generally supported the 'Abbasids. New elements entered the picture in the 860s, when imperial authority dissolved during a decade of conflict in the new 'Abbasid capital of Samarra.

On the one hand, Ahmad Ibn Tulun, a Turkish warlord, took com-mand in Egypt, theoretically on behalf of the caliph, and extended his authority into the Levant by crushing local usurpations in Palestine and interior Syria. This inaugurated competition between Egypt and Iraq, especially when Ibn Tulun and his successors asserted leadership of the "holy war" on the Byzantine front and seized Raqqa in the Jazira. On the other hand, the nomadic tribes of the Syrian steppe began to play a larger role in the politics of the region, after prolonged quiescence. The mixture of ambitious Turkish soldiers, the backbone of Muslim armies after the 830s, with Arab tribal reassertion, proved a destabilizing com-bination for the Levant.

In the late ninth century, new tribal groups moved out of northern Arabia to establish themselves in the interior of Syria and Palestine. The Kilab entered the area between Aleppo and Homs, and took the leadership of the Qaysis. Simultaneously, the Tayy entered Transjordan and Palestine, identifying as Yamanis. In between, the older Kalb con-federation maintained their hold on the surrounds of Damascus. Local tribes contested the Kilabi and Tayy intrusions, in fighting that dam-aged settled agriculture, and the Kilabis assisted the Tulunids to suppress a revolt in Homs in 882. In the 890s, the Tayy Arabs disrupted Tulunid control of Palestine. Both the Kilabis and Tayy were increasingly under the influence of the Qarmati (plural Qaramita) Isma'ili Shi'ites of northeast Arabia,[73] who opposed all established Muslim authority.

The Caliph al-Mu'tadid took advantage of Tulunid distress to restore 'Abbasid control of the Jazira and to recover command of the summer raids against Byzantium.[74] In the late 890s the Tulunids gave up all aspirations north of Homs, indicating their desperation about their inability to secure Palestine against the desert. In 902–903, the Qaramita launched tribesmen against Damascus, Homs, and Ba'albak, repeatedly defeating Tulunid troops.[75] The situation was only salvaged by an 'Abbasid army that hastened across the Jazira from Iraq. The 'Abbasid forces smashed the Qaramita near Shayzar and went on to depose the Tulunids in Egypt in 905.

Renewed Abbasid direct rule in Syria and Egypt was, however, short-lived. In 906, the Caliph al-Muktafi' oversaw the defeat of another Qarmati invasion of Palestine and Syria, but not before the Qaramita had sacked Tiberias and devastated the Hawran.[76] After al-Muktafi's death in 908, the 'Abbasid Caliphate went into terminal decline, with the exhaustion of its Iraqi resource base. The early tenth century witnessed a decisive split in the Levant, with Damascus and Palestine subject to Egypt and northern Syria under local control.

In a repeat of the Tulunid adventure, an Iranian soldier by the name of Muhammad Ibn Tughj ascended from 'Abbasid governorships in the *ajnad* of Palestine and Damascus to command of Egypt in the mid-930s. In 937, he successfully defended Egypt from the Fatimid Isma'ili Shi'ites, who had seized much of North Africa. The caliph granted him the Persian royal title of "Ikhshid," and thereafter his family and followers asserted autonomous authority over Egypt and Syria as the Ikhshidids. In these circumstances, the southern Levant guarded Egypt from the east, whether from Baghdad or the Qarmati Isma'ilis, while the northern Levant represented a base for projection of influence toward Iraq. As with the Tulunids, the Ikhshidid claim to the Levant derived from the 'Abbasid practice of joining Egypt and Syria under a super-governor.

In the event, the Ikhshidid representative in Aleppo was overthrown by a Kilabi tribal invasion and in 944, after several years of alternating 'Abbasid and Ikhshidid control, Kilabi leaders offered the Twelver Shi'ite Hamdanid family in Mosul an alliance for ruling northern Syria. The Hamdanids were Arabs from the Taghlib tribe of the Jazira, but relied on Turkish troops. Like the Tulunids and Ikhshidids they had risen in 'Abbasid service and turned a governorship into a de facto principality—in this case Mosul and the Jazira after 935. The ruler of Mosul sent his brother, Sayf al-Dawla, to establish himself in Syria. The infuriated Ikhshidids marched against Sayf al-Dawla as soon as he arrived in Aleppo.

Between 944 and 947, the two sides warred for the Levant. Sayf al-Dawla occupied Damascus, but he was not popular with the towns-folk[77] and the Ikhshidids expelled him and pushed him out of Aleppo as well. Like the Tulunids, however, the Ikhshidids did not have the resources both to hold the northern Levant and to maintain defenses against their Isma'ili Shi'ite enemies—in this case the Fatimids as well as the Qaramita. They negotiated a peace with Sayf al-Dawla by which the Hamdanids kept Aleppo and Homs.

Islamic Fragmentation

By the mid-tenth century, splintering in the Levant was not simply a matter of the Hamdanid-Ikhshidid division. Insecurity in Iraq and the Persian Gulf together with the Byzantine recovery brought the Eurasian trade back to the Red Sea and the Mediterranean, and the old Levantine coastal towns began to re-emerge. North of Aleppo, the fortresses of al-'Awasim and the Thughur also became more self-governing, though with Hamdanid coordination against the mounting Byzantine challenge. To the northeast, Mosul competed with Kurdish chiefs for command of the Jazira. In Palestine and Syria, the tribal confederations of the steppe continued to menace the urban authorities.

This was all part of the broader disintegration of the Islamic Middle East into regional principalities and tribal regimes, as Iran, Iraq, Arabia, the Levant, Egypt, and North Africa each became distinctive arenas. There was a clear contrast here with the survival of Byzantium as a centralized state, after the mid-ninth century reaching out from its Anatolian core to restore its hegemony in territories stretching from the Danube and southern Italy to Syria and the Caucasus.

Any treatment of the geopolitics of the Levant at the end of the first millennium of the Common Era should consider the difference between the Islamic and Byzantine trajectories at this time. The contrast affected Middle Eastern power relations for about a century after 950, with Syria on the front line. It also illustrates facets of the geography of state and society in the Levant and the wider Middle East that have longer-term significance.

The ultimate Byzantine advantage over the Umayyad and 'Abbasid regimes derived from more robust administrative machinery, the supremacy of orthodox religion in most of the empire, the subordination of the armed forces to the Byzantine state (if not to individual emperors), and the virtually impregnable military position of the Byzantine capital (here the contrast between Constantinople and Baghdad is particularly stark). The advantage also reflected the geographical continuity of settlement across Byzantine territory, through the Balkans and Asia Minor. There were no great wastelands equivalent to the deserts separating the fertile regions of the Middle East. Indeed, the medieval Byzantine advantage can be summarized in one word—coherence. Any survey of the religious diversity, recalcitrant Turkish and tribal soldiery, and bureaucratic disunity of the tenth century Levant, separated from Iraq and even Egypt by extensive wasteland, indicates the vulnerability of Syria to a strong power in Anatolia.

In this context, Ibn Khaldun's depiction of the rise and decay of medieval Middle Eastern regimes is of limited usefulness in understanding the Levantine situation as the Caliphate fragmented into local principalities. Ibn Khaldun describes the initial vigor of tribal or clan solidarity (*'asabiyya*) in establishing medieval Muslim states.[78] Rather than developing enduring institutions, these states remained dependent on such *'asabiyya*, which tended to dissipate after a few generations. Hence the relatively swift succession of Umayyad, 'Abbasid, Tulunid, Ikhshidid, and Hamdanid authorities in Syria between the seventh and tenth centuries is neatly explained.

There are two defects with this simplification of history. First, the *asabiyya* model is inadequate for interpreting 'Abbasid difficulties in maintaining central Islamic authority. The complexity of the 'Abbasid elite and governing institutions cannot be reduced to the workings of "tribal solidarity." Second, the failure of the various regimes owed more to weakness in mobilizing resources, maintaining cohesion among civil and military elements,[79] and coping with religious opposition than to decline in the "solidarity" of a ruling group. It is here that the comparison with the Byzantine recovery that paralleled the Islamic fragmentation is more instructive than Ibn Khaldun. This has relevance for the modern Levant because of some similarity in the circumstances and suggestion of an updated version of Ibn Khaldun for interpreting late twentieth century states in the Arab Levant.[80]

The Byzantine-Fatimid Standoff

Map 6 depicts the political configuration of the Levant in 1000. The 'Abbasid provincial system shown in map 5 survived into the early tenth century, preserved by the Tulunids. It finally disappeared with the Hamdanid-Ikhshidid division, the Byzantine breakthrough in the Thughur, and the resurrection of the port cities. In 969 the new order, which was to persist for one century, took shape with the Fatimid capture of Egypt at the same time as the Byzantines seized Antioch and coastal Syria. The northern Levant came under Byzantine influence, while the Fatimids moved into Palestine and Damascus. Autonomous local rulers, including the Hamdanids in Aleppo and the emir of Tripoli, maneuvered under the umbrella of the two great powers. The Byzantines and Fatimids tested each other, and in the eleventh century established a truce. Byzantium was the stronger of the two, but it had preoccupations in the Balkans and Italy and was satisfied with its frontiers in the Levant after the recovery of Antioch and Ladhiqiyya.

Byzantine advances into the Thughur began in 900–902, when the Emperor Leo VI extended imperial territory into Muslim-aligned Armenia in the north and raided through Cilicia in the south, temporarily capturing Tarsus. The basis for expansion in the east was the growth in Byzantine resources gained through advances in the Balkans after 805, along with initiatives by the capable Macedonian emperors

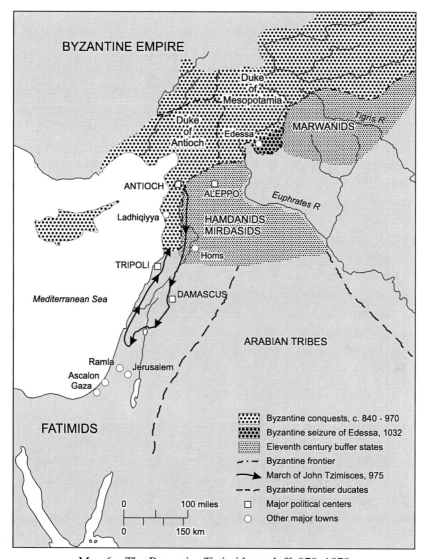

Map 6—The Byzantine/Fatimid standoff, 970–1070

Data sources: Haldon, 1999; Ostrogorsky, 1968; Treadgold, 1997; Parker, 1993; Whittow, 1996.

after 867. In the 930s, the Byzantines received important reinforcement when 12,000 of the Taghlib Arab tribesmen of the Jazira crossed
the frontier, fleeing from the taxes of their Hamdanid kinsmen.[81]

In 934, a Byzantine army captured Malatya, linchpin of the Thughur
of the Jazira. Through the 940s, Sayf al-Dawla of Aleppo earned
renown in the Muslim world for stemming the tide. However, apart
from the continued arrival of volunteers, he received no support from
Iraq or anywhere else. It was, therefore, a hopeless holding operation
against the most formidable army in the tenth century world.

Between 957 and 969, the Muslim front collapsed under Byzantine
hammer-blows. Hadath and Samosata fell in 957–58, and in 962 the
Byzantines marched 150 miles into Syria to sack Aleppo and chase
Sayf al-Dawla out of his own capital. In August 965, the Emperor
Nicephorus Phocus accepted the surrender of Tarsus after a "textbook"
siege,[82] and then overran Cilicia. The fall of the greatest Muslim frontier city reverberated through the Islamic world, but efforts to raise
relief armies only caused strife in Baghdad and the Jazira. From 965 to
969, the Byzantines extended their control down the Syrian coast as far
as the Homs gap, recovered Antioch, and established themselves in the
Orontes valley. Sayf al-Dawla died in 967, and under his son, Hamdanid Aleppo became a Byzantine protectorate, paying an annual tribute.

Sometime in the late tenth century, the Byzantines decided to shift
from conquest to consolidation in the Levant. Whittow attributes this
to a transfer of power in the Byzantine state from the Anatolian military families to the civil aristocracy of Constantinople under the
Emperor Basil II (975–1025).[83] There were, however, indications that
the change in emphasis occurred earlier, under the Emperor John
Tzimisces. In 975, Tzimisces took the main field army south to
Caesarea, in central Palestine, and accepted the submission of Beirut
and Damascus. He then returned to Byzantine territory without dis-
playing any serious wish to annex Mount Lebanon or southern Syria.

The disincentives were considerable. First, Byzantium already had
a well-stocked larder of acquisitions. Second, further seizures of lands
with Muslim majorities or large numbers of non-Greek Christians
posed demographic problems.[84] Third, pushing toward the southern
Levant meant an exposed flank against Muslim Iraq as well as perpet-

ual hostilities with Egypt. Byzantium had other enemies on other fronts, and knew about strategic overstretch. Jerusalem, more than three centuries after it had been lost, did not entice the leaders of the world's major Christian power.

Nicephorus Phocas inaugurated a demographic transformation in the northern Levant that continued under his successors. Muslims departed, and Christians flocked north from the Muslim Levant. In addition, many Armenians moved from eastern Anatolia into Cilicia[85] —a planned migration that inadvertently laid the foundations for a new Armenian state. Throughout the eastern Mediterranean, Byzantium beckoned as the superpower of the age, a remarkable comeback for the East Roman state. Jews as well as Christians left Palestine and Egypt,[86] attracted by the relative tolerance and commercial opportunities under Basil II, and hastened on their way by persecution by the Fatimid Caliph al-Hakim.

The Byzantine alignment in the Levant was stable from 969 to 1071. It comprised two geographical elements. First, the boundary of the new imperial territories bisected northern Syria, as indicated in map 6. The Byzantine government organized these territories into eighteen small military provinces (*themes*) along the Syrian coast and on either side of the Euphrates, grouped into three ducates. The ports of Ladhiqiyya and Baniyas flourished under Byzantine authority. Second, given the lack of defensible topography on the north Syrian plain away from the coastal ranges, the Byzantines used neighboring Islamic principalities—particularly Hamdanid Aleppo and Marwanid Mayyafariqin—as buffer states.

Détente in the Eastern Mediterranean

While the Byzantines consolidated their position in the north, the situation in Damascus and Palestine was in turmoil for a decade after the Fatimids displaced the Ikhshidids in Egypt in 969. Fatimid Egypt, with its Isma'ili Shi'ite caliph challenging his Sunni counterpart in Iraq, could not afford to leave the southern Levant open to its rivals.

Qarmati Shi'ite tribesmen filled the vacuum in Palestine left by the Ikhshidid collapse, and a Turkish chieftain, Alptakin, took charge of

Damascus and the Lebanese coast. In 978, the Fatimid Caliph al-'Aziz led an army into Palestine and defeated Alptakin and his Qarmati allies. Thereafter the Qaramita broke up, while Alptakin entered Fatimid service with a large Turkish retinue, introducing a balance to the North African Berber troops. The Fatimids, however, then had to deal with insubordinate Tayy Bedouin tribesmen within Palestine, an incursion into the Levant by 'Uqayl Arab tribesmen from Mosul, and defiance from the townspeople of Damascus, who reacted badly to their initial taste of Berber rule.

These troubles indicated the danger to Fatimid Egypt in the event of any challenge from the Twelver Shi'ite Buyids in Iraq, who guarded the 'Abbasid caliph after descending on Baghdad from the Iranian plateau in the 940s. In 980–81, the Fatimids exploited the old Yamani-Qaysi tribal rivalry to overturn the Tayy hold on rural Palestine with the assistance of the Qaysi Bedouin rivals of the Tayy. At the same time, they sent an army to Damascus. The Damascenes submitted when they saw that a Turk rather than a Berber was in command.

Fatimid rule of the southern Levant rested as much on naval forces as on land power. The revival of Mediterranean trade proceeded apace in Fatimid times, with triangular commerce linking Fatimid Egypt, Byzantium, and the rising Italian cities. For the first time since the Islamic conquest, the old coastal towns of Palestine and Lebanon resumed their role as the economic hinge of the Levant. The Fatimids established bridgeheads in Gaza, Ascalon, Sidon, and Tripoli, supplied by sea from Egypt. These made difficulties in the interior, especially in Damascus, easier to confront. Fatimid governors were based in the main ports as well as in Damascus and Ramla, a novelty when compared with the Umayyad and 'Abbasid periods. Under the Fatimids, Tripoli became a military and political center equivalent to Damascus.

Away from the coast, the Fatimids sought to keep the tribesmen subdued and to maintain a firm grip on such towns as Jerusalem, Tiberias, Ba'albak, and—above all—Damascus. Much of Palestine prospered, but Bedouin penetration damaged some areas; Ramla steadily declined and the Crusaders found it deserted when they reached the town in 1099.[87] Peasants around Damascus also suffered from depredations by desert nomads, but the city itself survived in a reduced condition. The

Fatimids had to rule Damascus if they were to dominate the region south of the Byzantine alignment—or even defend Palestine.

Hamdanid Aleppo was the most prosperous town in the interior in the late tenth century. It was also a potential foothold for any challenge to the Fatimids from Iraq. In the early 990s, the Caliph al-'Aziz decided on an aggressive policy north of Damascus; Fatimid troops seized Homs from its local ruler and advanced into the Orontes valley and toward Aleppo. This led to the first clash between the Fatimids and Byzantines. Aleppo appealed to Constantinople, and in 995 Basil II came in person, forcing the Fatimids to retire to Damascus. In 999, the Fatimids again threatened Aleppo, and this time Basil II responded with a punitive expedition. The Byzantine emperor ransacked Homs and the Lebanese coast, and Tripoli narrowly escaped the same fate.

In 1001, the Fatimids recognized the limits to their capabilities vis-à-vis Byzantium, and negotiated a ten-year truce, accepting Byzantine supremacy in the Orontes valley. Apart from the continuing interference of both powers in Aleppo, the Byzantine-Fatimid status quo became the overriding feature of the geopolitics of the Levant until the arrival of the Seljuk Turks from the east in the late eleventh century. This early version of "détente" suited commercial interests and allowed the Fatimid Caliph al-Hakim to pursue his eccentric religious predilections.

Even when al-Hakim ordered the destruction of the Church of the Holy Sepulchre in Jerusalem in 1009, the Byzantines confined their response to trade sanctions. Of course, the Byzantines may have had a hand in the 1012 Tayy uprising in Palestine, during which the rebels offered to rebuild the Church of the Holy Sepulchre,[88] but al-Hakim restored Fatimid control by bribing the Tayy leader. Between 1015 and 1023, the Fatimids even managed to subject Aleppo to a Fatimid governor, by exploiting factional conflict after the death of the last Hamdanid prince. Basil II was preoccupied in the Balkans.

Al-Hakim's legacy in the Levant was the Druze sect, named after a follower of the caliph who propagated the idea that al-Hakim was more than the normal Isma'ili concept of a divinely guided Imam—that he was in fact God descended to earth. Al-Hakim himself was careful not to become publicly associated with such notions, but his disappearance in 1021, with no body ever found, buttressed the convictions of his devotees. Missionaries from Cairo converted mountain peasants in parts of the Galilee, the Lebanon and Anti-Lebanon ranges, and northern Syria. These peasants were probably already Isma'ili or Twelver Shi'ites. The Druze may have been useful to the Fatimid regime in keeping Mount Lebanon quiet, though there is little indication that the mountain communities were of much interest in the Fatimid period. Al-Hakim's successors frowned on their beliefs. Salibi's work remains the best guide to Fatimid and Seljuk Syria, but his hint that al-Hakim may have deployed the Druze to extend Fatimid influence is probably unsustainable.[89]

Soon after the demise of al-Hakim, the Fatimids faced the most severe tribal challenge to their position in the Levant. In 1023, the Kilabi chief Salih al-Mirdas expelled the Fatimid governor from Aleppo and founded the Mirdasid principality, backed by the Byzantine duke of Antioch. The Kilabis, dominant on the steppe east and south of Aleppo, then established an alliance with the Tayy, who once again seized most of Palestine. Nonetheless, the Fatimids retained Damascus and Tripoli, thereby holding a powerful wedge between the Kilabis and the Tayy. In 1029, the Turkish commander of the Fatimid army, Anushtakin, defeated the Bedouin forces when they came together near Tiberias. Salih al-Mirdas died in the battle, the nomad coalition fell apart for good, and Anushtakin became governor of Damascus.

The main consequence of these developments, apart from confirming Fatimid hegemony from Palestine north to Homs, was to drive Mirdasid Aleppo into the arms of the Byzantines. This occurred despite an incompetent foray against Aleppo by the Emperor Romanus III in 1030, against the advice of his generals. According to the Byzantine historian Michael Psellus, Mirdasid envoys told the emperor "that they had not wanted this war, nor had they given him any pretext for it."[90] Local Byzantine forces, minus the emperor, performed more impressively in the Orontes valley the next year, gaining some outposts. Thereafter Aleppo resumed tribute payments to the Byzantines while the emir of Tripoli, who had just rebelled against the Fatimids, requested an alliance with the empire. Through most of the 1030s the Mirdasid ruler of Aleppo favored the Byzantines and local Christians, which irritated many of his Muslim subjects.[91]

Meanwhile, Byzantine command of the Nusayriya hills provided a protective umbrella under which local 'Alid Muslims gravitated toward a new religious doctrine. In 1032, al-Tabarani, a religious scholar from Aleppo, settled in Ladhiqiyya.[92] He brought the teachings of his grandfather al-Khashibi, a follower of Muhammad Ibn Nusayr, a disciple of the last revealed Shi'ite Imam, Hasan al-'Askari, in Baghdad. Al-Tabarani propagated a fringe Iraqi Shi'ite concept of the divinity of the Caliph 'Ali and the Imams[93]—heretical to both Sunni and Twelver Shi'ite Muslims. Halm notes that through the mid-eleventh century al-Tabarani and his assistants won over the 'Alid peasants of Byzantine coastal Syria,[94] apparently without imperial interference. Byzantium thus played an interesting "godfather" role in the emergence of the Alawite (Nusayri) sect of modern Syria.

Seljuk Turkish Intervention

The mid-eleventh century was at once the high point and the twilight of the Byzantine-Fatimid political order in the Levant. The Christian Empire and the Isma'ili Caliphate were the wealthiest powers of the Middle East, especially compared with the relative poverty of Iraq and Iran. It is certainly worth noting that the Byzantine-Fatimid century in the Levant coincided with a period of passive authority to the east. At the height of their prosperity, however, the Byzantines and Fatimids were themselves politically adrift, with a dangerous slackening in military muscle.

For a time, the two powers had capable commanders in the Levant. On the Fatimid side, Anushtakin provided Damascus with a welcome interlude of competent administration through the 1030s. In 1038, he took advantage of discontent with the Mirdasids in Aleppo to restore Fatimid authority—yet another round of "musical chairs" with Byzantium. On the Byzantine side, George Maniaces guarded the frontier *themes* in the Jazira, reaching across the Euphrates to seize Edessa in 1032. Anushtakin secured Syria and Palestine while intrigue enveloped the boy-Caliph al-Mustansir in Egypt. Maniaces added victories in Sicily to his achievement in the Jazira, and finally marched against Constantinople, infuriated by the subversive behavior of the central government.

Anushtakin died in 1041 in faithful service, while Maniaces was killed during his rebellion in 1043. The Byzantines exploited Fatimid disarray to bring the Mirdasids back to Aleppo, in the final such oscillation. Otherwise, however, strategic conditions swiftly deteriorated for both the Empire and the Caliphate.

To the north, the Byzantines were over-extended toward the Caucasus. The large standing army bequeathed by Basil II may not have been the best instrument for countering the small groups of Turcoman nomads troubling the empire in the east.[95] Whatever the case, in the early 1050s the Emperor Constantine IX demobilized tens of thousands of Armenian provincial troops,[96] the backbone of the Anatolian forces, at the same time that new waves of highly mobile Turcoman horsemen infiltrated eastern Anatolia. Constantine forcibly moved many of the Armenians to Cilicia and the Jazira.[97] From the 1050s, Byzantium maintained defenses facing southward in Syria and the Jazira that were exposed both to invasion of their rear by the Turcomans and to local subversion by the Cilician Armenians.

In the meantime, a new power appeared to the east. In the 1040s, the Seljuk Turks, recently converted to Sunni Islam, overran Iran, and in 1055 they captured Baghdad. The 'Abbasid caliph, for more than a century little more than a figurehead, was now in the hands of committed and dynamic Sunni Muslims. For the first time, the Fatimid Levant faced the prospect of serious pressure from Iraq. This coincided with conflicts in Cairo among military leaders of Berber, Turkish, Arab, and Armenian origin, reflected in political disintegration in Syria and Palestine. Through the 1060s, Aleppo and Damascus slipped out of the Fatimid sphere, while on the coast Tripoli and Tyre asserted themselves as autonomous principalities.

Ironically, Turcoman chiefs entered the Levant by invitation. In 1064, the Mirdasid ruler of Aleppo appealed for Turcoman assistance to offset an influx of Kilabi Arabs, themselves displaced by Turcomans in the Jazira. In 1070, Aleppo formally accepted Seljuk Turkish overlordship, giving the Seljuk Sultan Alp Arslan a forward position in Syria. (On the distinction between "caliph" and "sultan," see p. 197.)

In parallel, Damascus, where the Sunni Muslim townsfolk had never been enthusiastic about the Shi'ite Fatimids, rose in rebellion against Cairo.

Everything came to a head in 1071, a revolutionary year for the Levant. First, the Fatimid commander in Palestine, faced with Arab tribal uprisings as well as the defiance of the Damascus citizenry, invited the Turcoman chief Atsiz into Syria. Atsiz himself laid siege to Damascus, which fell to him in 1075. Second, a disgruntled Berber faction in Cairo invited Alp Arslan to overthrow Fatimid rule in the Levant. The Seljuk sultan crossed the Euphrates in the summer of 1071. Third, as soon as Alp Arslan reached Aleppo he heard that the Byzantine Emperor Romanus IV was leading the main Byzantine field forces against the Turcomans in eastern Anatolia. Alp Arslan immediately marched north and defeated the Byzantines at Manzikert, near Lake Van.

The sultan preferred to give Romanus a generous truce, so that he might return to unfinished business against the Fatimids, but the Constantinople elite foolishly deposed the emperor. Alp Arslan then renewed the war in eastern Anatolia, and Seljuk forces and Turcoman tribes surged through the broken Byzantine lines to the main part of the Anatolian plateau, where the Byzantines had disbanded the provincial defenses.

For the remainder of the eleventh century, the main Seljuk expansion was diverted from the Levant to Anatolia, where the new Seljuk Sultanate of Rum (i.e. "Rome") emerged. This allowed a variety of authorities to continue their competition in Syria and Palestine, and a brief survival of Byzantine and Arab tribal rule in a belt from Cilicia through Aleppo to the Jazira. Antioch and the Byzantine frontier districts had the Turks to their rear and no land connection with the rest of Byzantine territory, while the Arab 'Uqaylids of Mosul administered Aleppo for a few years, with the acquiescence of the Seljuk Sultan Malikshah, based in Isfahan. In 1085, the Anatolian Seljuks seized Cilicia and Antioch in a sweep down from the Taurus, prompting Malikshah's brother Tutush, who had taken Damascus from Atsiz, to march north to prevent his Anatolian rivals from capturing Aleppo. Tutush defeated the Rum Seljuks, but then had to defer to Malikshah, who put Aleppo and Antioch under Seljuk governors.[98]

Seljuk diversion gave the Fatimids the opportunity to recover some-what in the southern Levant, retaking Jerusalem from the Turcomans in 1098 and keeping a Mediterranean beachhead from Gaza as far as Beirut. This maintained cover for Egypt. Tripoli stayed autonomous under Twelver Shi'ite jurists, and the Seljuks dominated Damascus and Aleppo. When Tutush died in 1095, his two sons (Duqaq in Damascus and Ridwan in Aleppo) and the Seljuk lord of Antioch fought for Syria. The First Crusade—a complete surprise for the Muslim Levant—inter-rupted these hostilities among Damascus, Aleppo, and Antioch.

Conclusion

In the nearly twelve centuries that separated the arrivals of the Roman and Crusader armies in Cilicia, the Levant was invaded by land from every conceivable direction, and attracted the close attention of every major power in the eastern Mediterranean and southwest Asia.

Events amply demonstrated both the vulnerability and the centrali-ty of the Levant. Romans, Byzantines, and Seljuk Turks came from the north over the Taurus mountains; Arab nomads and the Islamic con-quest came from the south and east out of Arabia and the Syrian steppe; Persians and Seljuk Turks came across the Jazira grasslands from Iraq; and Tulunids, Ikhshidids, and Fatimids came through Sinai from Egypt. For the Romans, the Levant covered the land approaches to the Mediterranean from the east, and connected Anatolia with Egypt. For the Umayyads and 'Abbasids, it linked the Asian and North African wings of the Islamic world. For the Fatimids, Palestine guard-ed the gateway to their center of power in Egypt. For the Byzantines, northern Syria offered a buffer zone for Anatolia.

Through most of these twelve centuries, the Mediterranean ports and the coastal mountains did not play a significant role in the geopol-itics of the Levant. In Syria, political competition principally involved the eastern frontier in the Jazira and on the steppe margins, the moun-tain borderlands of Anatolia, and the interior cities, especially Damas-cus and Aleppo. In Roman times, this reflected the deep expansion of settled territory eastward into the steppe. Thereafter, it involved the interactions of Syria and Iraq, Syria and Anatolia, and Syria and

Arabia, encompassing power struggles within the Islamic world and the "holy war" between Islam and Byzantium.

As for Palestine, from late Roman times the main concern of the authorities was the penetration of desert nomads into the zone of towns and settled agriculture, including the coastal plain. At first, coping with Arab tribesmen entailed policing the Transjordan plateau, arranging alliances with amenable tribal confederations, and assimilating those who infiltrated westward. After the final Roman-Persian war and the Islamic conquest, which decisively weakened the towns and the settled peasantry, it was a matter of juggling powerful tribal groups who often dominated most of Palestine. Islamic authorities from the Umayyads to the Fatimids had to deal with Yamani-Qaysi feuding, the incursions of the Qarmati Shi'ites from Arabia, and the truculent Tayy tribes, who ravaged the coastal plain and were prepared to conspire with anyone, even the Byzantines.

The Mediterranean ports and their mountain hinterlands figured prominently only in the early Roman period, when the mountain communities challenged imperial rule, and at the very end, under the Byzantines and Fatimids, when Mediterranean commerce recovered after half a millennium of depression. The Romans had to subdue the Jews of Judea and the tribes of Mount Lebanon to secure the Levant, and this enhanced the significance of the coastal road and coastal bases like Beirut. The Fatimids used the reviving ports as a naval bridgehead in the region, particularly when the interior slipped out of their hands. Otherwise, the mountain people featured only occasionally in the historical record, when the Mardaites assisted the Byzantines against the Umayyads, or the Maronites rebelled against an 'Abbasid governor, or the Shi'ites linked with the invading Qarmati Isma'ilis. The Jews ceased to be a significant political factor in Palestine after Christians overtook them as the largest local community by the early fifth century.

Nonetheless, between the fifth and eleventh centuries the inhabitants of the coastal mountains acquired the sectarian diversity that was to prove of more importance later. This applied to the mountains from the Galilee northward into Syria and Cilicia, because the Palestinian hills of Judea, Samaria, and Transjordan became and remained Sunni

Muslim, apart from minorities of Jews, Orthodox and Jacobite Christians, and Shi'ites. In the early Islamic centuries, Maronites and Shi'ites laid claim to parts of Mount Lebanon. Under Fatimid and Byzantine rule, the Druze appeared in Galilee and Mount Lebanon, the Alawites established themselves in the Nusayriya range, and Armenians moved into the Amanus hills and Cilicia.

The complex geopolitics of the Crusader and Mamluk periods continued to bypass the mountain communities, apart from the Isma'ilis and the Armenians, who paid for their salience. The mountains themselves became of vital strategic significance through the twelfth and thirteenth centuries, but their communities shuffled only slowly onto the political stage.

CHAPTER THREE

CRUSADERS, MAMLUKS, AND OTTOMANS

Crusaders and Muslims

At first sight, the march of the First Crusade through Byzantium and Seljuk Anatolia into northern Syria in 1097, taking Antioch in June 1098 and moving south toward Palestine, resembles Pompey's descent on Cilicia in 63 B.C.E. Once again, Europe reached into the eastern Mediterranean and, once again, this was part of a general Western European assertion, with the forces of Western Christendom taking the offensive against Islam in Spain and Sicily.

Otherwise, however, the circumstances were different. Rome came to the Levant after a methodical expansion, with continuity of territory under its control across Anatolia and the Balkans back to Italy. Western Europe was then well on the way to becoming a single entity under Roman hegemony. In cultural terms, Rome, by incorporating Greece, had come to share the Hellenistic civilization of the urban population of most of the Levant. Rome thus arrived in the Levant with the advantages of overwhelming power, unified command, secure logistics, and cultural compatibility. Apart from a fleeting possession of the military initiative, the Western Crusaders had none of these assets.

The Crusader enterprise expressed the disorderly dynamism of a potpourri of unstable kingdoms, baronies, and other authorities in the medieval West, briefly pulled together by the Papacy to recover Jerusalem from Islam. It was a response to an appeal in 1095 by the Byzantine Emperor Alexius Comnenus for assistance against the Turks in Anatolia. Pope Urban II called on Western monarchs, lords, and knights to proceed to Constantinople, and thereafter to Jerusalem, to restore Christian control of the Holy Sepulchre, the tomb of Christ. The extraordinary response in Western Europe reflected medieval religious devotion.

The precariousness of the Western European presence in the Levant between 1097 and 1291 raises the question of how it endured for almost two centuries. First, there was no coherent plan for conquered lands. When the leaders of the First Crusade assembled in Constantinople en route to Palestine, they acknowledged the Byzantine emperor's claim to the Levant even while some of them intended to establish their own lordships.[99] This led to tension in Crusader-Byzantine relations when the Crusaders carved out new states on an ad hoc basis in the early twelfth century. Troubled relations with the Byzantines had disturbing implications because the Crusaders were at the end of long supply lines without any command of land routes to their homelands. Through the twelfth century the Byzantine Empire, resurgent under the Comneni emperors, could interfere with land and sea communications. In 1148, Manuel Comnenus colluded with the Seljuks to frustrate the progress of the Second Crusade through Anatolia.[100]

Second, at the same time the Crusaders confronted a mounting Muslim recovery they were themselves divided and dependent for reinforcement on mutually suspicious European monarchies. In particular, the Crusader states were chronically short of military manpower; in the thirteenth century events sometimes hinged on the chance arrival of willing pilgrims. Under medieval conditions, Western reaction to contingencies, for example the 1187 disaster at Hattin, took months at best. Further, it was often mediated through Italian city-states like Venice and Genoa which could mobilize ships and finances when the monarchies came up short, but which also had interests of their own with the Muslims and Byzantines.

Third, "Outremer"—the Latin Levant—was an alien implantation in the eastern Mediterranean that lacked cultural commonality with the local Muslims and Christians. For the Muslims, the Franks were a force of nature that burst out of nowhere. In some ways their appearance resembled that of the waves of Turkish nomads from Central Asia—another barbarous horde from the twilight zones of northern

Eurasia. Unlike the Turks, however, the Franks were adherents of the enemy religion. In this situation, they could not be assimilated as a political presence.

Although murderous rampages were standard practice after medieval sieges (in 1077 the Turcoman warlord Atsiz massacred Jerusalemites of all three religions[101]), the Crusaders started badly. The killing of thousands of Muslims and Jews when Jerusalem fell in July 1099 was not forgotten in the Islamic world. After its establishment, the Kingdom of Jerusalem excluded Muslims and Jews from residing in the Holy City, but in other respects displayed a relaxed attitude toward them. In addition, many Franks adopted local customs and Muslim leaders in Aleppo and Damascus allied with Crusaders against Muslim rivals.

Nonetheless, there was always a chasm between Crusaders and Muslims in the Levant. The Crusader perspective was that Jerusalem belonged to Christians and had been unjustly usurped. In the eyes of most of the Levant's Muslims, the Franks occupied the Dome of the Rock and the Aqsa mosque on Jerusalem's Temple Mount, an unacceptable situation. The Crusader presence also restricted communications between Syria and Egypt and impinged on the pilgrimage route between Damascus and Arabia. In short, Frankish existence in the Levant represented a standing invitation to hostilities.

The Crusaders survived so long, despite their bickering, their distance from Western Europe, their problems with the Byzantines, and Muslim opposition, because there were qualifications to these elements. The Crusader states had local strategic advantages. In the twelfth century, they commanded the coastal mountains and had mainly decent relations with the Christian, Druze, and Shi'ite communities of the hills. Their armies were more homogeneous than the generally short-lived Muslim coalitions mobilized against them.[102] Despite limited manpower, the combination of mobile field forces, religious orders of knights, and great castles proved resilient. In the thirteenth century, even after geographical shrinkage, they retained powerful fortified towns on the coast that generated considerable wealth.

For a long time, Western Europe maintained its interest, came to the rescue, and generally displayed sustained Crusading fervor. Notwithstanding its contempt for the West, Byzantium also sometimes buttressed the Crusaders. On the Muslim side, disunity prevailed until Salah al-Din combined Damascus with Egypt and mounted an offensive in the late twelfth century that almost overturned the Latin Levant. The Third Crusade enabled Outremer to outlast the challenge, and the Muslims fragmented once more.

The Crusader presence went into terminal decline after the 1240s, as the circumstances offsetting its precariousness fell away. For better or worse, Byzantium ceased to be a factor after the Fourth Crusade stormed Constantinople in 1204—the Crusaders themselves removed the major Christian power of the eastern Mediterranean. Further, Western Europe tired of propping up the distant holdings clinging to the coast of Palestine and Syria, especially after the final loss of Jerusalem in 1244. The Papacy remained absorbed in its confrontation with the Holy Roman Empire, and a fierce struggle for Norman Sicily preoccupied Europeans.

Within the Levant, the Mamluk Sultanate applied superior numbers and stern Sunni Islamic revivalism to a systematic campaign to reduce Crusader strongholds. The Mongol threat only galvanized the new Islamic power to remove the danger on its flank represented by the remnants of Outremer. In their last years, the Crusader coastal towns were wracked by civil strife, involving local factions and the Italian merchant communes, as the Mamluks closed in on them.

The Crusader Apogee

Map 7 indicates the Crusader alignment at its maximum extent in the 1140s. At this point, the Levant was entirely occupied by local principalities. The four Crusader states held the coast and parallel mountains, with the greatest depth in the south, where the Kingdom of Jerusalem pushed into Transjordan, and in the north, where the Principality of Antioch and the Frankish-Armenian County of Edessa reached west and north of Aleppo. In the center, the County of Tripoli shared Mount Lebanon with the Kingdom of Jerusalem, connecting the northern and southern wings. The Kingdom of Jerusalem became the leading Crusader power, and was particularly involved in Antioch, beset by the

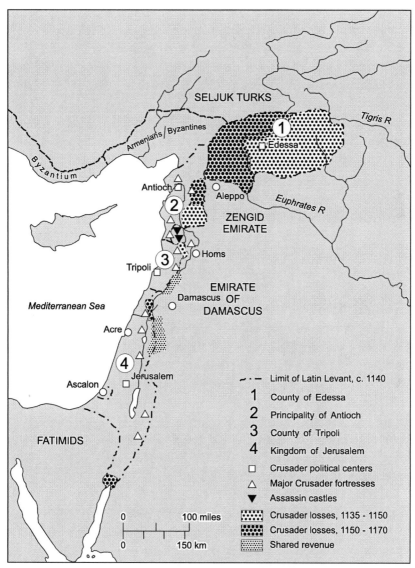

Map 7—Crusader alignment, 1130–1170

Data sources: Hooper and Bennett, 1996; Hamilton, 2000; Lilie, 1993; Moore, 1981; Parker, 1993; Richard, 1999; Smail, 1995; Vilnay, 1968; Westermann's Grosser Atlas, 1966.

Muslims and Byzantines.

The Crusaders did not fully secure the coast until more than twenty years after the First Crusade; they captured Tripoli in 1109 and Tyre in 1124. Naval interventions from Venice, Genoa, and Pisa offset Fatimid sea power in the critical process of seizing the Levantine ports,[103] and the Italians acquired trading privileges amounting to "states within the state."

Muslim rule in the Levant contracted to interior Syria, comprising the Emirates of Aleppo and Damascus. Aleppo went through a confused period until 1128, when it was united with Mosul under Zangi, son of a former Seljuk governor of Aleppo. Zangi had the resources of the Jazira, which enabled him to keep Aleppo out of Crusader hands, check Crusader expansion toward Hama, and detach Homs from the Emirate of Damascus. When Zangi was killed in 1146 and Aleppo and Mosul separated under his sons, Nur al-Din in Aleppo had the advantage over his rivals in Damascus, and united the two cities under his authority in 1154.

At first, the Muslims were on the defensive against the Crusaders in Syria, especially as long as Aleppo and Damascus were divided. The Emirates acknowledged the suzerainty of the Seljuk sultan in Iraq but, far from being helpful, Muslim rulers in Iraq and Anatolia were predatory toward Syria. In 1115, an invasion of Syria by the sultan's army from Baghdad, supposedly against the Crusaders, provoked fear in the Jazira and Damascus that the real purpose was to end local Muslim autonomy. The rulers of Mardin and Damascus occupied Aleppo, where a local leader had appealed to Baghdad, and allied with Crusader Antioch to repel the intrusion from Iraq.[104]

In this situation, the Crusaders had an early opportunity to break what was left of the Muslim Levant. Interior Syria was a threat because of its resources and the Muslim advantage of shorter lines of communication. Muslim forces could strike with little warning at any point in the stretched Crusader alignment—south against northern Palestine, west against Tripoli or Antioch, or north against Edessa.

Damascus was the key, and the Crusaders had the choice of detaching it as a friendly buffer state, as the Byzantines had done with Hamdanid Aleppo, or conquering it. Despite overtures from the ruling clique in Damascus, the Crusaders never seriously pursued the first option. Given the staunch Sunni Islamic loyalties of the Damascus townspeople, an alliance could not have lasted long. In 1144, however, when Zangi overran most of the County of Edessa, the Latin Levant had to forestall unification of Damascus with Aleppo.

The Second Crusade attacked Damascus in 1148, but Crusader dissensions and the approach of an army from Aleppo led to the siege being broken off. This setback proved a turning point in the Latin-Muslim power balance. From the 1150s, Nur al-Din's command of Damascus as well as Aleppo propelled him toward intervention in the faction-ridden affairs of Fatimid Egypt, which eventually led to the combination of Syria and Egypt under Salah al-Din Yusuf ibn Ayyub (Saladin).

To face interior Syria, the Crusaders sought to offset their numerical deficiencies by fortifying the natural lines provided by the mountains. As indicated by Smail, Crusader castles integrated local "maintenance of Latin overlordship" with "frontier defense."[105] Map 7 displays the distribution of the major fortresses, which remain landmarks of a defunct strategic geography.

Karak and Shawbak in Transjordan gave the Crusaders positions in the highlands east of the Jordan Valley. They flanked the desert route linking Syria to Arabia and Egypt, and therefore disrupted communications between Muslim centers.[106] Belvoir, Tiberias, and Safed covered the eastern approaches to the Galilee gap and the port of Acre. Beaufort, used in recent times by both the Palestinians and Israelis, guarded the access from the Biqa' around Mount Lebanon to the Lebanese coast. Gibalcar and Crac des Chevaliers watched over the Homs gap and the main route from the interior to Tripoli. Safita, Margat, and Sahyun ensured territorial continuity between Tripoli and Antioch and contained the Isma'ili Assassins. Although the mountain castles had local functions—Beaufort, for example, secured the farmlands and revenues of the Marj 'Uyun plain—they provided the Latin Levant with critical geographical depth.

In the Crusader period, the Levant was for the first time divided between a coastal power holding the hills and a hostile interior power. In such conditions, the integrity of each of the Crusader states depended on fortification to the rear—on the coast and the coastal plains—as well as on the frontier. Latin settlers were a minority and, apart from Jerusalem, overwhelmingly resident in the ports. The native population of Muslims and Christians had to be overawed from strong points throughout Crusader territory. Further, distances were short and warning time limited, and if the frontier was penetrated, hostile forces could be on the coast quickly. In spring 1137, for example, a force from Damascus, guided by local Christians, raided across Mount Lebanon to the outskirts of Tripoli.[107]

The geopolitics of the Latin-Muslim confrontation gave the mountain communities a new salience. In Mount Lebanon, the Crusaders relied on understandings with Maronite, Shi'ite, and Druze chiefs to secure the hills behind Tripoli, Beirut, and Sidon. There were no major Crusader fortresses on Mount Lebanon between Gibalcar and Beaufort—a distance of more than 100 miles. The mountain chiefs, particularly the Druze in the Shuf hills,[108] maintained relations with both sides, and in the twelfth century the Biqa' was a marchland between the Crusaders and Damascus, with revenue sharing arrangements. Rugged topography, sectarian sensibilities, and winter snows affected the strategic balance between the coast and Damascus, at the center of the Latin Levant. After 1167, when Nur al-Din seized the cave redoubt of Tyron, above Sidon, the Druze and the Buhturid lords in southern Mount Lebanon became more troublesome as they sensed Frankish weakness.

To the north, the Isma'ili Assassins established themselves in the Nusayriya uplands in the 1130s after being driven out of Aleppo and Damascus. They created a mountain principality based on the fortresses of Masyaf and Qadmus.[109] They had bad relations with the Muslim interior, which was becoming emphatically Sunni under Zangi and Nur al-Din. In 1176, Salah al-Din tried unsuccessfully to destroy them. However, though the Assassins paid tribute for Crusader protection, many Crusaders, particularly their Templar neighbors, distrusted them. Like the Druze in Mount Lebanon, they were positioned awkwardly from the Latin perspective, wedged between Tripoli and Antioch.

To the south, the Kingdom of Jerusalem had direct control of the Palestinian hills. Nonetheless, the kingdom had to deal carefully with the Sunni peasantry of northern Samaria, around Nablus. In 1113 and 1187, when Muslim armies broke into northern Palestine, the Nablus peasantry rose to support them.[110]

Although the Seljuk Turks and the Crusaders had replaced Byzantium and the Fatimids in the Levant, the latter powers played a significant role from the margins in the twelfth century. The interplay of forces was most intricate in northern Syria and Cilicia, where the Crusader Principality of Antioch indulged in risky provocations. The reviving land trade across the Jazira to the Mediterranean made this corner of the Levant a desirable possession for all parties. Asbridge's study of the first decades of the principality illustrates sharp fluctuations in its territorial extent before and after defeats by the Muslims in 1104 and 1119.[111] By the 1140s, the principality was forced out of the Cilician plain by the Byzantines and local Armenian lords. To the east, Antioch threatened Aleppo by holding the Talat hills, and menaced Muslim Shayzar by expanding into the Summaq upland on the inland side of the Orontes Valley.[112] For a while, Aleppo and Shayzar paid tribute to Antioch, but Zangi forced Antioch onto the defensive when he seized Edessa.

Antioch was unstable because of its large Armenian and Muslim populations and the immediate proximity of unfriendly neighbors. Through much of the 1120s and 1130s, for example, Antioch's affairs required the attention of Kings Baldwin II and Fulk, diverting them from their Egyptian front. In 1137–38, the Byzantine Emperor John Comnenus appeared in Cilicia, extracted homage from Antioch, and ordered local Crusader leaders to join him against the Muslims. According to the Crusader chronicler William of Tyre, John campaigned inconclusively against Shayzar while the disgruntled Crusader chiefs played dice.[113] For their part, Anatolian Turkish rulers only intermittently joined the power play in northern Syria, clashing or allying with the Antioch Franks, the Cilician Armenians, and the Syrian Muslims. Their own dissensions and complicated interactions with the Byzantines often preoccupied them.

On the Egyptian front, the Fatimids retained a foothold in southern Palestine until the Crusaders captured Ascalon in 1153. Ascalon gave the Fatimids a forward base from which to invade the Kingdom of

Jerusalem. For the Crusaders, the struggle for Ascalon indicated the importance of neutralising Egypt. Chaotic intrigue in Cairo under child Fatimid caliphs after 1150 invited intervention. Through the 1160s, Muslim Damascus and Crusader Palestine competed for domination of Egypt—a reversal of the relations between Egypt and the Levant through the 'Abbasid and Fatimid periods. The competition for Egypt promised to determine the power balance of the Levant.

Crusader losses in the northern Levant in the 1150s and 60s made the Egyptian question more urgent and more difficult. The Kingdom of Jerusalem did not have the manpower to conquer Egypt while propping up the lesser Crusader states. Nur al-Din led a Sunni Islamic revival in interior Syria, after 1154 deploying the joint capabilities of Damascus and Aleppo. He pushed the Principality of Antioch out of the Orontes valley, captured Afamiya, and threatened the County of Tripoli. Meanwhile, the Anatolian Turks eliminated the remnants of the County of Edessa.

King Amalric of Jerusalem led three land invasions of Egypt between 1163 and 1168. For his part, Nur al-Din took advantage of disputes in the Egyptian regime to have his Kurdish subordinate Shirkuh, with Shirkuh's nephew Salah al-Din, installed in top military positions in Egypt. Shirkuh's opponents in Cairo appealed to Amalric, who marched into Egypt to keep it out of the hands of Muslim Syria. Amalric's efforts might have borne fruit if the Kingdom of Jerusalem had been able to concentrate on one front—many Fatimid officials were wary of Nur al-Din, and Coptic Christians were still a large part of Egypt's population. Amalric, however, failed because he had to divide his forces between initiatives in Egypt and defenses against Syria. In 1169, Shirkuh and Salah al-Din became the Fatimid caliph's chief ministers, and in 1171 Salah al-Din took command of Egypt, terminating the Fatimid Caliphate and ordering acknowledgement of the 'Abbasid caliph in Friday prayers.

In the late 1160s, the Crusaders turned to Byzantium for help. Manuel Comnenus had become more sympathetic to Westerners, and fear of Byzantine intervention deterred Nur al-Din from assaulting Antioch. The Byzantine option, however, involved submission to the emperor, and in 1169 a joint Crusader-Byzantine operation against

Egypt came unstuck.[114] Plans for a similar attack in 1177 also unravelled, while a Byzantine fleet waited in Acre, because of disputes involving the kingdom's grandees, newly arrived Crusaders, Byzantium, and the northern Frankish states over leadership and whether or not the Egyptian project should override action in Syria. If executed, the project could have jeopardized Salah al-Din's hold on Cairo.[115]

Thereafter, Byzantine capability contracted. Manuel died in 1180, whereupon factional conflict engulfed Constantinople, and in 1185 the Sicilian Normans sacked Thessalonika, second city of the empire. Relations between Constantinople and the Latin Levant cooled as Orthodox-Catholic religious hostility surged. In the 1180s, the Byzantines cheered Salah al-Din, while the Anatolian Turks favored the Franks against the rising Muslim power in Syria and Egypt.

When Nur al-Din died in 1174, Salah al-Din extended his authority to Damascus, responding to local appeals. Aleppo, however, refused to accept Salah al-Din and aligned itself with the Crusaders, who did their best to keep Aleppo and Mosul from uniting with the Ayyubid. It took Salah al-Din a decade to assert his leadership in northern Syria and the Jazira; Aleppo only submitted in 1183 and both the caliph in Baghdad and the Anatolian Turks suspected the Ayyubid's ambition.

Undoubtedly, Salah al-Din's ability to coordinate Egyptian and Syrian armies against the Kingdom of Jerusalem presented a grave threat to the Latin Levant. In his *Chronicon*, William of Tyre records Salah al-Din's efforts in Syria after 1174 with clear apprehension.[116] On the other hand, Salah al-Din was also in a precarious situation—he had only a limited time to prove himself as the champion of Islam against the infidel if he was to sustain his overlordship of the Muslim warlords of Syria.[117]

Salah al-Din therefore ignored the lesser Crusader states and concentrated on his main opponent, the Kingdom of Jerusalem, in the most critical sector—the wheat-producing lands around Lake Tiberias (the Sea of Galilee) that also commanded the Galilee gap, the approach to the main Crusader port at Acre.[118] In 1177, Salah al-Din tried to surprise the kingdom by thrusting across Sinai from Egypt. This led to a Muslim defeat in southern Palestine. He then moved to Damascus, scoring limited successes in the eastern Galilee in 1179.

After 1180, dissension over the succession to the young leper king, Baldwin IV, destabilized the Kingdom of Jerusalem. Prince Reynald (formerly of Antioch), lord of Transjordan and the king's confidant and distant relative, countered Salah al-Din's pressure on the kingdom and its Muslim allies in Aleppo by adventurous probes into Arabia, including a naval raid down the Red Sea to Jedda, the port of Mecca, in 1183. The raid infuriated Salah al-Din, because Reynald showed up the Ayyubid as neglecting the protection of Muslim pilgrims while he attacked Muslim rivals in the Jazira.[119] Reynald, who spoke Arabic, also deployed a Bedouin spy network that balanced Salah al-Din's espionage system.

Richard and Hamilton doubt that Reynald's activities gave any special impetus to the Islamic "holy war."[120] Overall, Baldwin IV successfully resisted Muslim offensives in the Galilee gap and against Karak and Beirut until his death in 1185. Cross-frontier commerce continued, Muslim neighbors supplied grain when needed, and Salah al-Din could not take territory or any major stronghold.[121]

In 1186, Salah al-Din exploited a truce with the kingdom to subordinate Mosul, giving him the prospect of campaigning against the Franks with maximum resources and without diversion. In April 1187, he refused to renew the truce, citing Reynald's seizure of an armed caravan heading from Cairo to Damascus. He led a large army into Transjordan and the Galilee. Crusader leaders, in disarray after Baldwin's death, hastily assembled their forces to block him.

In the heat of summer, the Crusaders made the fatal error of separating themselves from water supplies, and Salah al-Din forced their surrender at Hattin, above Lake Tiberias, on 4 July 1187. After Hattin the kingdom had no field army and collapsed within a few months. Salah al-Din marched to Acre, secured the Palestinian coast, and then took Jerusalem.

Although by the standards of the age Salah al-Din behaved decently toward the Frankish settlers, he made it plain that they were to be deported or enslaved, and that the Latin presence was to be eliminated. Ironically, this policy ensured that the Latin Levant outlasted him. First, it stiffened resistance in the frontier castles, which survived the rest of the kingdom, as well as in the coastlands north of Acre. Over

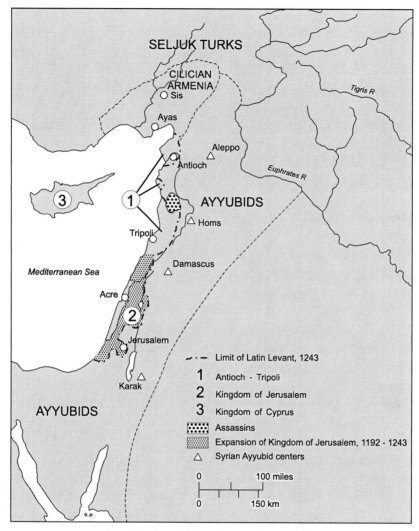

Map 8—Ayyubids and Crusaders, 1240s

Data sources: Moore, 1981; Marshall, 1992; Richard, 1999; Vilnay, 1968.

two years Salah al-Din overcame the fortresses in the Palestinian and Transjordan hills, but the long siege of Beaufort and failure to take Tyre allowed the initiative to pass to the arriving contingents of the Third Crusade.[122]

Further, Salah al-Din's stance galvanized the West. Three Western monarchs—Richard of England, Philip Augustus of France, and the Emperor Frederick Barbarossa—led armies to the east in 1190/91, though Frederick was drowned in Anatolia. The English and French forces came by sea, using their own shipping and that of Genoa and Pisa.[123] This demonstrated improved logistical capability in the West since the First Crusade. The Crusaders recaptured Acre, reconstituted a reduced Kingdom of Jerusalem, and in 1192 forced Salah al-Din to accept the Latin presence. Salah al-Din bitterly contrasted his difficulties in mobilizing support from the Islamic world with the Western effort.[124]

Crusader-Ayyubid Coexistence

Map 8 indicates the Latin alignment that came out of the 1190s and expanded up to about 1240. Jerusalem was only briefly retaken, between 1229 and 1244, and most of interior Palestine was lost. However, the Crusaders restored their command of the coastline, and from the Galilee north the Latin Levant retained or regained strong hill positions. A number of factors favored the Crusaders in the first half of the thirteenth century. First, seaborne expeditions illustrated European commitment until the 1250s. Second, increased revenues from the Eurasian trade through the Levant ports attracted the Italian city-states, which ensured Western naval supremacy. This was important because of the disappearance of Byzantine support. Third, after the death of Salah al-Din in 1193, the Ayyubid domain in Egypt and Syria was divided among members of his family, and the Muslim Levant again fragmented into Damascus, Aleppo, and lesser lordships in places like Hama and Homs. The Crusaders were able to exploit Ayyubid rivalries until the Mamluks seized Egypt in 1250.

In the north, contests involving Tripoli, Antioch, and the Cilician Armenians reached resolution through the early thirteenth century without the neighboring Muslims taking advantage of the situation. The principal new element after the 1190s was the conversion of de facto domination of Cilicia by Armenian warlords into a new Armenian kingdom.[125] This culminated the Armenian movement into the area from eastern Anatolia that Nicephorus Phocas had begun two centuries previously. The Armenians profited from the Byzantine recession of the late twelfth century, after the death of Manuel Comnenus, and the weakening of the Crusader Principality of Antioch in its conflicts with Muslim Aleppo.

The shrewd Armenian leader Leon took the opportunity of Salah al-Din's blows against the Latin Levant to ingratiate himself with the Italian city-states and the Papacy. He made trade concessions to the Venetians and Genoese,[126] and his port of Ayas became the entrepôt of the Levant while Acre was out of commission. His expressions of allegiance to Rome were enough to gain Western recognition of his coronation as king by the Armenian Catholicos in Tarsus in 1198.[127] Armenian Cilicia was to outlast the Crusaders by almost a century.

Leon entered a twenty-year conflict with Count Bohemond of Tripoli for the Principality of Antioch. Leon, hoping to unite Cilicia and Antioch as an Armenian-led state that would rival the Ayyubids and Anatolian Seljuks as a regional power, asserted the claim of his infant grandnephew Raymond-Rupen, son of the deceased heir of Prince Bohemond III of Antioch, who himself died in 1201. Bohemond of Tripoli, second son of Bohemond III, contested the claim.

The great orders of knights, who manned the major castles of Crusader Syria and were more powerful vis-à-vis Tripoli and Antioch after the 1187 collapse of the Kingdom of Jerusalem, took opposite sides. The Templars, furious at Leon's failure to return the fortress of Baghras in the Amanus Mountains, which was lost to Salah al-Din in 1188 and then occupied by the Armenians, supported Bohemond. The Hospitallers, who commanded Crac des Chevaliers, were promised lands on the Antioch-Tripoli border by Leon and favored the Armenians. The Frankish and Greek inhabitants of Antioch disliked the Armenians and looked to Bohemond.

Both sides enrolled Muslim allies in the same way the Muslims enrolled Crusaders in their own disputes. Bohemond appealed to the Anatolian Turks, while the Hospitallers probably hired the Isma'ili Assassin who murdered Bohemond's son in Tartus in 1213.[128] The affair ended in 1219, when Bohemond expelled Raymond-Rupen from Antioch. This confirmed Antioch and Tripoli as a single realm under Bohemond IV (1219–33), though with separate legal and administrative arrangements. The autonomy of the Templars and Hospitallers qualified the political significance of the union. The struggle for Antioch between Leon and Bohemond illustrated the complexity of interactions in the northern Levant in the early thirteenth century, involving Armenian, Crusader, Ayyubid, and Seljuk interests.

To the south, the Holy Roman Emperor Frederick II, who was by marriage regent of the Kingdom of Jerusalem, arrived in 1228 after many delays to regain Jerusalem from the Ayyubids. Frederick was a cynical statesman, opposed by the nobility of the kingdom. He brought an army, but sought to prevail by diplomacy.[129] Ayyubid princes had already offered to restore pre-1187 Crusader holdings in Palestine in exchange for alliances against their rivals. The Ayyubid sultan of Egypt, al-Kamil, was prepared to do a deal with Frederick—both men wanted stability in Palestine. In February 1229, they made an arrangement for joint sovereignty in Jerusalem that has resonance for the Israeli-Palestinian circumstances of the early twenty-first century.

Under the 1229 Treaty of Jaffa, the Crusaders acquired Jerusalem except for the Herodian Temple platform (*al-haram al-sharif*) and al-'Aqsa mosque, which remained under Muslim sovereignty. Frederick also received Bethlehem and a corridor from Jerusalem to the coastal plain. Muslims had access to Bethlehem while Christians did not have such rights to the Temple platform. The treaty was unclear about Crusader rebuilding of the walls and it left most of the town's surrounds in Muslim hands. It was badly received on both sides; the contemporary Muslim chronicler Ibn al-Athir called on God to "humiliate" al-Kamil, while a crowd "pelted" Frederick with "guts and offal" on his departure for the West from Acre.[130] In subsequent years, local Muslims attacked Frankish residents in Jerusalem and ambushed pilgrims in the corridor from the coast.[131]

Frederick's treaty demonstrated the limitations of negotiation in a conflict inflamed by religion, the dangers of what today's diplomats term "creative ambiguity," and the likely isolation of compromisers—all relevant to the geopolitics of the modern Levant.

The Crusader recovery reached its peak in the early 1240s, assisted by hostility between the Ayyubids of Syria and Egypt. In 1240, the ruler of Damascus handed over former Crusader positions in the hills of southern Lebanon and the Upper Galilee, including Beaufort and Safed, in exchange for an alliance against Egypt.[132] This enabled the Crusaders to restore their influence over the Druze chiefs of Mount Lebanon, and to re-establish their command of the eastern approach to the Galilee gap.

In 1243, the Ayyubids of Egypt, Transjordan, and Damascus, wishing to preserve alliances with the Latin Levant, agreed to cede the Muslim sector of Jerusalem.[133] Here, however, the Crusaders had to choose between the Emperor Frederick II's 1229 arrangement with the sultan of Egypt, which Frederick considered vital to Crusader security in Palestine, and the preference of the anti-imperial majority of Frankish leaders for the alliance with Damascus. Muslim conflicts now became a trap for the Latin Levant.

Fearful of the alignment of the Ayyubids of Syria and Transjordan against him and calculating that the Crusaders would join his enemies, the Sultan Ayyub of Egypt requested assistance from the Khawarizmian nomads of the Caucasus, displaced by the advancing Mongols. Since Hattin, the Crusaders had avoided concentrating their forces, wary of risking everything in one encounter.[134] In 1244, their alliance with the Muslims of Damascus, Homs, and Karak against Ayyub and his dangerous new friends gave them no choice but to commit most of their field capability.

The Khawarizmians crossed Palestine to join the Egyptians near Gaza. On the way, they stormed Jerusalem, still inadequately garrisoned. This ended the Latin presence in the Judean highlands. In October 1244, the Egyptians and Khawarizmians defeated the Latin and Muslim Levant at La Forbie, outside Gaza. The Crusaders lost 2,000 knights, a disaster equivalent to Hattin.

Ayyub, however, was no Salah al-Din, the Khawarizmians disintegrated, and little impetus existed for continued warfare with the Franks. Instead, Ayyub extended his rule into the Palestinian interior, detaching Judea and Samaria from the territory of his cousin in Transjordan, and took control of Damascus.[135] In the late 1240s, the Egyptian Ayyubids, represented by Turkish Mamluk soldiers, dominated Transjordan and southern Syria, and faced the rival Ayyubid regime of al-Nasir Yusuf in Aleppo.

In 1249–50, King Louis IX of France led an abortive seaborne invasion of Egypt, the last major European effort to secure the Latin Levant. The landing at Damietta precipitated a crisis in Cairo that resulted in the overthrow of Ayyubid rule by Turkic Mamluk military leaders. Mamluk ascendancy in Egypt, though initially chaotic, represented a new Muslim power and, ultimately, a mortal threat to the Crusaders. The defeat and capture of King Louis, ransomed at great expense, also discouraged European adventures in the eastern Mediterranean. Again, the consequences were masked by the French king's investments in fortifying Caesarea and Sidon and reinforcing Crusader field capability.[136] The 1256–58 war of St. Sabas, in which rivalry between the Venetian and Genoese merchant communes escalated into fighting that destroyed much of Acre, indicated the Frankish malaise while the wider regional power balance shifted.

Mamluk Supremacy

After 1243, when the Mongols subjugated the Seljuk Turks in Anatolia, a new threat to the Levant loomed, as when the Seljuks themselves had appeared. Unlike the Seljuks, however, the Mongol power that established itself in Iran, Iraq, and Anatolia did not initially adopt Islam. Its rulers, who used the title "Ilkhan," meaning deputy of the supreme Khan in Central Asia, held to their Shamanist and Buddhist traditions until Ghazan in 1295. Their demand that Muslim princes should bow to Mongol claims to universal sovereignty therefore meant a religious as well as a political confrontation. Until its elite became Islamized, the Mongol Ilkhanate represented an existential challenge to the Islamic world. It had access to a host of Central Asian cavalry troops, as well as to the resources of extensive conquered lands.

The most dangerous phase began in 1258, when the Mongol commander Hülegü Khan sacked Baghdad and destroyed the 'Abbasid caliphate. In 1259 he led a huge army through the Jazira, crossed the Euphrates, and seized Aleppo. Hülegü intended to conquer the Levant en route to Egypt, the last redoubt of Muslim power in the Middle East. From Aleppo, however, he unexpectedly reversed course and led the main part of his army back to northern Iran. He left his subordinate

Ketbugha, a Nestorian Christian, to take a smaller force deeper into the Levant. Amitai-Preiss suggests several explanations for Hülegü's decision, including the death of his older brother Möngke, the supreme Khan, a dispute with the Golden Horde Mongols over rights in Azerbaijan, and underestimation of Egyptian strength.[137]

Through the 1250s, the Syrian Ayyubids were divided on whether or not to resist the Mongols, but al-Nasir Yusuf of Damascus was ready to submit and the ruler of Transjordan wavered. To the north, the Cilician Armenians and the Franks of Antioch aligned themselves with the Mongol regime in Anatolia in the late 1240s. The new Mamluk rulers of Egypt therefore faced the risk that the Mongols would have a comfortable passage through Syria and Palestine to the gates of Cairo.

The Mamluk leaders Qutuz and Baybars took advantage of the division of Mongol forces and the fact that the combination of their own army with refugee Muslim troops from Syria gave them a numerical edge. While Ketbugha took Damascus, welcomed joyously by the native Christians, and raided into Transjordan and Palestine, the Mamluk army moved up the Palestinian coast. The Crusaders of the southern Levant hedged their bets,[138] receiving Ketbugha at Safed and supplying the Mamluks at Acre. On balance, however, they feared the Mongols more and expressed their disapproval of Antioch's alliance with them.

In September 1260, the Mamluks smashed Ketbugha's army at 'Ayn Jalut, in the Jordan valley south of Tiberias. This was the third decisive battle at the eastern entrance to the Galilee gap after the Fatimid defeat of the Mirdasid-tribal coalition (1029) and Salah al-Din's victory at Hattin (1187), emphasising the significance of this gateway to Palestine from Syria.

'Ayn Jalut inaugurated Mamluk rule in the Muslim Levant, but it was some time before firm control from Cairo was established in the interior from Transjordan to Aleppo. Most immediately, Baybars arranged the assassination of Qutuz, became sultan, expanded the Mamluk army, and instituted rapid communications from the Levant to Cairo as early warning for Egypt.[139] A second Mongol incursion from the Jazira was broken up by the Ayyubid emirs of northern Syria in 1261, but not before it had penetrated as far as Homs. The Mongols received assistance from Antioch and Cilicia, and the Crusaders of Acre took advantage of Mamluk preoccupation with the situation around Aleppo to raid the Golan Heights. The Crusaders suffered a reverse, but the intrusion was uncomfortably close to Mamluk Damascus.

These experiences confirmed for Baybars that securing the Levant was vital for the Mamluk Sultanate. No other power should be allowed a foothold in the region, and the challenge from the Ilkhanate in Anatolia and Iraq should be met by vigorous forward defense.

Removing the Crusaders

Confrontation with the Ilkhanate made sharing the Levant with the bridgeheads of the Christian West intolerable, even apart from the religious imperative of the zealously Sunni Muslim Mamluks. After 'Ayn Jalut, Baybars was slow to act because he needed to consolidate his power in Egypt, while famine in the Syrian interior in the early 1260s made it politic to ensure supplies continued to flow through the Crusader ports.[140] Several factors, however, made Mamluk assaults on the Latin Levant inevitable.

First, the Crusaders held rich farmlands and had a stranglehold on Syria's access to the Mediterranean, commanding revenue from the trade routes. Acquiring these resources would benefit the Sultanate. Second, the Frankish territories in Palestine flanked the shortest route from Syria to Egypt, through the Galilee gap to Gaza via the coastal plain. Third, the Tripoli-Antioch state had already declared itself in favor of the Ilkhanate. Fourth, in the late 1260s the Ilkhanate openly sought European intervention in the eastern Mediterranean, whether in the form of reinforcement of the Franks or an attack on the Egyptian coast. Baybars faced the possibility of being squeezed between two fronts in Syria, combined with a threat to Egypt.

After initial raids against Antioch and its port, the Mamluk offensive began with the seizure of Caesarea and Arsuf in 1265, extending Mamluk control of most of the Palestinian coastal plain northward to beyond Caesarea. Baybars intensified the Ayyubid policy of destroying captured coastal fortifications, in places even blocking harbors with debris, to make it difficult for any new Crusade to regain old footholds.

Ayalon argues that Mamluk devastation of the Palestinian coast, because of fear of Western naval superiority, left coastal areas under-populated for centuries, until Jewish settlement in the early twentieth century.[141]

The tempo of Mamluk action against the Latin Levant depended on the situation on the Euphrates front with the Ilkhanate. Mongol invasion scares brought Mamluk armies from Egypt, and if there was no real Mongol threat these armies could be used against Crusader fortresses.[142]

Baybars' investment in his field forces meant that the Mamluks always had numerical superiority against the Franks.[143] Between 1265 and 1270, he concentrated on the southern and northern extremities of the Latin Levant. He drove deeply into the Galilee gap toward Acre, taking the castles of Safed and Beaufort. He also captured Jaffa. This consolidated Mamluk command of Palestine excepting the coast from Caesarea to Acre. In the north, Baybars took Antioch in 1268, which left Cilician Armenia exposed to the Sultanate.

By 1270, Crusader holdings were reduced to the coastlands of North Palestine, Mount Lebanon, and the Nusayriya range, and the redoubts in the Homs gap. These were, however, at the core of the region. Prince Edward of England's arrival in 1271 and his contacts with the Ilkhanate demonstrated the ongoing risk for the Mamluks. Baybars made an advance in 1271, before Edward landed, when he broke open the Homs gap by taking Crac des Chevaliers and Gibalcar. Otherwise, Mamluk raiding weakened Crusader control of the countryside.

Between 1271 and 1285, the rump of Outremer had a respite. Baybars was busy with his campaigns into Cilicia and Anatolia until his death in 1277, and thereafter the Sultanate's affairs were confused until Qalawun became sultan in 1280. The fact that the Mamluks faced no challenge from Western Europe in this period, when they could have been embarrassed in the Levant, demonstrated their good fortune. The Papacy and European monarchs were immersed in Italian affairs; no impetus existed for a new thrust into the Levant. Despite Mongol appeals to the West, the intervening distance made combined operations unlikely. An exchange of plans between Prince Edward and the Ilkhan in 1271 opened the sole practical opportunity for Mongol-

Crusader collaboration, but the Mongols themselves botched it by withdrawing prematurely from northern Syria.[144]

Italian traders maintained the Western linkage to the Latin Levant through the thirteenth century. After the 1240s, they became a dubious asset for the Franks. The conflicting interests of the Italian communities in Crusader ports contributed to destructive factionalism in Acre and Tripoli, while the Mamluks could play Italian interests against those of the Franks.

As regards commercial affairs, the Mongol invasion of the Middle East helped the Mamluks, because the lucrative Persian Gulf–Levant trade of the early thirteenth century was damaged by the Mongol occupation of Iraq and the Jazira. Egypt, eclipsed by Acre since the Third Crusade, benefited from renewed Red Sea commerce in the late thirteenth century. Trade with Mamluk Egypt attracted the Venetians, weakening their commitment to their co-religionists. Even the Genoese, more hostile to the Mamluks, profited by carrying slaves to the Sultanate from the Black Sea. By the 1270s, the last opportunity for Crusader revival, the European sea powers of the Mediterranean had no interest in confronting Mamluk Egypt.

The denouement was inevitable. In 1285, freed from the preoccupations with the Mongols and Armenians of his first years as sultan, Qalawun attacked the northern territories of Crusader Tripoli. Margat and Ladhiqiyya fell, and in 1289, possibly prompted by Genoese designs on Tripoli,[145] the sultan besieged and took the city. This left Acre, which fell to Qalawun's successor al-Ashraf in 1291 in an elaborate siege by the main Mamluk field army.[146] After nearly four centuries of division, the Levant was again dominated by a single power, though that power still faced enemies in Cilicia, Anatolia, and the Jazira.

Outlasting the Mongols

Considering that demolition of the Franks coincided with the Sultanate's efforts to stabilize the Muslim Levant and confront the Mongols, the Mamluk achievement was formidable. Although Baybars made sure of Damascus from the outset, the Sultanate had to impose itself on a patchwork of local princes, nomadic tribes, and mountain sects. In Transjordan and Palestine, Baybars forced the Ayyubid lord of Karak out of his fortress and did deals with the tribes for revenues, thereby securing territorial continuity between Damascus and Egypt. In northern Syria, he displaced the Ayyubid lord of Aleppo, did a deal with Hama, and in the early 1270s pressured the Isma'ili Assassins into submission.[147]

The erosion of the Crusaders indicated the consequences of defiance. Nonetheless, after the dearly bought 1281 victory over the Mongols, the Mamluk regime's weakness led to northwestern Syria becoming autonomous under Sunqur al-Ashqar, based in the old Crusader castle of Sahyun, and to tribal rebellions in Palestine. Restoration of Mamluk authority took several years.

On the desert frontier, the Mamluks used a mixture of carrot and stick to prevent the nomads giving the Mongols a foothold west of the Euphrates. Baybars patronized the al-Fadl branch of the Tayy Bedouin, who held the vital space east of Hama toward Palmyra and the enemy boundary.[148] The Banu Kilab north of Aleppo were initially difficult, but were quietened by Baybars' punitive expeditions against the Armenians.[149]

Even after the Mongol setbacks at 'Ayn Jalut and Homs, Mamluk Syria was vulnerable to challenges from the Ilkhanate and Armenian Cilicia. The Armenians and Mongols held territory in the Amanus mountains and the Jazira plains, threatening Aleppo. In the early 1260s, King Het'um of Armenia seized several fortresses between the Amanus range and the Euphrates,[150] improving his communications with the Ilkhanate.

Baybars reacted quickly. First, he secured the Euphrates forts of al-Bira and Rahba for the Sultanate. This gave Syria buffering to the east, and made the Euphrates a military boundary between the Levant and Iraq for the first time since early Roman times. In 1265, al-Bira proved its worth when it delayed a Mongol attempt to cross the Euphrates into Syria.

Second, after establishing good relations with the Golden Horde Mongols, who distracted the Ilkhanate in the Caucasus, Baybars sent an army through the Amanus gate into Cilicia in 1266. The Mamluks

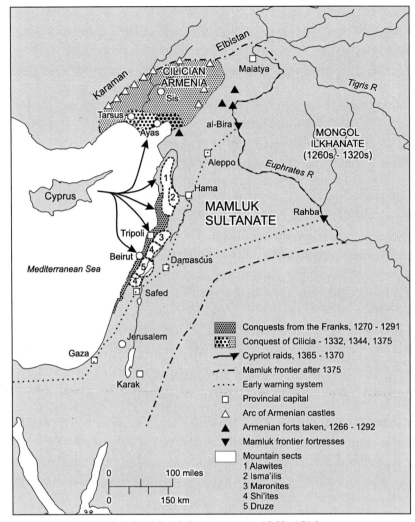

Map 9—Mamluk supremacy, 1260–1516

Data sources: Amitai-Preiss, 1995; Ayalon, 1977; Boase, 1978; Edwards, 1987;
Irwin, 1986; Parker, 1993.

brushed aside defending forces, sacked the Armenian capital at Sis,
and pillaged the upper Cilician plain. The raiding army withdrew after
a few weeks, but Het'um had to hand over the fortresses east of the
Amanus. Baybars thus exposed the unreliability of the Ilkhanate to its

Armenian friends. He also showed the limitations of the defensive arc of Armenian castles in the Taurus and Amanus mountains (map 9) against a major power.[151] Restricted Armenian manpower meant that the Mamluks could break the arc and cripple the Armenian economy, even if most of the mountain recesses remained as refuges.

The change in the strategic situation in favor of the Mamluks allowed Baybars, in his final campaign in 1277, to march north into Anatolia, bypassing Cilicia. Turkish discontent with Ilkhanid domination enabled him to carry the war to the Mongols. He defeated a Mongol army in Elbistan and captured Kayseri, a major Seljuk-Mongol center. The local Turks, however, were unwilling to risk a decisive rupture with the Ilkhan, and the Mamluks had to return to Syria. Thereafter, Syria's northern and eastern fronts stabilized with the Mamluks holding the advantage. The principal victims of the stalemate were the Armenians, repeatedly pummelled by the Mamluks.

Mamluk military effectiveness reflected the fact that the stakes were higher for the Sultanate. The Ilkhanate had greater strategic depth and could not be overthrown from the west. On the other hand, a defeat in Syria might lead to the unravelling of the Mamluk regime. On two occasions, the Mamluks narrowly avoided such a catastrophe. In 1281, the Mongols left al-Bira in the rear, seized Aleppo, and were turned back only with difficulty. In December 1299, provoked by Mamluk raids into Cilicia and the Jazira and subversion of the Anatolian Turks, the Ilkhan Ghazan launched an invasion that marked the central crisis of the war.

Taking advantage of conflict in Cairo and the desertion of the Mamluk governor of Damascus, the Mongol army rushed past al-Bira and Aleppo, risking harassment to the rear for the sake of speed and surprise. The Mamluks were perhaps caught off guard by the winter timing[152]—medieval armies usually avoided winter warfare, especially in northern Syria, because of storms and cold. The Ilkhan overcame the disordered Mamluks at Wadi al-Khazindar, near Homs, and entered Damascus. This was a desperate moment for the Sultanate, but it soon passed. The Mamluks retained the main Syrian fortresses and Ghazan found Damascus difficult. Within a few months the Mongols withdrew.

A further Mongol winter expedition in 1301 was aborted by storms

south of Aleppo. In 1303, shortly before Ghazan's death in the following year, the Mamluks defeated an Ilkhanid army outside Damascus. In
1312, the Mongols tried and failed to take the Mamluk Euphrates fort
of Rahba, their last attempt to enter Syria. Hostilities petered out under
the Sunni Muslim Ilkhan Abu Sa'id after 1316, with peace agreed in
1322. The eastern front once more became an open frontier between
Muslim states, while the Anatolian Turks shook off Ilkhanid control.

Strategic Consolidation

Within the Levant, the Mamluks consolidated provincial military
governments based on urban citadels and former Crusader castles. After
the wars against the Franks and the Ilkhanate, the Mamluk military
caste provided a strong authority under which the civilian population
experienced an economic and cultural revival in the early fourteenth
century. Muslim refugees fleeing the Mongols reinforced the Levant in
economic, cultural, and military terms. They encouraged interaction
with Iraq and Iran when the Ilkhanate fragmented after the 1320s.

The Sultanate managed the Levant from seven provincial centers
(map 9), where the governors or *nuwwab* (singular *na'ib*—"deputy")
were almost always directly responsible to Cairo.[153] In Syria, it used the
Ayyubid citadels of Aleppo, Hama, and Damascus, to which it added
Crusader Tripoli as its principal center on the coast. It commanded most
of Palestine from the great Crusader redoubts of Safed and Karak, with
Gaza as the link to Egypt. Away from Gaza, the Mamluks feared that
the openness of the Palestinian coastal plain might make it difficult to
dislodge intruders; hence they razed port facilities. Frankish pirate
excursions from the Kingdom of Cyprus, which continued to claim
"Jerusalem," through the fourteenth century, demonstrated that this was
not mere paranoia.

Port activities continued from Lebanon northward, where the close-
ness of the hills to the sea and the military presence in Tripoli facilitated monitoring of the coastline. Beirut became the main shipyard and
entrepôt, though the local defenses could not prevent Frankish raiding,
or even raids by Venetian, Genoese, and Catalan traders on one another.[154] The Mamluks had "an alarm system of carrier pigeons by day and

signal fires by night to summon help from Damascus."[155] The provincial capital was rarely able to respond, but at least there was quick news of trouble.

Mamluk concerns within the Levant after the Crusader collapse differed between the coast, the coastal mountains, and the interior plains. On the coast, the main interests were twofold—to frustrate any landing or attempt to subvert the mountain communities, particularly from Cyprus, and to encourage revenues from trade. The first replicated Umayyad/'Abbasid concerns vis-à-vis Byzantium while the second echoed Fatimid commercial interests. The Levant trade with Europe in Mamluk times was secondary to that from Egypt, and not a mainstay of the Syrian economy. The southwest Asian trade routes, diminished by the Mongol advance, were further disrupted by the Mamluk capture of the Crusader ports, when the papacy embargoed commerce with the Sultanate. Nonetheless, European links with Egypt were too profitable to be overridden by religion, and this guaranteed a return of Italian and Catalan merchants to the Syrian ports. Even in their absence, the financial adviser of Sultan al-Nasir Muhammad, Karim al-Kabir, planned in the 1320s to develop Ladhiqiyya, possibly for trade with Italy through Cyprus.[156] Venetian convoys sailed to Beirut after Venice concluded new treaties with the Mamluks in 1355 and 1361.[157]

Guarding the Mediterranean flank of Syria depended on securing the coastal hills, particularly Mount Lebanon. While they destroyed coastal fortifications, the Mamluks strengthened those in the uplands, including Safed and Crac des Chevaliers.[158] In Palestine, Baybars reinforced Qaqun, in the Samarian hills above the coastal plain, and established Turcoman settlers in the western fringes of Judea and Samaria.[159]

The main task, however, was the subjugation of the Maronites, Druze, Twelver Shi'ites, and Alawites of Mount Lebanon and the Nusayriya range, on account of their religious distinctiveness and suspect relations with the Franks. Qalawun began the process by raiding the Maronite clans inland from Tripoli in 1283. In 1292, after the fall of Acre, the Mamluks moved against the Twelver Shi'ites and Maronites of the Kisrawan and Jubayl districts north of Beirut. This expedition became a fiasco; it was ambushed, and only extracted after negotiation. Further, when the Mongols seized interior Syria in 1299,

Druze from Mount Lebanon plundered retreating Mamluk forces.

Vigorous Mamluk reaction was inevitable. In 1300, the governor of Damascus attacked the Druze. The leading Sunni Muslim scholar Ibn Taymiyya accompanied the governor,[160] excoriating the mountain heresies. The punishment proved insufficient. In 1305, the Kisrawan Shi'ites rose in rebellion and were suppressed with much bloodshed. The governor then settled loyal Turcomans in the Kisrawan and the coastal margins of the Nusayriya hills,[161] to watch the sea, the roads, the Shi'ites, and the Alawites.

Thereafter, the Sultanate settled into a policy of "divide and rule," tolerating the Maronites, establishing better relations with the Druze chiefs, and repressing the Shi'ites and Alawites. The distribution of landholdings to soldiers in the 1317 property survey (*rawk*) of Tripoli province was apparently organized to facilitate supervision of these two communities.[162] Mamluk targeting of the Kisrawan Shi'ites had important implications—it eased Maronite migration south into the Kisrawan in early Ottoman times. By the nineteenth century, a few villages inland from Jubayl were all that remained of the old Shi'ite presence in the coastal mountains north of Beirut. After 1300, the Mamluks turned against the Maronites only when provoked by Christian enemies, most notably after Peter of Cyprus sacked Alexandria in 1365.

As in Umayyad and 'Abbasid times, the interior provincial centers were the backbone of the Mamluk position in the Levant—in the Mamluk case, the line through Aleppo, Hama, Damascus, and Karak. Wars with the Franks and Mongols impelled the Mamluks to fortify their nerve centers, not just their frontiers. Conflict in the Levant through the Fatimid and Crusader periods left many towns and strategic locations with defensive works, which the Mamluks extended.

The interior cities had never before been so thoroughly garrisoned in any period of rule by a single power. The Romans concentrated their forces on the eastern frontier after suppressing the Jews in Palestine, and the Arab Caliphate concentrated on the northern front with Byzantium. Although senior Mamluks preferred to live in Cairo and regarded the Levant as peripheral, provincial governors had significant Mamluk retinues. In addition, interior Syria provided the Sultanate's main infantry force, mobilized from the freemen of the towns and the desert tribes. Ayalon cites figures that indicate substantial contingents in Aleppo, Damascus, Tripoli, and Safed.[163]

Defense in depth enabled the Mamluks to survive the Mongol penetration of 1299–1300, and this experience conditioned Mamluk rule through the fourteenth century, the height of the Sultanate's power. Timurlane's brief seizure of Damascus in 1401 gave another lesson of the uncertainties of a region so exposed to the north and east, even when occupied by a militarized state based in Egypt. Timurlane, after all, only replicated the incursions of the Ilkhan Ghazan and the Byzantine Emperor John Tzimisces, and was a harbinger of the Ottoman Sultan Selim the Grim.

Tenacity and Adversity

After 1320, Mamluk geopolitical concerns in the Levant projected northward into Cilicia and the Anatolian margins, with the distractions of piracy on the Syrian coast. Unlike the 'Abbasids, however, the Mamluks did not face a regional power like Byzantium, but local Turks and Christians (map 9)—the Turcoman rulers of Karaman and Elbistan,[164] the Cilician Armenians, and the Frankish Kingdom of Cyprus, last relic of the Latin Levant. This was the situation from the Ilkhanid recession in the early fourteenth century to the Ottoman domination of Anatolia in the late fifteenth century.

The Armenian position was increasingly desperate with the loss of Ilkhanid cover. Between 1290 and 1320, the Mamluks consolidated their influence in the upper Jazira, taking the last Armenian strongpoint of Qila'at al-Rum on the Euphrates north of al-Bira and installing a governor in Malatya. This outflanked Cilicia to the east. Thereafter, the Armenians also faced the Turcomans to the north, no longer restrained by the Ilkhan. The Turcomans initially had friendly relations with the Mamluks.

The Sultanate wanted Cilicia's timber and iron, as well as the revenues of the port of Ayas, the main outlet from central Anatolia to the Mediterranean.[165] Through the early fourteenth century, the Mamluks got what they required by exacting onerous tribute payments from the

Armenians, without direct occupation.[166] In 1322, 1332, and 1337, the Mamluks raided Ayas, destroying its defenses and in 1332 installing Mamluk officials to collect half the customs revenues.[167] The last attack came after local people murdered two officials,[168] and it inaugurated permanent occupation. In 1344, the Armenians surrendered Adana and Tarsus, giving the Sultanate much of the Cilician coastal plain.

Squeezed between the Mamluks to the east and the Karamanid Turks to the west,[169] the Armenians got help from Frankish Cyprus to keep their access to the Mediterranean. In the 1360s, the Armenians joined Peter of Cyprus in his war against the Mamluks, which involved the attack on Alexandria and raids against the Syrian ports. The Sultanate, lacking naval capability, was unable to do much about Cyprus and negotiated a peace after Peter's death in 1369. This finally isolated the Armenians, and in 1375 the Sultanate despatched an army to Sis and extinguished the kingdom.

In the late fourteenth century, the Mamluks faced difficulties in maintaining their supremacy on the Anatolian margins. The resources of the Sultanate were weakened in the late 1340s by the Black Death, which may have killed up to one-third of the population of Egypt and the Levant, devastating both the cities and their rural surrounds.[170] In particular, it took a heavy toll among the Mamluk soldiery, who remained in their urban barracks.[171] Plague seems to have been less severe on the Anatolian plateau, away from the trade routes.[172] This heightened the challenge to the Mamluks from the Ottoman Turks, who unified much of Anatolia under their rule after 1380. The Ottoman rise also coincided with political turbulence in the Mamluk territories, as the Qalawunid dynasty lost its grip on the Sultanate and gave way to Circassian Mamluks in the 1380s.

The deterioration can be traced in the affairs of the Levant. Under al-Nasir Muhammad, competent governors in Damascus and Aleppo gave Syria stability after the wars against the Franks and Mongols. Tankiz, the governor of Damascus between 1312 and 1340, implemented a major program of urban development and waterworks.[173] In the early 1340s, however, a deposed sultan held the fortress of Karak, threatening Egypt's link with Damascus. Al-Nasir's son, al-Nasir Hasan, revived central authority in Syria in the 1350s. He appointed non-Mamluks as his representatives in Aleppo, Damascus, and Safed. In contrast, when Barkuk seized power in 1382, the Levant became a base for rebellion against Cairo. In 1389, the governors of Malatya and Aleppo seized Syria and invaded Egypt, temporarily deposing the sultan.

In the meantime, the Mamluks failed to hold onto Cilician Armenia. In 1378, after only three years of direct rule, the Sultanate transferred Cilicia to a tributary Turcoman chief, Ramadan, who asserted his autonomy. Karaman came under pressure from the Ottomans, who annexed it in 1397. By the late 1390s, Mamluk influence on the Levant's Anatolian frontier contracted to Elbistan, north of Malatya. In 1399, after Barkuk's death, the Ottomans thrust into the Jazira, briefly capturing Malatya.

Timurlane's assault on the Ottomans rescued the Mamluks. Although Timurlane devastated Syria in 1400–1401, to overawe Cairo before he marched against the Ottoman Sultan Bayezit I,[174] his intervention postponed the decisive Ottoman-Mamluk clash. Timurlane's defeat of Bayezit allowed the eastern Anatolian chieftains to recover their autonomy, and the Ottomans did not reappear for half a century. Timurlane's own swollen domains collapsed after his death, apart from eastern Iran.

At first the Mamluks drew little benefit from such good fortune. Mamluk dissidents in Aleppo and Damascus rose in revolt in 1405. The Sultan al-Nasir Faraj made expeditions into the Levant against rebels, falling victim to al-Mu'ayyad Shaykh in Damascus in 1412. Shaykh himself faced revolts in Syria, and was unable to turn to the Anatolian front until 1417. He then assaulted the resurgent Turcoman principalities. He expelled the Karamanids from Tarsus in Cilicia, and reduced both Cilicia and Elbistan to their previous vassal status.[175]

The last great Mamluk sultan, al-Ashraf Barsbay, secured this situation into the 1430s. Unlike his predecessors, Barsbay also had the time and energy to deal with Cypriot piracy. Between 1424 and 1426, he sent three expeditions to the island from Egypt, one of which collected Syrian troops in Tripoli.[176] He forced the Franks into a tributary relationship. Toward the end of his reign, in 1437, Barsbay mobilized the forces of the Syrian governors for an attack into Elbistan to humble a Mamluk rival who was inciting Turcoman leaders to invade the Levant.

Developments on the Anatolian frontier went against the Mamluks after the Ottoman capture of Constantinople in 1453. This time there was no relief from the Ottoman ascent. In the late fifteenth century, the Mamluks were even more disadvantaged than in the 1390s by the impact of violence and disease on their resources. Further plague epidemics caused a sustained population decline, with royal Mamluk recruits being repeatedly decimated.[177] The Mamluks also failed to adopt the new muskets and infantry tactics deployed by the Ottoman janissary corps.

In 1475, the Ottomans absorbed Karaman in their renewed expansion through eastern Anatolia. As in the 1390s, only Cilicia and Elbistan were left as a buffer for Syria. The Mamluk position suffered from tussles with the Ottomans over the succession in Elbistan in the 1470s, which pulled the Mamluks into an expensive frontier war in the 1480s.[178]

The time of reckoning came after Selim I, later named "the Grim," displaced his father Bayezit II as Ottoman sultan in 1512. Selim checked the new Iranian Safavid regime at the battle of Çaldiran in 1514, thereafter eliminating Elbistan's autonomy. The Mamluk Levant now had no cover to the north. In summer 1516, when Selim again led his army into eastern Anatolia, the Mamluk sultan advanced north through Syria. Selim, perhaps initially undecided as to whether he would strike into Syria or Iran, decided he had best secure his southern flank and invaded the Jazira. He hurried past Malatya and shattered the Mamluk army north of Aleppo in August 1516, then taking Aleppo and Damascus.

Like John Tzimisces and Timurlane before him, Selim did not plan to move further south, and was wary of logistical overstretch. Mamluk dissidents, however, persuaded him to take Palestine and invade Egypt. He reached Cairo in January 1517, eliminating the Mamluk Sultanate and unifying the eastern Mediterranean under a single authority for the first time since the Romans.

The Ottoman Levant

The Ottomans found the Levant exhausted. By the early sixteenth century, the population of Syria and Palestine, estimated at about 1.2 million for the 1340s,[179] before the Black Death, was below one million. Indeed, the fifteenth and sixteenth centuries were probably the demographic nadir of the past two thousand years. In Cilicia and on the Anatolian margins, the Armenian population dwindled in the face of incursions by nomadic Turcomans and Kurds through the fifteenth century. The Palestinian and Cilician coastal plains were mainly wilderness at the outset of Ottoman rule.

In 1521, the Ottoman government established one province for the Levant, including Cilicia, which was run from Damascus, with division into *sanjak*s (sub-provinces).[180] In 1568, Aleppo became the center of a separate province. Two more provinces, based on Tripoli and Adana (Cilicia), were carved out of the territories of Damascus and Aleppo respectively in the 1570s. The fact that all four governors resided in what is now Syria, Lebanon, and southern Turkey reflected the economic and political realities of the sixteenth century. Aleppo and Damascus, each down to around 60,000 inhabitants,[181] were nonetheless the major towns of the Levant, with Tripoli as the primary coastal settlement.

For the Ottomans, the strategic axis of the region passed south from Anatolia through Aleppo and Damascus, then bifurcated—one branch continuing via the desert margins of Transjordan to Mecca and Medina, and the other passing via the Palestinian hills to Jerusalem and Hebron and thence to Gaza and Egypt. This axis connected the Anatolian core of the empire with Arabia, where Ottoman overlordship was critical to the sultan's claim to paramountcy in the Islamic world, and Egypt, as in Roman times critical for its grain and tax revenues.

Later in the sixteenth century, after Süleyman the Magnificent conquered Iraq in the 1530s, the route from the Persian Gulf through Baghdad and Aleppo, bifurcating to the Syrian coast or through Anatolia to Istanbul, increased in significance.[182] Aleppo thus became the nexus of the major communication lines of the Ottoman Middle East. For its part, Damascus represented the meeting point of the routes

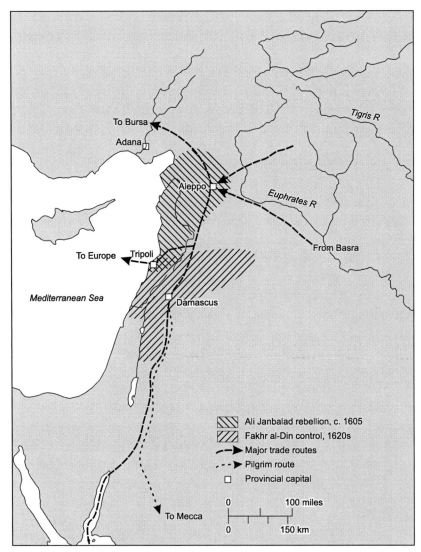

Map 10—The Ottoman Levant, early seventeenth century

Data sources: Abu-Husayn, 1992; Inalcik and Quataert, 1994; Salibi, 1988.

linking Anatolia, Arabia, and Egypt (map 10).

Until the mid-seventeenth century, the Ottoman emphasis in the east was continental, directed toward holding Iraq against the Iranian Safavids, protecting the land caravans, and guarding the pilgrimage route to Arabia. Nonetheless, precisely because Aleppo, Damascus, and the axis linking them were so crucial to this geopolitics, the Ottomans also had to safeguard their western rear—the coastal hills.

For more than a century after they first rebelled in 1518, the Druze of Mount Lebanon presented the principal problem. The Druze had had government favor in late Mamluk times, resented the new order, and maintained connections with the Venetians who replaced the Franks in Cyprus.[183] Maronites and Shi'ites were initially quiescent, but became difficult later. Further north, the Alawites had no external relations and Turcoman landholders contained them easily. The Mamluks had already subdued the Armenians and Isma'ilis.

The troubles with the Mount Lebanon Druze were the nearest Ottoman equivalent to Rome's difficulties with the Jews of Judea. Sunni judges and scholars in Ottoman Damascus took the same belligerent attitude toward them as their Mamluk predecessors had taken toward the Kisrawan Shi'ites. Major Druze clans, with the advantages of rugged topography, intelligent leadership, and Venetian muskets, rejected Ottoman attempts to command the mountain. They rebelled for decades, and the Ottoman conquest of Cyprus in 1571 made no difference. The central government, heavily committed against the Habsburgs in Hungary, was concerned about European interest in Mount Lebanon. In 1585, Istanbul ordered the governor of Egypt, Ibrahim Pasha, to repress the Druze. Ibrahim Pasha assembled forces from Egypt, Syria, and Anatolia for the task, and after a successful campaign was made first minister in the Ottoman regime.

Away from Mount Lebanon, the Ottomans had firm control of the Levant through the sixteenth century. From the 1530s to the 1590s, the unification of the Levant, Iraq, Arabia, and Egypt under Ottoman control led to a surge of trade through Aleppo and Damascus. Ottoman sea power restricted Portuguese ability to divert the Indian Ocean trade to the Atlantic. Portuguese based in Hormuz themselves profited from the Persian Gulf route to the Levant. Spices came to Damascus from the

Red Sea, and silk, spices, pearls, and other goods to Aleppo from Basra. Low ship taxes and convenient access from Damascus and Aleppo through the Homs gap made Tripoli the main outlet to the Mediterranean,[184] while land caravans proceeded from Aleppo across Anatolia to Bursa. In 1599–1602, the Aleppo customs generated two-thirds of the Ottoman revenue surplus in Syria.[185] Ottoman power deterred the desert nomads and after 1585 Mount Lebanon's turbulent affairs were contained for a while.

In the early seventeenth century, the Ottoman practice of appointing local chieftains to administrative positions destabilized the Levant. In Mount Lebanon, the Druze leader Fakhr al-Din Ma'n controlled his community satisfactorily as sub-governor of the *sanjak* of Beirut-Sidon after 1593. In 1598, he expelled the governor of Tripoli, a Turcoman chief, from the district of Kisrawan.[186] Thereafter, Fakhr al-Din acquired the *sanjak* of Safed from the governor of Damascus and developed an interest in political autonomy. In 1605, he linked with 'Ali Janbalad, governor of Aleppo, a Kurdish chief who wanted to make his own state in northern Syria.

This was a dangerous moment for the empire (map 10). First, unemployed soldiers disrupted communications across Anatolia to the Levant—the Celali rebellions. The Ottoman state was no longer advancing in Europe, and faced a financial shortfall. Second, both Fakhr al-Din and Janbalad had strong relations with Western Europe. Tuscany promised Janbalad backing in return for trade privileges, and Fakhr al-Din contacted the Papacy. In 1598, the Vatican upgraded its links with Mount Lebanon's Maronites by establishing a college in Rome to train Maronite priests. Fakhr al-Din had a close synergy with leading Maronite clans.

Janbalad declared his independence in Aleppo, and in 1607 overthrew the governor of Tripoli. He campaigned jointly with Fakhr al-Din, who took the opportunity to seize Beirut. Reacting swiftly, the Ottomans sent an expeditionary force to Aleppo, and Janbalad fled into Anatolia. His family married into the Mount Lebanon Druze community, and their descendants, the Junblats, became the most influential Druze family in modern Lebanon. In 1613, an Ottoman expedition forced Fakhr al-Din into exile in Tuscany, but the authorities allowed him back in 1618 because they could not control the Druze.

In the 1620s, Fakhr al-Din deposed the governor of Damascus and extended his influence to Palmyra. This coincided with the occupation of Iraq in 1624 by the Iranian Safavid ruler Shah 'Abbas, who expressed his intention to march to Aleppo and take over the Persian Gulf–Levant trade.[187] The conjunction of an Iranian Shi'ite challenge from the east with defiance in Mount Lebanon threatened to sever the Aleppo-Damascus axis, and the Ottomans could not permit Fakhr al-Din to command interior Syria. For the Ottomans, the spectres of Druze recalcitrance, Maronite ties with Western Europe, and the special relationship of Mount Lebanon's Shi'ites with Iran, converted to Twelver Shi'ism by the Safavids with Lebanese assistance, made it imperative that Fakhr al-Din's "principality" be demolished. In 1633, a large Ottoman army invaded Mount Lebanon and captured Fakhr al-Din, who was executed. In 1638, the Iranian danger ended with the Ottoman recapture of Baghdad.

Although the Ottomans recovered their position in southwest Asia, the Persian Gulf–Levant trade began to decline. While the Ottomans were preoccupied with Iran, the Dutch and English pushed aside the Portuguese in the Indian Ocean. The Ottomans and their Muslim allies in southeast Asia could not now hinder diversion of trade toward the Cape of Good Hope. Süleyman the Magnificent's vision of Ottoman global power,[188] via domination of Eurasia, was long gone by the mid-seventeenth century. The Levant lost its status as a transcontinental hinge and became a side-route in commerce between the Indian Ocean and Europe. The Venetians and other Italians diminished with it. For the next century and a half, the Levant was part of an Ottoman world of more limited horizons.

Management Dilemmas

Between the mid-seventeenth and late eighteenth centuries, the international balance shifted against the Ottoman Empire. The Ottomans were almost continuously at war against one or more of Habsburg Austria, Tsarist Russia, Safavid Iran, Venice, and Poland, and despite some success, they lost territory in the Balkans and north of the

Black Sea. They preserved the Iranian frontier, but the fighting represented a costly distraction. In this environment, the Ottomans wanted
peace in the Levant, with remission of taxes to Istanbul and respect for
imperial sovereignty.

To prevent a recurrence of the Janbalad and Fakhr al-Din episodes,
the central government imported governors from other parts of the
empire, rotated them rapidly, and divided provincial government
responsibilities among officials. The purpose was to limit local power
bases. The problems included lack of local knowledge by the governors, and weakened capability for action. It worked for a few decades
while the desert tribes remained quiet, the Druze were divided, and
Aleppo still prospered.

In the early eighteenth century, however, conditions changed.
During the struggle with the Habsburgs between 1683 and 1699, the
Ottomans neglected security for the desert caravans,[189] including the
Damascus-Mecca pilgrimage, at the same time that the 'Anaza tribal
confederation of Arabia moved toward the Levant.[190] In 1701, Bedouin
plundered the Mecca pilgrimage caravan, killing 30,000 pilgrims.

A new force also appeared in Mount Lebanon. In 1697, the Shihab
family took over the Druze "principality," reduced to the hills south of
Beirut since the 1630s. Allied with the Junblats, in 1711 the Shihabs
defeated Druze opponents at 'Ayn Dara. The latter migrated to hills
south of Damascus, henceforth known as the Jabal al-Druze. The
Shihabs and Junblats extended their sway in Mount Lebanon in the following decades.

To the north, Aleppo remained the dynamo of the Levant into the
eighteenth century, with local production compensating for losses in
long-distance trade.[191] The city's population grew to about 115,000 in
1683,[192] ahead of Damascus. In the late seventeenth century, however,
disturbances in Iran and the desert hit the silk trade, and led to its diversion from Aleppo to Izmir.[193] Depredations by Kurdish, Turcoman, and
Arab tribesmen also caused rural depopulation around Aleppo.

The threat to the pilgrimage and failure to maintain security led the
Ottomans to revise their methods. In 1713, the government appointed
a member of the prominent al-'Azm family of Hama as governor of
Damascus. This marked a return to local expertise, with the governor

again being given broad authority.[194] The Damascus governor, for example, was made personally responsible for the annual pilgrimage to Mecca. Governors were no longer asked to lead armies to the imperial frontiers, a practice that had disrupted provincial administration. There was also a preference for appointing local notables (*Ayans*) who had good connections in Istanbul. Several al-'Azms served as governors in the eighteenth century.

Efforts to strengthen government authority worked reasonably up to the 1750s. In Damascus and Aleppo, the governors had difficulty balancing amid janissary troops, guilds of tradesmen and craftsmen, and the religious elite.[195] Nonetheless, factional diversity split opponents and governors created their own retinues. The central government used appointments and patronage to bind local notables into Ottoman networks, and to convert prominent Sunni Muslim religious families from the Shafi'i tradition (*madhhab*) to the official Hanafi rite.

On the desert margins, the governors sought to contain tribesmen in Transjordan, the Hawran, and the interior plain north from Homs to the Jazira. They failed to turn Kurds and Turcomans into settled peasants,[196] but were temporarily successful in buying off the 'Anaza Bedouin. The governors used subsidies and employment of tribesmen in the pilgrimage guard to assimilate Bedouin into settled society. The Ottoman authorities also renovated the dilapidated fortresses on the pilgrimage road,[197] particularly in Transjordan.

Through the eighteenth century Mount Lebanon and northern Palestine became more prosperous, which diminished the domination of Damascus. This reflected a shift in foreign commercial interest, particularly by the French, from the caravan trade to local production of silk and cotton.

Silk cultivation lay behind the rise of the Shihabs in Mount Lebanon and the increasing numbers of Maronite Christians within the resurgent mountain "principality." French cultural influence and Vatican-instigated church reforms encouraged Maronite assertiveness. After 1770, the Shihabi domain extended to northern Lebanon, wresting the hinterland of Tripoli from a Shi'ite tax farmer.[198] The Shihabs carefully respected Ottoman sovereignty, represented after 1660 by the province of Sidon. However, the conversion of leading Shihabs from Sunni

Islam to Maronite Christianity in the late eighteenth century indicated coming difficulties.

Developments in northern Palestine had more immediate impact.[199] Encouraged by the French, Zahir al-'Umar, a Galilee tax farmer, promoted cotton cultivation around Acre in the 1750s. Al-'Umar created a productive fiefdom, fortifying Acre as his headquarters and bringing Palestine out of political obscurity. From the outset, al-'Umar subverted the authority of the governor of Damascus. He imported rifles, and the desert tribes used Ottoman subsidies to buy them from him.[200] This demonstrated the risks in the Ottoman methods of assimilating the Bedouin. In 1757, half a century of administrative reform went to waste when 'Anaza tribesmen destroyed the pilgrimage caravan, with 20,000 pilgrims killed.

In 1769, in the midst of a disastrous war with Russia, the Mamluk strongman of Egypt, 'Ali al-Kabir, rebelled with Russian encouragement. He established links with al-'Umar and the Shi'ite leader in southern Lebanon, Nasif al-Nassar, and sent an army into Palestine that advanced as far as Damascus. Fortunately for the Ottomans, the Egyptian commander deserted. The Ottomans made al-'Umar governor of Sidon to salvage the situation, but deposed and executed him soon after the 1774 Küçük Kaynarca settlement with Russia.

While Mount Lebanon and the Galilee advanced, conditions in Syria worsened. Aleppo's population slipped from a peak of perhaps 130,000 in the early eighteenth century to under 100,000 by 1800,[201] with famine, plague, and nomad attacks devastating its hinterland. Tripoli also suffered as shipping turned south to Sidon and Acre. Damascus held up better as the main administrative center, but disruption of the Mecca pilgrimage damaged its economy.

The new salience of the Levant's central coast became clearer in 1776 when the Ottomans sent the Bosnian Ahmad Jazzar to restore order around Acre and among the Shi'ites. Jazzar repressed the Jabal 'Aamil Shi'ites, who had prospered from cotton,[202] so thoroughly that the community disappeared from the political landscape until the mid-twentieth century. As governor of Sidon, Jazzar converted Acre into a political center equivalent to Damascus, and tried to subordinate the Shihabi emirate. He built up his own army of Albanians, Moroccans, and other mercenaries in Mamluk style, and became the key player in the Levant. He failed, however, to subdue Bashir II Shihab in Mount Lebanon, or to impose his hegemony in Damascus.[203]

The late-eighteenth-century Levant presented an extraordinary picture of provincial warlords in Syria and Palestine and autonomous politics in Lebanon, as if the empire had dissolved. Nonetheless, there was no Janbalad-style rebellion against the Ottomans. Jazzar, the Shihabs, and others acknowledged the sultan and remitted taxes. The imperial framework had become looser than its Roman counterpart, but it persisted.

The Return of the West

Bonaparte's occupation of Egypt in 1798 and invasion of Palestine in 1799 coincided with transformation in the Levant. Ahmad Jazzar's fiefdom, combining Acre and Tripoli, and the rise of Bashir II Shihab in Mount Lebanon, represented a shift in political weight from Aleppo and Damascus toward a Tripoli-Sidon-Acre axis.[204] Although the cotton and silk trade from Palestine and Lebanon to Europe collapsed through the Napoleonic wars, the resources of local strongmen sustained the shift.

The Aleppo-Damascus axis was also subverted from the east in the 1770s, when the 'Anaza Bedouin pushed into the territory of the Mawali tribal confederation, which had stabilized the Syrian steppe on behalf of Mamluk and Ottoman authorities from the time of Baybars. Disorder in the steppe produced the late-eighteenth-century crises for settled farming in interior Syria and the pilgrimage route through Transjordan.

Jazzar's fortifications in Acre shielded Damascus from the French when Bonaparte led his army from Egypt into Palestine in 1799. The Ottomans, however, needed British assistance to recover Egypt in 1802, and by 1807 Cairo was in the hands of the Albanian adventurer Muhammad 'Ali. The empire also lost control of Mecca and Medina to the puritanical Wahhabi movement, which meant suspension of the Damascus-Mecca pilgrimage caravan from 1809 to 1813.

Istanbul had to call on Muhammad 'Ali to remove the Wahhabis, which he achieved in 1815, and to help against the Greek rebellion in the 1820s. This established Egypt, where Muhammad 'Ali reformed the army, bureaucracy, and tax collection with French advice, as a rival to Ottoman Anatolia. Although the whole eastern Mediterranean was still under Ottoman sovereignty, in practical terms the Levant fell between competing authorities in Cairo and Istanbul, as in the Fatimid-Byzantine phase.

In the early nineteenth century, the Ottomans had mixed fortunes in Syria and Palestine. Jazzar died in 1804, and after 1812 imported governors gave Istanbul a firmer hold on Damascus. The disruptive struggle between Damascus and Acre waned because of economic exhaustion. On the other hand, local strongmen and Mawali tribesmen commanded the environs of Aleppo and Hama. The Mawali, under pressure from the 'Anaza, invaded the agricultural zone as far as the Nusayriya hills.[205] Further, the Ottomans could not displace members of Jazzar's retinue as governors of Sidon, or return Tripoli to its subordination to Damascus. In the 1820s, for example, 'Abdullah Pasha of Sidon defied dismissal.

The hills proved intractable. In Mount Lebanon, Bashir II Shihab consolidated his command of the Druze and Maronite areas and played between Egypt and the Ottomans. In 1825, he defeated his former Druze ally, Bashir Junblat, with Ottoman blessing—the Ottomans mistakenly calculated that he might be an amenable agent, even after he had spent the early 1820s in exile in Cairo. In the Nusayriya range, Alawite strongmen mobilized armed followings, for example Saqar al-Mahfud of Safita in the early 1800s and Uthman Khayr, who controlled the hill country north of the Homs gap in the late 1820s.[206] Similar militias dominated the 'Akkar, south of the Homs gap, and Hebron and Nablus in the Palestinian uplands.[207]

Egyptian influence in the Levant strengthened through the 1820s. Bashir II Shihab and the military commander of Tripoli both had good relations with Muhammad 'Ali. In 1831, following the path of the Fatimids and Mamluks, Muhammad 'Ali sent his army into Palestine. His move redrew the regional map. Only 'Abdullah Pasha of Sidon, based in Acre, resisted. The Egyptians demolished Acre's fortifications and established a single capital at Damascus. The Ottomans retreated into Anatolia, and Syrians initially welcomed the law and order brought by the Egyptians.

Egyptian rule, from 1832 to 1840, had three consequences. First, it suppressed the local autonomies of the preceding half-century. Muhammad 'Ali imported Europeanized bureaucrats backed by disciplined force. Second, it intensified European interest in the Levant. The French saw openings for cultural and commercial penetration, and the British saw a threat to their strategic position as patrons of the Ottomans. Third, Egyptian policy exacerbated Muslim-Christian tensions provoked by Maronite assertion and European favors to Christian merchants. The Egyptian regime established equality in legal status and taxation, and deployed Maronites against rebellions.

The Ottomans recognized Muhammad 'Ali as governor of "Syria," but they and the British were determined to remove him at the earliest opportunity. The local people soon tired of heavy taxes, weapons confiscations, and military conscription. In 1840, Mount Lebanon's Maronites and Druze briefly united in insurrection, and the British landed troops near Beirut. Egyptian rule in Damascus collapsed, and the Ottomans returned, courtesy of the British.

Sunni Muslim leaders in Damascus and Aleppo aspired to a measure of autonomy under the Ottoman restoration, more successfully in Damascus. After 1840, according to Thompson, reformed provincial advisory councils offered local representatives an opportunity to press community interests.[208] Damascus maintained a fully Muslim council through most of the 1840s, but it took care in handling Christian and Jewish affairs. It also had to watch impotently while local industry succumbed to French price-rigging for silk and British dumping of textiles, exercised via Beirut and the local Christians.[209] The Ottoman Empire could survive only by adjusting to European global supremacy, adjustment that involved economic subordination and suspension of the old religious pecking order.

Aleppo was worse hit. In addition to the decline of traditional crafts, it lost much of its regional trade to Beirut. Harel comments that the Sunni Muslim majority bore the brunt of the economic contraction while the Christians, principally the Greek Catholics, flaunted their new social equality in religious processions.[210] In these tense times, the Ottoman "millet" system of separate legal compartments for Muslims, various Christian groups, and Jews reinforced social and residential segregation, and provided "front lines" for sectarian assertion.

In October 1850, Muslims assaulted the Christian quarters of Aleppo. They did not attack the Jewish quarter, despite the fact that Jews prospered as much as Christians.[211] The Jews were a smaller minority, did not provoke the Muslims, and were not yet considered a threat. The Sunni Muslim elite of Syria supported the Jews when the latter were subjected to virulent Christian prejudice.[212]

The Aleppo riots gave the Ottomans an opportunity to demonstrate their determination to uphold law and order. They punished the Aleppo Muslims severely, which stabilized the Syrian towns and satisfied the European powers.

In Mount Lebanon, however, the Ottomans' administrative failure between 1840 and 1861 compromised their overall position in the Levant. The Ottomans abolished the Shihabi "principality" that had caused them such trouble. They played leading families against peasants and Maronites against Druze. Maronites resented the return of exiled Druze landlords and control of the Kisrawan district by the al-Khazen family. Druze feared Maronite numbers and resented Christian wealth in the mountain villages. In the 1850s, the Ottomans lacked the resources for direct control, and could not handle sectarian jealousies.

Ferment among Maronites, with an uprising against the al-Khazens, mutated into Maronite-Druze fighting in 1860. The outnumbered Druze defeated their disorganized opponents and massacred Christians, including many non-Maronites. Druze success stimulated Sunni Muslim mobs to attack Catholic and Orthodox Christians in Damascus. Several thousand died in each eruption.[213] Ottoman inability to protect civilians precipitated another European naval landing in Lebanon, involving the British, French, Austrians, and Russians. In 1861, the European powers compelled the Ottomans to accept an autonomous province (*mutasarrifiyya*) of Mount Lebanon—a resurrection of the "principality" with defined boundaries, international cover, and a Christian governor from elsewhere in the empire.

Through the late nineteenth century, the Ottoman Levant experienced the effects of the "Tanzimat" reforms in Istanbul, as the empire adopted European laws, administrative methods, and technologies. Railways, the telegraph, and better-trained officials gave the government unprecedented capability in the Syrian interior. Agriculture expanded into the steppe, nomads and tribal chiefs were brought under control by the 1880s,[214] and the urban elite competed for government appointments. Transport improvements, more productive farming with secure private tenure for big estates after the 1858 land law, and foreign investment revived the economy. The price was foreign domination of infrastructure (for example, French investment in railways from the interior to the coast, port installations in Beirut, and private education[215]), and the differentiation of Lebanon and parts of Palestine from the rest of the Levant. In Palestine, Jerusalem and the ports of Jaffa and Haifa developed rapidly.

The greatest change was the rising port city of Beirut, which was the base for French influence on the Maronites and commercial penetration of Syria. In 1800, Beirut had a population of about 6,000.[216] In 1890, it eclipsed Sidon and Tripoli as a metropolis of 100,000, dominating the Levant trade and joining Aleppo and Damascus as one of the three main cities of the region.[217] It had a Christian majority after the 1840s and, with Mount Lebanon, provided a European bridgehead.

After 1865, the Ottomans tried to subordinate Beirut to Damascus by abolishing the coastal province.[218] Muslim and Christian merchants in Beirut protested, and in 1887 the Ottomans restored the city's status as a provincial capital. This episode emphasized the distinctiveness of Beirut and its mountain hinterland. It encouraged Maronites who wanted to see the city united with Mount Lebanon in an enlarged autonomous entity.

To the south, in Palestine, a new element appeared after 1880 with immigration and land settlement by Jews from Russia and Eastern Europe. The Ottomans at first encouraged such settlement, seeing economic benefits. The Jews were perhaps 5% of Palestine's population through the Caliphal, Crusader, Mamluk, and Ottoman periods—a remnant of the Jewish majority of early Roman times, resident in Jerusalem, Hebron, Tiberias, and Safed. This community was maintained by a continuous trickle of religious migrants from the diaspora, increasing in the mid-nineteenth century. Between 1880 and 1914, however, the Jewish proportion of the population of Palestine west of the Jordan River jumped to about 12% and became more dispersed, with agricultural settlements on the coastal plain and in the Galilee gap.

The immigration expressed the Zionist ideology articulated by Theodor Herzl, endorsed in 1897 by the first Zionist Congress in Switzerland. Zionism addressed the precarious situation of Jews in the face of new European nationalisms by proposing a Jewish national home in Palestine. Leading Muslim and Christian families in Palestine, who were increasingly dynamic in the new commercial environment and evolving their own local identity,[219] reacted quickly. In 1891, Palestinian Arab notables sent a petition against Jewish land purchase to Istanbul. As in Mount Lebanon, the Ottomans faced a potentially difficult communal problem, but one that they could hope to contain within the imperial framework.

Unlike the Roman Levant, where there was little relief from crises from about 540 through to the Islamic conquest, the Ottoman Levant never seemed more solid than in its final decades. The population of about 1.5 million in 1840, little different from the sixteenth century, tripled to 4.5 million by 1914,[220] in contrast to the late Roman decline. Considering the improved security on the desert frontier, the imperial command of the Aleppo-Damascus axis, and the broad harmony between Turks and Arabs, there was no reason to expect catastrophe in the early twentieth century.

The Levant appeared insulated from Ottoman difficulties with new states in the Balkans. There was no serious Maronite agitation for independence in Lebanon, and Arab-Jewish friction in Palestine hardly registered on the scale of the ethnic conflicts the empire faced elsewhere, for example with Armenians in Anatolia. Better government and improved economic conditions calmed Muslim-Christian relations in the Syrian interior.[221]

European education and influence brought new ideas about identity and political participation, but their effect should not be exaggerated. Arab nationalism, as an impetus for separation from the Ottoman Empire, was an offshoot of nineteenth-century European ethnic nationalism. It emerged among Christian and Muslim intellectuals in Beirut and Damascus in the 1860s. In the following half century, it never gained more than minority support in the urban bourgeoisie. It had little impact on the urban lower orders or on the peasantry—in this sense

Maronite assertiveness was a more potent phenomenon up to 1914.

As for political liberalism, the Arab elite of the Levant received equitable representation in the Ottoman parliaments of 1877 and 1908.[222] There was no serious discontent either with these arrangements or with the intervening authoritarianism of the Sultan Abdul-Hamid, who stressed Islamic fraternity.

Ottoman loss of the Levant came as a result of the empire's adherence to the losing side in the First World War in October 1914, and of the exposure of Palestine to British forces in Egypt. The 1916 British offensive, stalled near Gaza for more than a year, broke through to Jerusalem in December 1917, and to Damascus and Aleppo in October 1918. It succeeded where Bonaparte had failed, and surpassed the First Crusade in establishing European hegemony. Britain's victory caused a discontinuity comparable to the Islamic and Ottoman seizures of the region. Nonetheless, the Turks retained a presence on the northern margin, just as medieval Byzantium had managed in the seventh century.

Conclusion

The years 1097 and 1917 marked invasions of the Levant by Western European Christians, via Anatolia and Egypt respectively. Between the First Crusade and the First World War, the Levant was rarely free of violence and political change—the geopolitical energy of preceding times continued. This remained the case after the collapse of the Latin Levant in the late thirteenth century, regardless of the fact that the region was incorporated into the Mamluk and Ottoman states through the following six centuries.

Certainly the Levant of the twelfth and thirteenth centuries had its special features—political fragmentation, defense lines in the mountains and on the Euphrates, and frenetic struggles among Crusaders, Muslims, Mongols, and Armenians. Nonetheless, even after this phase the Mamluks and Ottomans still had to deal with desert tribesmen, mountain communities, urban factions, provincial warlords, and intrusions by external powers. The constant geopolitical flux makes nonsense of notions of static societies in the late medieval and early modern Muslim Levant.

117

Crusader, Mamluk, and Ottoman times illustrated the vulnerability and centrality of the Levant as well as its internal disunity. As before the Crusades, the Levant was invaded or threatened from every side through these centuries, sometimes on two or more frontiers at once. The Mamluks, Mongols, and Ottomans came in from Egypt, the Jazira, and Anatolia, while Frankish pirates and Bedouin tribesmen troubled the Mediterranean and desert margins. Later the Ottomans had to worry about collapsing security in the Syrian steppe, European influence on the coast, and challenges from the French, Muhammad 'Ali, and the British in Egypt.

The rising commercial and political significance of Western Europe through these eight centuries also heightened the centrality of the Levant within the Middle East, and between Europe and Asia. The Crusader experience accustomed Western Europeans to silks and other luxury items from East Asia. Until the decisive trade diversion in the late seventeenth century, the Levant functioned as a commercial hinge between the Indian Ocean and the Mediterranean, under Ottoman rule surpassing Egypt. Later, in the nineteenth century, global competition among European powers emphasized the Levant as a strategic hinge, with the British, French, and Russians staking out spheres of influence across southern Eurasia.

Within the Levant, the differentiation of the coast, the mountains, the interior cities, and the steppe continued to hamper political coordination, even at the height of Mamluk and Ottoman capability. The Druze and Maronites in Mount Lebanon embarrassed the Ottomans at the core of the region, adjacent to Damascus. The economic dynamism of Acre and Beirut in the eighteenth and nineteenth centuries was a headache because they were gateways for Europeans and new bases for political organization. Jewish immigration in Palestine complicated affairs in the southern Levant in the late nineteenth century.

Nonetheless, European methods and technologies transferred in the "first globalization" enabled the Ottomans to establish unprecedented control in their last decades. On the eve of the First World War the most likely outlook was for the Levant to remain Ottoman into the foreseeable future.

THE JEWS OF THE LEVANT
FROM THE ISLAMIC CONQUEST
TO ZIONISM

Between the Islamic conquest and late Ottoman times, the Jews preserved a presence in the Levant as a relatively small minority, mainly
based in a few towns. Under the Umayyads and 'Abbasids, the Galilee
continued as the principal area of Jewish settlement, with Tiberias as
its center. The growing Aleppo community eclipsed that of Antioch in
northern Syria, and Jews returned to Jerusalem. The only other notable
communities were in Damascus and Ramla, center of the *jund* of
Filastin. In these towns, Jews were perhaps 5–10% of the population
through the 'Abbasid period, higher in Tiberias. Jews, like Christians,
ran their own communal affairs as "dhimmis"—protected by Islamic
authority as "people of the book," but legally inferior to Muslims. The
Jews of the Levant were overshadowed by the larger Jewish population
of Iraq, which the 'Abbasids treated as the leading Jewish center of the
Caliphate.

Sometime before the tenth century, the Palestinian Academy, the
governing institution of Palestinian Jewry, moved from Tiberias to
Jerusalem.[223] In the tenth century, Jews prospered in Hamdanid Aleppo
and Fatimid Damascus, with an influx from Iraq,[224] where security and
economic conditions had deteriorated. The Fatimids promoted the head
of the Palestinian Academy (the "gaon") as leader of all Jews under
Fatimid rule,[225] as part of the broader political competition with the
'Abbasid Caliphate.

Jewish fortunes fluctuated in the fragmented Levant of the late
Middle Ages. The Crusader invasion brought both the destruction of
the Jerusalem community and the rise of new Jewish populations in the
coastal ports, particularly in the great Frankish entrepôt of Acre. Jewish

pilgrims came from Europe, and numerous French Jews settled in Acre in the thirteenth century. As for the Muslim interior, Benjamin of Tudela found a thriving Jewish population of more than 3,000 in Nur al-Din's Damascus when he visited in 1170.[226] Petahiah of Ratisbon estimated that there were about 1,500 Jews in Aleppo in the 1170s.[227]

The Mamluks massacred the Acre Jews together with the Frankish inhabitants when they captured the city in 1291. Otherwise, however, the Mamluks treated the Jews tolerably well. They reopened Jerusalem to Jewish settlement, and their conversion of Crusader Safed into a provincial capital made this town the focus of Jewish settlement in the Galilee.

The Ottoman conquest of the Levant, coming at about the same time that the Ottomans welcomed Jews expelled from Spain, meant an important reinforcement of the Aleppo Jewish community by Spanish Jews in the mid-sixteenth century. This reflected the importance of Aleppo as a trading center after the Ottoman seizure of Iraq, and its reputation as a center of Jewish religious scholarship. In Palestine, the Safed community particularly benefited from immigration from the Diaspora. By 1567, half the population of Safed was Jewish—945 households (4–5,000 people)[228] made the community the largest Jewish concentration in Palestine and at least comparable to the Damascus and Aleppo communities.

Poor economic conditions in Palestine through much of the seventeenth and eighteenth centuries apparently led to stagnation and even decline in Jewish numbers, because estimates for the Palestinian Jewish population in the 1830s were between 6,000 and 10,000, half in Jerusalem and 1,500 in Safed.[229] Pre-Zionist Jewish immigration through the mid-nineteenth century, mainly of religiously devout Orthodox Jews, raised the number to 25,000 by about 1875,[230] by which time Jerusalem had a Jewish majority.

In Syria, the Jews of Aleppo numbered about 4,000 in the 1840s,[231] rising to about 10,000 in 1879.[232] The similarly sized Damascus community had a nasty experience in 1840, under Egyptian rule, when some of its leading members were falsely accused of murdering an Italian monk. The French consul, in collusion with the local governor and police, targeted Damascus Jews for arrest and torture. The community gained relief only with the restoration of Ottoman control backed by Britain and Austria. Subsequent Ottoman and Muslim benevolence notwithstanding, the incident gave an early warning of the vulnerability of the Jews of the northern Levant.

Under the French Mandate after 1920, the Jewish population of interior Syria reached about 30,000, and that of Lebanon rose toward 10,000. Arab reactions to Jewish statehood in Palestine doomed these communities, though with a time-lag for Lebanon. In the late 1940s, hostility to Zionism stimulated attacks on Jews in Syria—more than half left, and the Aleppo community collapsed. Lebanese Jewry continued to live in a tolerant environment through the 1950s, but almost all migrated in the 1960s and 70s. In Damascus, a Jewish remnant faced tight restrictions by the Syrian Ba'thists through the late twentieth century, with more than 80% of the last 1,500 taking the opportunity to depart allowed them in 1994.

CHAPTER FOUR

THE MODERN LEVANT

The Levant's situation at the outset of the twenty-first century is as different from that of the late Ottoman era as the twelfth-century Crusader alignment was from preceding Islamic arrangements. The externally imposed unity of the Ottoman Levant, shattered with the Ottoman defeat in the First World War, was replaced by the emergence of a Jewish state in most of Palestine, three new Arab states at odds with one another, and domination of the far north by the new Turkish republic.

Britain and France, overlords of Palestine and Syria between the First and Second World Wars, oversaw the initial development of the new dispensation south of the Syrian-Turkish boundary. The outcome by the mid-twentieth century, after the Second World War and local aspirations made continued British and French rule unviable, was the most fractured and contested Levant since medieval times.

The new order encompassed the first Jewish political assertion since the Bar Kokhba rebellion against the Romans and, despite an Arabic-speaking majority in the Levant for more than a thousand years, the first Arab political regimes since the Mirdasids of Aleppo in the eleventh century. It also involved a wide variety of political systems. Israel established a multiparty democracy, limited by Jewish ethnic nationalism. Syria proceeded from unstable bourgeois republicanism to an intimidating autocracy dominated by members of a minority sect. Lebanon evolved a pluralist multisectarian regime that eventually fell under Syrian overlordship. Jordan emerged as an authoritarian monarchy, later with a representative parliamentary dimension.

None of the Arab regimes had secure legitimacy among their populations. The Palestinian Arabs, whether under Israeli occupation after

1967 or as refugees in the Arab Levant, were largely outsiders in this political landscape. When they finally acquired their own regime in fragments of the West Bank and the Gaza Strip in the 1990s, it proved controversial and inept. As for democratic credentials and human rights, it was roughly equivalent to Lebanon in the 1990s—glaringly defective, but creditable compared to Syria.

Through the late twentieth century, unprecedented pressure of people on resources, a widening technological disparity in favor of Israel, and the rigidity of a resented status quo exacerbated tension in the Levant. The Arab-Israeli dispute has overshadowed other conflicts, but it is only one of a variety of cleavages within and among the new states. At the same time, from its commanding position on the Anatolian margin, modern Turkey has loomed over the Arab Levant since the end of the Cold War, like medieval Byzantium during its tenth-century ascendancy.

Overview, 1918–2002

The Anglo-French "Mandatory" Regime, 1918–1947

As with the Islamic conquest and the Crusader invasion, the creation of the modern states of the Levant represented a radical shift in the history of the region. The abrupt disappearance of Ottoman authority in 1918 left the stage open to various sectarian and ethnic elements. The Anglo-French takeover crippled the pan-Arab nationalists of Damascus, who had hoped to substitute their own rule for that of the Ottomans.

Anyway, it is doubtful that the Levant's Sunni Arab elites could have sustained a regional regime. Common Arab identification in *bilad al-sham* was at first simply a reaction to the sudden replacement of Ottoman Islamic authority by European Christian domination. Among Arabic speakers it joined a variety of identities. From the outset, political coherence between interior Syria and Palestine was problematic, as was integration of the formidable minority communities of the coastal hills. Damascus did not provide a strong enough focus for a fractured region, and in the 1920s Sunni Arabs were not more than

60% of the population between the Anatolian margins and Sinai.

Even if the British had not made an arrangement to divide the Levant between themselves and France, and had not promised to sponsor a "Jewish national home" in Palestine, the best the bourgeois Arab nationalists could have hoped for would have been control of interior Syria, Transjordan, and Palestine. The French would have detached Mount Lebanon, Beirut, and the Alawite hills in any case.[233] Turkey would have made sure of Cilicia, most of the Jazira, and probably Alexandretta as long as it secured command of Anatolia. In other words, something resembling the Byzantine-Fatimid division of the Levant would have emerged, with a state incorporating Aleppo, Damascus, and Palestine facing a Lebanese/Alawite/Turkish arc to the west and north.

In the event, the intersection of Anglo-French intervention with local sectarianism and Arab, Jewish, and Turkish nationalism guaranteed a complex new geopolitics, more akin to that of the Crusader period. The 1916 Sykes-Picot discussions between Britain and France led to a north/south division of the Levant. France sought predominance in Lebanon and the Alawite hills, building on its economic and cultural investment in Beirut and among the local Christians. To secure the coastlands, the French also wanted to control Aleppo and Damascus.

To the south, the British sought to command an axis from the Mediterranean to the Persian Gulf, through Palestine and Transjordan to Iraq. Palestine also buffered British interests in Egypt and the Suez Canal, recently threatened from the east by the Ottomans.

Mustafa Kemal's success in removing the Greeks, Italians, and French from Anatolia led to inclusion of the far north of the region in the new Turkish republic, adding a third zone to those of France and Britain. The Turkish-French and French-British boundaries cut across the topography of the Levant and the aspirations of local Arabs, but they endured as international divisions after the British and French departures in 1946–48.

Britain, France, and Turkey also resuscitated the separation of the coast from the interior that had prevailed between the Latin Levant and the Muslim principalities in the twelfth century. In the early 1920s, the ambitions of the three powers led to the establishment of a line running from north to south on the inland side of the coastal hills, between thirty and fifty miles east of the Mediterranean shore. This line split the Levant at a right angle to the Turkish-French and French-British boundaries, and resembled the eastern frontier of the Latin Levant at the time of the Crusader apogee.

In the far north, Turkey insisted that Antakya (Antioch) and Iskenderun be separated from Aleppo as a special district within the territory awarded to France as a League of Nations mandate, because of the large local Turkish community. In the late 1930s, Turkey pressured France to cede this district, to the fury of Arab nationalists. In the remainder of their zone of influence, the French created an autonomous area for the Alawites incorporating the Nusayriya range,[234] and extended the limits of the Ottoman province of Mount Lebanon north and east to include Tripoli and the Biqa' Valley—the new state of "Greater Lebanon." These arrangements potentially prejudiced access from the interior cities to the sea.

In the south, the British similarly divided their zone between direct British rule in Palestine west of the Jordan River and a new principality in Transjordan, created to accommodate their Hashemite ally from Arabia, Emir 'Abdullah. As with French Syria and Lebanon, British legal authority in Palestine derived from a League of Nations mandate. Under the mandate, the British struggled to reconcile their promise to satisfy Jewish aspirations with their commitment to protect Muslim and Christian Palestinian Arabs. In the context of Jewish immigration and Zionist insistence on a Jewish state, this was an impossible contradiction. While the Jews strove to acquire land and build institutions and Jewish-Arab conflict relentlessly intensified west of the Jordan, 'Abdullah quietly established his own state on the Transjordan plateau.

Like the French and British zones, the coastal/interior division also outlasted French and British rule. It at least matched the topography and reflected sectarian heterogeneity. The line, however, was breached in the north, where the Alawite area lost its autonomy in 1936 in a treaty between France and the new Syrian state in Damascus. Damascus, Homs, and Aleppo secured their access to the sea, and the interests of the Alawites became integrated with the affairs of the Sunni Arab interior.

The coastal/interior separation also became messy in the south after the British departure, with the emergence of Israel as the Jewish state, Palestinian Arab rejection of Israel, and the uneasy coexistence of Palestinian Arabs with the Jordanian monarchy.

Ironically, while the Turkish-Syrian and coastal/interior lines became unsettled, the most artificial boundary of all—that bisecting the Levant between French and British authority—became the least controversial. This boundary cut off Damascus from its Ottoman tributary areas to the south. However, despite the pan-Arab and Greater Syrian ambitions of the Hashemites of Transjordan and the rulers of the new Syrian republic, neither seriously disputed the line between them.

Anglo-French control of the Levant between 1918 and the 1940s incubated four new territorial states within the compartments set by the east/west and north/south demarcation lines established by the "mandatory" powers (map 12). Apart from Lebanon, these states bore no relationship to the late Ottoman provinces (map 11).

French interaction with the Maronites of Mount Lebanon and the Arab nationalists of the Syrian interior produced modern Lebanon and Syria. Syria had a particularly painful birth. The elites of Damascus and Aleppo had to cooperate against French "divide and rule" policies, a new experience for cities that had usually been political rivals. Aleppo's loss of its Anatolian hinterland to the Turkish republic was a more grievous blow than Damascus suffered from truncation of its sphere of influence by the British Mandate to the south and Lebanon to the west. France downgraded both cities in favor of Beirut, headquarters of the French High Commission for Lebanon and Syria.

In parallel, two states also emerged in the British zone. The Jews achieved economic and military superiority over the Palestinian Arabs, which enabled them to convert most of Palestine west of the Jordan into the new state of Israel when the British withdrew after the Second World War. The horror experienced by the Jewish people in the Nazi Holocaust intensified Jewish determination, and assured Israel of widespread international support. The highlands of Judea and Samaria, however, remained in Arab hands until 1967, secured in 1949 by 'Abdullah of Transjordan as the "West Bank" of his Kingdom of Jordan.

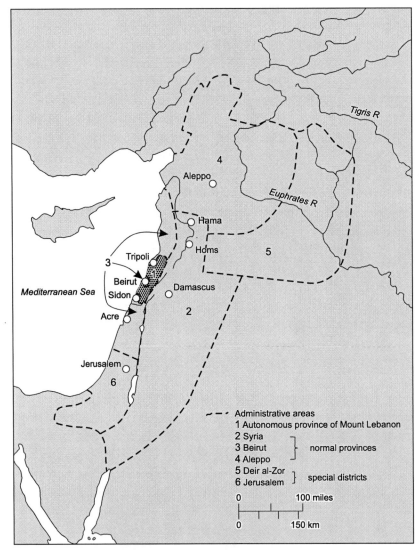

Map 11—The Ottoman Levant, 1900

Data sources: Akarli, 1993; Tibawi, 1969; Tübinger Atlas, 1974.

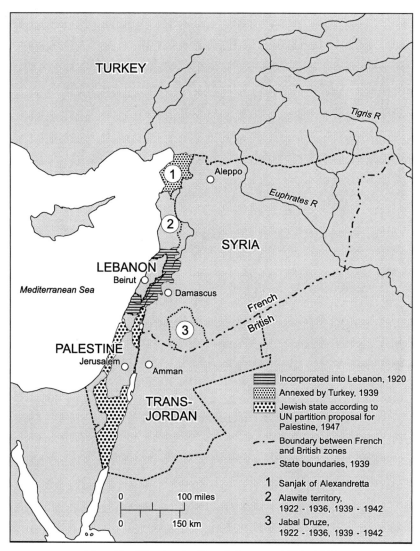

Map 12—The Anglo-French Levant, 1920–1947

Data sources: An Atlas of Palestine, 2000; Khoury, 1987; Shambrook, 1998.

129

Independence, Fragmentation, and Turbulence, 1948–2000

The fracturing of the Levant into Israel and three Arab states (map 13) encouraged interventions by surrounding countries after the British and French withdrawals. The flight of most of the Arab population of the 78% of Palestine that became Israel guaranteed transformation of the Jewish-Arab conflict within Palestine into a confrontation between Israel and the Arab Levant, which contested the legitimacy of the Jewish state. Egypt and Iraq joined Jordan, Syria, and Lebanon in fighting the Israelis in 1948–49, and Egypt retained a toehold within the Levant by occupying a small coastal strip including Gaza.

Egypt and Iraq competed for leadership of the Arab world as it emerged from British and French domination. Command of the Arab Levant was crucial to the outcome of this competition. In the mid-1950s, Gamal 'Abd al-Nasir's Egypt gained the upper hand, but lost ground when the 1958–61 Egyptian-Syrian union collapsed in recrimination.

Syria attracted international interest as inter-Arab affairs became bound up with the Cold War between the US and the Soviet Union. Syria, where Arab nationalism and hostility to Western colonialism encouraged relations with Moscow, attracted the Soviet Union because it outflanked Turkey, a member of NATO. The Turkish-Syrian boundary thus became a Cold War frontier, and in the late 1950s Turkey joined the US and Britain in pressuring Syria and bolstering conservative regimes in Lebanon and Jordan.[235] Up to 1967, the Arab-Israeli dispute generally took second place to these maneuvers, apart from its contribution to estranging Arabs from the West, which was seen in the Arab Levant as patronizing the Jewish state.

The June 1967 Arab-Israeli war represented the greatest shock to the modern order in the Levant in its eighty-year existence. Israel occupied the remainder of former Mandatory Palestine, removing Jordan from the West Bank and Egypt from Gaza, as well as seizing the Sinai Peninsula and the crest of the Syrian Golan plateau covering the approaches to Damascus. The upheaval elevated Israel as the major power of the Levant, and made Arab-Israeli affairs the primary dimension of regional geopolitics.

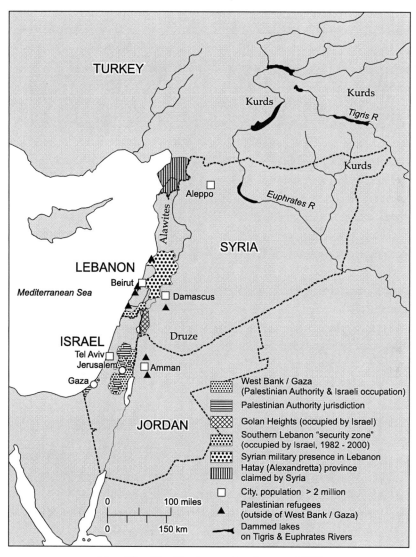

Map 13—The Contemporary Levant, 2000

In particular, Israel's exposure of the military bankruptcy of Arab states brought the Palestinian Arabs, quiescent in their refugee camps and remaining towns and villages since 1949, back into the picture. Direct Israeli rule of all Palestinian Arabs west of the Jordan River, combined with claims to a "Greater Israel" buttressed by Jewish settlement in the newly occupied territories, guaranteed a violent confrontation.

Palestinian guerrilla attacks against Israel from Jordan in the late 1960s, and from Lebanon between the late 1960s and 1982, destabilized Jordan and Lebanon but failed to move Israel. The Palestinians had more success when they rebelled within the West Bank and Gaza in the late 1980s—the first *intifada*. In the 1990s, the Israelis acknowledged the burden of controlling more than two million hostile Palestinians, and allowed self-rule in parts of the occupied territories. Self-rule, however, did not answer Palestinian demands for an independent state in the whole of the West Bank and Gaza, sovereignty in East Jerusalem, an end to Jewish settlement in the occupied territories, and a solution for Palestinian refugees scattered throughout the Arab Levant.

Apart from giving renewed emphasis to the Israeli-Palestinian conflict, the June 1967 war transformed the circumstances of the three existing Arab states of the region. Syria's loss of the Golan paved the way for a strong authoritarian regime under Hafiz al-Asad after 1970. Asad ended the instability bequeathed by the French to the independent republic in 1946, and converted Syria into a leading Arab power.

Lebanon and Jordan had to deal with the new assertiveness of Israel, the Palestinians, and Syria. Lebanon's open politics, and the delicate sectarian balance left by France when it added Sunni and Shi'ite Muslim areas to Mount Lebanon in 1920 at the insistence of its Maronite friends, could not accommodate the new strains. From 1975 to 1990, the country was a war zone as factional and sectarian disputes became intertwined with Palestinian, Israeli, and Syrian interventions.

Lebanon only re-emerged as a functioning state in the 1990s at the cost of subservience to Syria. This restored the Syrian-Lebanese linkage of the French mandatory period, but the linkage was now commanded from Damascus—not Beirut. Seventy years after the contested creation of "Greater Lebanon," the Syrian interior had its revenge.

Like Lebanon, Jordan found itself sandwiched between Israel and Syria as the ascendant regional powers. Between 1949 and 1967, Jordan's topographic advantage in the West Bank buffered it vis-à-vis Israel, while the monarchy concentrated on surviving pan-Arab nationalism promoted by Nasir's Egypt and the Syrian Ba'thists. The June 1967 war discredited Nasirism and pan-Arabism, but the Israeli conquest of the West Bank put Jordan in the shadow of Israel. Israeli security interests prevented Asad's Syria from overawing Jordan from the north, though Syria's preoccupation with Lebanon also gave King Husayn room for maneuver in inter-Arab affairs.

Otherwise, Jordan had no choice but to bow to Israeli domination of the southern Levant, especially after Egypt ended its confrontation with Israel in the 1978 Camp David accord. As soon as Israel concluded the 1993 Oslo agreement with the Palestinians, Jordan negotiated a peace treaty with the Israelis, signed in October 1994.

Jordan's relations with Israel in the 1990s differed from Lebanon's subordination to Syria. In the southern Levant the coastal state dominated the interior, the reverse of the situation between Lebanon and Syria. Israel has not needed Jordan for access to the sea or to water resources—as an inland state on the steppe margin Jordan is the disadvantaged party. Jordan is vulnerable to Israeli diktat, including for the security of its port on the Gulf of Aqaba. Israel, however, has no vital interest in Jordan beyond security requirements.

In contrast, Syria has had concerns in Lebanon beyond the security sphere. Syria has shown interest in Lebanon's water surplus, expressed in the 1990s by an agreement guaranteeing Syria 78% of the flow of the Orontes River, which originates in Lebanon.[236] Beirut is also the closest and cheapest port for Damascus. Further, as a long-standing beachhead for the West, Lebanon has offered Syria financial services at the same time as it hosts unsettling cultural influences. In these respects, Lebanon is Syria's "Hong Kong"—but in relative terms, a much bigger "Hong Kong."

Beyond the incentives to steer Lebanese politics and to profit from the Lebanese economy, Syria deployed familiarity as a "sisterly" Arab state sharing the common Arabic dialect and culture of *bilad al-sham*. This familiarity does not exist between Israel and Jordan, and Israel cannot achieve serious penetration of Jordan.

In the late twentieth century, complicated interactions among Israel, Jordan, and the Palestinians characterized the former British zone of the Levant. On the one hand, the emergence of a Palestinian administration under Yasir Arafat in Gaza and parts of the West Bank, by agreement with Israel, indicated potential for an alignment of Israel, Jordan, and "Palestine." This prospect aroused unease in Damascus, which opposed separate Palestinian and Jordanian arrangements with Israel as breaking Arab solidarity, strengthening Israel, and damaging Syria's prospects for regaining the Golan Heights. Syria also feared that Lebanon might drift out of its orbit in the event of a settlement in the southern Levant.

Everything, however, hinged on a compromise between Israel and the Palestinian Arabs. Israel's severance of the West Bank and Gaza from existing Arab states in June 1967 provided the arena for a Palestinian state, but Israel's security and historical claims to the highlands of "Judea and Samaria," lost by the Jews to the Romans, pre-empted this arena. The 1993 Oslo agreement was only a starting point—Arafat's new Palestinian Authority was not prepared to consider partial transfer of the West Bank, creating a collection of Palestinian "islands" surrounded by Israeli settlements, roads, and military areas, as a long-term solution.

In 2000–2001, the Israeli Labor government of Ehud Barak came closer than any preceding Israeli administration to Palestinian requirements, but not close enough from the Palestinian perspective. After September 2000, the second Palestinian *intifada* brought the worst violence in thirty-three years of Israeli occupation to the West Bank and Gaza, and the replacement of Barak by the hard-line Ariel Sharon as prime minister of Israel.

At the Turn of the Millennium

The main feature of the Levant at the outset of the twenty-first century is the imbalance between the non-Arab countries—Israel and

Turkey—and the Arab Levant. Israel, with 6.6 million people, has greater economic and military capability than the three Arab states and the Palestinians combined, representing 29 million people. Turkey is the most powerful state in the surrounding neighborhood. It is linked to the West through its membership in NATO, and in the 1990s developed military ties with Israel. In particular, Turkey commands Syria's main water source—the Euphrates River.

The Arab Levant is disadvantaged by internal fracturing—involving not just three states and the Palestinians, but also secular, Islamic, pan-Arab, and communal identities. Lebanese and Palestinian "national" identities are relatively strong, the former because of the legacy of autonomous Mount Lebanon and the latter because of the struggle with Zionism. The Lebanese, however, remain handicapped by sectarian jealousies, and Palestinians are divided among factions.

The Syrian and Jordanian states are twentieth-century creations. In the Syrian case, the population readily expresses Arab and Islamic identification above and beyond attachment to "Syria." There is also a sectarian cleavage between the Sunni majority and the Alawites who have held power since the mid-1960s. For the moment, regime solidarity, attention to Arab-Islamic sensitivities, and strenuous public denial conceal this cleavage. For its part, the Jordanian monarchy has to balance between the indigenous Arabs of Transjordan, who provide its basic support, and Palestinian Arabs who have become the majority of the population and the underpinning of the economy.

Looking ahead, how might interactions among the Arab, Jewish, and Turkish "Levants" develop in the coming two decades? Continuation of conflict in the West Bank and Gaza promises to complicate Israel's recent alignment with Turkey. Israeli-Palestinian hostilities are embarrassing to Turkey as an overwhelmingly Muslim country. Much, however, depends on affairs between Turkey and Syria, as the allocation of Euphrates waters becomes a supply crisis for Syria in the next few years. More broadly, Israeli intractability would reinforce Islamic radicalism in the Arab Levant.

As for external forces, the Levant entered a new phase in the late twentieth century. With the exception of Turkey, which extends into the northern Levant, surrounding Arab and Middle Eastern states became less important in the Levant's affairs. This was a marked change from the interventions of Egypt and Iraq in the 1950s, and the participation of Egypt in the 1967 and 1973 Arab-Israeli wars. It involved Middle Eastern developments, such as Egypt's withdrawal from the Arab front facing Israel in the late 1970s and Iraq's adventures against Iran and Kuwait. However, it also reflected the solidity of the post-Ottoman states in the Levant by the late twentieth century, most notably Israel and Syria as regional powers. Only twice in the preceding 2,000 years, during the apogees of the Umayyads and Crusaders, did states based within the Levant have such capability.

The contemporary order also incorporates a new feature—the strengthening of "international legitimacy," represented by the United Nations, since the Second World War, and its aversion to the overthrow of states or boundaries by force. This ensured that Lebanon came out of fifteen years of turmoil in 1990 unchanged as a territorial state. It also enabled the setting of guidelines, however vague, for an Arab-Israeli settlement, primarily the principles of "land for peace" and "inadmissibility of the acquisition of territory by war" in UN Security Council Resolution 242 of November 1967, following the June 1967 war.

Certainly, the limited influence of surrounding states on the contemporary Levant does not mean that Israel, Syria, Jordan, Lebanon, and the Palestinians are insulated from the winds of the world. On the contrary, the impotence of Egypt, the absence of Iraq, the minimal "hard power" of the Arab oil states, and the dabbling of Iran as a "partner" of Syria, together highlight the immensely superior role of the US in the affairs of the region.

The United States increasingly intruded into the Levant after the departure of the British and French. It sought to exclude the Soviet Union, secure predominant influence in the Arab hinterland of the Persian Gulf, and buttress Israel as an outlier of the West. These goals were contradictory because of Arab hostility to Israel, especially as the US armed and subsidized the latter from the 1970s on. Nonetheless, as the US became the hegemonic global power in the late 1980s, the Arabs had to work with Washington if they wanted concessions from Israel, economic support, or technological updating.

In the contemporary Levant, as elsewhere, the US is the gatekeeper for the favors of the capitalist West. The Europeans, whatever their pronouncements on Arab-Israelis issues, do not violate US parameters. The US is also the ringmaster of the Levant. It has buttressed Israel, Turkey, and Jordan. Syrian mastery of Lebanon depended on US acquiescence, which has been withdrawn since the US overthrew Saddam Husayn in 2003. Variations in the vocabulary of senior American officials can give Israel a chill sense of its vulnerability. Above all, the US can redraw the map of the Levant in the early twenty-first century—by patronizing "Palestine," or by conclusively constricting the Syrian regime for "rogue state" behavior or "harboring terrorists."

Israel, the Palestinians, and the Arabs

Crusader Precedent?

Arabs frequently compare the Zionist enterprise and the state of Israel to the Crusader invasion of the Levant. In strategic terms there are similarities, but, as already noted, these are offset by the demographic and technological differences, and by the new global political environment. Israel occupies roughly the same space as the Crusader Kingdom of Jerusalem, the leading state of the medieval Latin Levant. It has the same preoccupation with topographic defense lines facing the interior, where modern Syria takes the place of the medieval emirates of Damascus and Aleppo. It also has the same interest in preventing Egypt from combining with its opponents within the Levant.

Further, like the Kingdom of Jerusalem, Israel has the problem of containing an alien population within its security perimeter, whether in the Palestinian hills of Judea and Samaria, covering the approaches from Transjordan, or in the surrounds of Gaza, on the main route from Egypt. The Nablus district, for example, has had a long history of recalcitrance—rising to support Salah al-Din as it has recently participated in the Palestinian Arab *intifada*. For its part, Palestinian Gaza has a strategic position similar to that of Fatimid Ascalon.

Despite being a respectable regional power through most of the twelfth century, however, the Kingdom of Jerusalem always had a precariousness that does not really apply to Israel, at least since the 1980s. At the outset of the twenty-first century, Israel's resources relative to those of the Arab Levant are far superior to anything achieved by the Crusader states relative to their Muslim neighbors. Israel's physical entrenchment in the territory under its control surpasses the wildest dreams the rulers of the Latin Levant might have had for their own reinforcement. Israeli Jews have a deeper commitment as an indigenous population than was the case for most European residents in the Latin Levant.

The preference of many Arabs to conceive Israelis simply as usurping settlers, by implication without serious roots, invites miscalculation on the Arab side. Above all, the tenuous logistical links of the Latin Levant with Western Europe cannot be compared with the Israeli-US relationship in an age in which distance means little to the US as the global hegemonic power.

On the one hand, the fractured political geography of the Crusader period has echoes in the contemporary Levant, both in the Arab-Israeli confrontation and in the affairs of the Arab states. Medieval precedent also provides warnings about the delicacies of alliance management, divergent interests between allies, and the intractability of a conflict reduced to irreconcilable religious visions of holy lands and places. Nonetheless, Arab-Israeli developments are almost certainly heading toward an outcome different from the medieval period, when the Muslims eliminated the Crusader states. That is not to say that the outcome will be a happy one, for either Israel or the Arabs.

False Dawn, 1990–96

The late twentieth century witnessed a partial breakthrough toward détente in the southern Levant. Three developments assisted the establishment of interim peace arrangements between Israel and the Palestinians, and a treaty between Israel and Jordan, in the early 1990s.

First, the decline of the Soviet Union in the late 1980s followed by the US defeat of Iraq in the 1991 Gulf War gave the US supremacy in the Middle East. In this context, Washington moved to stabilize the Levant, the hinterland of the Persian Gulf oil reservoir.

Second, Israel's difficulties between 1987 and the early 1990s in suppressing the first Palestinian *intifada*, after twenty years of easy control of the West Bank and Gaza, persuaded many Israelis that concessions should be offered. A pragmatic Labor-led government in Israel from 1992 to 1996 interrupted the post-1977 pattern of Likud-dominated coalitions opposed to Israeli retreat within geographical Palestine. This opened a window of opportunity.

Third, Israel's increasing military edge over the Arabs, and its entrenchment in the territories it occupied in 1967, persuaded the Palestine Liberation Organization (PLO) that it should take advantage of US amenability to establish itself in the West Bank and Gaza while part of Palestine might still be salvaged.

These circumstances led to the September 1993 Oslo agreement between Israel and the PLO. As a result, the PLO was able to set up infrastructure for a Palestinian state—the Palestinian Authority (PA)—in parts of the West Bank and Gaza. In 1994, the Israelis transferred administrative and security control of about 70% of the cramped Gaza Strip, including the teeming, poverty-stricken refugee camps near Gaza City, Khan Yunis, and Rafah, to the PA. On the West Bank, the PA only acquired Jericho in 1994, with extension of its rule to the main towns of the West Bank highlands in 1995–96. By 2000, after difficult negotiations with Israel, the PA fully controlled about 18% of the West Bank, with administrative but not security authority in a further 23%. The Israelis, however, did not concede sovereignty in either the West Bank or Gaza.

During the Israeli-Palestinian "honeymoon" in 1993–96, wide possibilities for rapprochement between the two peoples seemed to be opening. The southern Levant settled into stability unprecedented since the 1920s. Peaceful exchanges among Israelis, Palestinians, and Jordanians contrasted with the continuing confrontation on Israel's northern front. Fighting persisted in southern Lebanon, where Israel held a "security zone" on Lebanese land and faced mounting resistance from Lebanese Shi'ite Islamic fighters (Hizballah). Israeli and US attempts to draw Syria into an arrangement for full peace in exchange for staged Israeli withdrawal from the Golan Heights led nowhere. The Arab Levant appeared to be splitting between the PA and Jordan, prepared to link with Israel in advance of a final Arab-Israeli settlement, and tightening Syrian-Lebanese opposition to "separate deals."

The stabilization of the southern Levant, however, proved unsustainable. There was too much ambiguity among Palestinian and Israeli supporters of the Oslo arrangement, and too much opposition to it on both sides, for proper development of the peace process. The sincerity of the PLO commitment not to look for a "Palestine" beyond the West Bank and Gaza, and of Israel's willingness for fundamental concessions over "final status" issues—Jerusalem, Israeli settlements in the West Bank and Gaza, and Palestinian refugees—were both dubious.

A succession of shocks in 1995–96 caused the peace process to stall. These included the November 1995 assassination of Israeli Prime Minister Yitzhak Rabin by a militant young Israeli opponent of the Oslo deal, Palestinian suicide bombings in Tel Aviv and Jerusalem in early 1996, and the return of the hard-line Likud to power in Israel in May 1996.

Treading Water, 1996–2000

In the late 1990s, the limited trust established between Israelis and Palestinians in 1993 dissipated. Between the 1996 and 1999 elections, Israel was again led by a government that did not believe in "land for peace" in the West Bank and Gaza, despite acceptance of the Rabin-PLO fait accompli. Likud Prime Minister Binyamin Netanyahu declared that the PA did not deliver "security" for Israel, and adopted a rigid stance on transferring territory to the PA. This devalued the crackdown against the Hamas and Islamic Jihad organizations implemented by Palestinian leader Yasir Arafat after the 1996 suicide bombings. It also left the PA restricted to segments of the West Bank, hemmed in by the Israeli army and Jewish settlements. Palestinians watched the continuing growth of the settlements. They felt cheated over the "land" dimension of the Oslo formula, just as Israelis felt let down over "peace," because of PA shortcomings in curtailing Islamic militants.

I have followed the steady expansion of the Israeli settlements on the West Bank, under whatever Israeli governments, since writing the first academic analysis of this phenomenon in 1980.

It is true that in 2003 the built-up area of the settlements was perhaps 2% of the West Bank, but settlement boundaries encompassed about 10% of the territory, widely dispersed geographically, with further expanses foreclosed for buffer zones and access corridors. From the perspective of the UN and all Western states apart from Israel and the US, the settlements are illegal under international law.

The Israeli authorities have sequestered land mainly by declaring areas "state property," and putting the onus on Palestinians to hire lawyers to prove otherwise. Throughout the West Bank, Israeli settlers live amid fiercely hostile Palestinian Arabs. Violence by Palestinian gunmen and Israeli settler vigilantes has become routine.

It should be noted that the current Jewish-Arab land conflict in the southern Levant is not "age-old," as frequently indicated in the media, for example in the CNN website "Centuries of Conflict." It began in the late nineteenth century and had no antecedents. Historically, the Jews resisted Roman encroachment in Judea, and Arab Muslims under Turkish and Kurdish rulers confronted European Crusaders. Although Jews and Arabs both have long-standing stakes in the southern Levant, they did not confront each other over territory before the modern period.

The Jewish settlers across the 4 June 1967 lines—by 2000 including 150,000 in East Jerusalem housing estates, 200,000 elsewhere on the West Bank, 17,000 on the Golan Heights, and 7,000 in the Gaza Strip—were the touchstone of the opposed nationalist assertions. For most Israelis, the settlements either gave a political hold on strategic hills—the margins of the coastal plain, the Jordan Rift, and the Golan—or represented the national claim to Judea and Samaria, the ancient Jewish core territories.

Even Israeli moderates mainly thought in terms of giving up "isolated" settlements—involving the extraction of perhaps 50,000 people—but retaining the principal settlement clusters in East Jerusalem and the West Bank. Any significant retreat compromised Zionist fundamentals and promised confrontation with Israel's religious nationalist minority.

Palestinians, however, found the notion of compromise within the territories Israel conquered in 1967 difficult to countenance. From the Palestinian perspective, the West Bank, Gaza, and East Jerusalem represented the last 22% of historical Palestine available for a Palestinian Arab state. The PLO regarded its 1993 recognition of Israel's 1949 borders as its concession.

As for the Islamic militants of Hamas and Islamic Jihad, a minority that attracted more support in the PA areas after 1995 as discontent with PA incompetence and corruption increased, compromise meant Israel would get a temporary truce in exchange for total withdrawal from the West Bank and Gaza. Mamluk truces with the Latin Levant were the model. Like their Jewish counterparts, the Palestinian Islamic radicals had a rigid religious bond to territory—the whole of Palestine as a usurped portion of *dar al-Islam.*

In this context, the suspension of the peace process in the late 1990s had dangerous implications. In 1993–95, the Israelis allowed the PA to import light weaponry for its security agencies on the understanding that the PA would contain Islamic opponents of peace and help give Israel "security." In the late 1990s, the continued dissemination of arms in the West Bank and Gaza, facilitated by radical Islamic networks and Israeli mafias, created an explosive situation in the absence of progress between Israel and the PA.

Arab-Israeli developments through the 1990s demonstrated the potential and limitations of US leadership after the Cold War. The US could bring Israel, the Palestinians, Jordan, Syria, and Lebanon into peace discussions beginning with the October 1991 Madrid conference because all feared to offend Washington and either depended on US assistance or desired US rewards. The US also facilitated the 1993–95 agreements among Israel, the Palestinians, and Jordan. Nonetheless, much of the progress in the southern Levant was actually achieved between the parties themselves, with the Norwegian channel between Israel and the PLO surprising Washington.

US limitations became more apparent after 1996, when the time came to deal with core issues put aside in the initial Israeli-PLO rapprochement, and the parties had less interest in further concession. It was no coincidence that faltering US leadership, with the diversions of President Clinton's reelection and the Monica Lewinsky affair, ran together with deterioration in Israeli-Palestinian affairs. Even obtaining the October 1998 "Wye River agreement" for further Israeli withdrawal from about 13% of the West Bank required Clinton's intense personal involvement.

The constraints on US power became most exposed when the environment briefly improved in 1999–2000. Shifting Israeli public opinion produced a new Labor prime minister, Ehud Barak, in the May 1999 elections, and President Clinton was able to make Arab-Israeli issues his top foreign policy priority.

Barak aimed at an Arab-Israeli settlement acceptable to Israel by playing between the Palestinian and Syrian-Lebanese negotiating "tracks." Here he differed from Rabin, who turned away from Syria because of problems in coordinating Israeli withdrawal from the Golan with steps toward a full Israeli-Syrian peace, and concentrated on the Palestinians. Barak hoped to hasten the Palestinians toward "final status" arrangements by opening the prospect of an Israeli-Syrian deal that might sideline Arafat's PA. Similarly, he could pressure Syria by switching back to the Palestinian "track."

In addition, Barak promised the Israeli electorate that he would evacuate the Israeli-held security zone in southern Lebanon within one year after forming his coalition government in July 1999. This reflected Israel's difficulties with Hizballah, but also represented pressure on Damascus, because Israel's presence in Lebanon was the main justification for Syria's post-1990 hegemony in Beirut. If Israel withdrew unilaterally, Syria would face problems with Lebanese opinion regarding its own presence in the country. Israel's proposed territorial retreat thus doubled as a threat.[237]

Barak's zigzag tactics between the Palestinians and Syrians and his alternation between toughness and conciliation confused both Arabs and Israelis. The US joined Barak in a push on the Syrian "track" in late 1999. Israel offered withdrawal to the 1923 international boundary and the Syrians seemed ready for a deal on security and normal relations, but the US could not complete the jigsaw. Clinton hosted Barak and Syrian Foreign Minister Faruq al-Shar'a, and met Hafiz al-Asad in Geneva in March 2000, but the Syrians demanded their 1967 positions on the shore of Lake Tiberias—Israel's main water reservoir.

Asad would not accept an inch less than what Egypt had got in Sinai. His worsening health, fears for his regime's stability, and concern for a trouble-free leadership transition to his son, Bashar, negated all pressures from Barak and Clinton. For their part, Arafat and his advisers were unmoved by Barak's maneuvers with Syria. They saw no Israeli proposals justifying Palestinian declaration of "an end to the state of conflict." They preferred to extract more territory in interim accords without final commitments.

Israel therefore implemented its withdrawal from Lebanon in late May 2000 in the absence of progress with either the Palestinians or Syria. Hafiz al-Asad's death only two weeks later eliminated any chance of an early Israeli-Syrian accord, because of Syrian preoccupation with domestic affairs. Within Israel, Barak's position became increasingly problematic in mid-2000 as the governing coalition unraveled in the Knesset and the prime minister's popularity plummeted.

President Clinton, who had staked his reputation on achievements between Israel and the Arabs, faced leaving office in early 2001 with the Israeli-Palestinian relationship in tatters and no advance between Israel and Syria. Clinton decided to rush the Israelis and Palestinians into a "final status" agreement. He requested that Barak and Arafat meet him at Camp David, where Jimmy Carter had mediated the Israeli-Egyptian breakthrough in 1978.

Barak accepted, because the US agreed that Israel should get an end to "the state of conflict" while retaining basic assets in the West Bank and East Jerusalem. He knew that he would have to make concessions over Jerusalem, hitherto unthinkable for an Israeli government, but believed he could rally Israeli opinion for the prize of Palestinian commitment to a final peace. The PA was unenthusiastic, complaining about lack of preparation and fearful of being pressed to the wall.

Barak's position at the July 2000 Camp David talks, developed further in assent to President Clinton's December 2000 proposals and in Israeli-Palestinian discussions at Taba in January 2001, expressed the outer bounds of Israeli flexibility. This position went beyond what the Israeli majority considered acceptable concessions. Barak's concept of "final status," fleshed out by the US, addressed core issues.

First, Palestinian administration would extend to Arab neighborhoods in East Jerusalem, including parts of the Old City and the upper surface[238] of the Herodian Temple platform (*al-haram al-sharif*), site of the Dome of the Rock and the renowned al-Aqsa mosque. Israel would retain the Jewish quarter of the Old City, including the Western (Wailing) Wall of the Temple platform, and the Jewish neighborhoods created after 1967. In December 2000, Barak accepted that Palestinian administration meant sovereignty.

Second, Israel would eventually hand over 90–95% of the West Bank and all the Gaza Strip to the PA, retaining 5–10% of the West Bank that contained Jewish settlement concentrations.[239] Barak was willing to make a border adjustment south of Gaza to compensate the PA for West Bank changes. The PA would declare a Palestinian state on its territories, but agree to an Israeli military presence in the Jordan Rift, weapons limitations, and Israeli supervision of military links with Arab states to the east.

Third, Israel would take in about a hundred thousand 1949 refugees and their descendants, mainly from Lebanon, on "family reunions."[240] Those who left the West Bank in 1967 could return. Israel, however, would not accept a general Palestinian "right of return" to its territory, because this threatened the demographic foundations of the Jewish state.

The Israeli evolution was not enough for the Palestinians, and Clinton's Camp David gamble failed. First, the PA would not endorse Israeli sovereignty across the pre–June 1967 lines in East Jerusalem, especially when Camp David did not deliver a satisfactory solution for the *haram al-sharif*. Second, Barak's ideas for the West Bank almost split Palestinian territory north and south of Jerusalem, with Israeli rule to extend from Jewish housing estates in East Jerusalem to beyond the large Ma'ale Adumim settlement in the Jordan Rift.[241] Palestinian negotiators wanted viable contiguity within their new state. Third, the PA was prepared to discuss options for the refugee population outside geographical Palestine, but refused to abandon the "right of return."

Not even Clinton could cajole Arafat into taking risks with his Palestinian constituency, especially when Saudi Arabia and other Western-aligned Arab states advised Arafat to be cautious. From the US and Israeli perspectives, the Palestinians should at least have reacted positively, assisting further negotiation. For the PA, the Camp David proposals were simply unacceptable. Arafat's resistance boosted his Palestinian popularity. It did not suit him to indicate flexibility when holding out might induce the US president to seek more Israeli concessions. The US could not discourage such calculation, because it was a logical interpretation of Clinton's personal stake.

The Palestinian Armed Uprising, 2000–2003

Whereas the first Palestinian *intifada* of 1987–92 was a spontaneous uprising that remained the preserve of stone-throwing youths and produced political compromise, the second uprising of September 2000 followed a different course. After the Camp David failure, the idea of leverage through violence gained ground among Palestinians. Lebanon's Hizballah vigorously incited the Palestinians to emulate its own success in hastening Israel out of southern Lebanon.[242] The rioting sparked by Likud leader Ariel Sharon's tour of the Temple platform (*al-haram al-sharif*) on 28 September 2000 was probably pre-planned, and it soon mutated into an armed insurrection. Because it came after Israeli concessions, it produced Israeli hardening rather than softening.

Palestinians misjudged Israel's determination when challenged at its core rather than on its periphery—the Hizballah precedent was misleading. The more appropriate precedent was the 1936–39 Palestinian Arab armed revolt against the British Mandate, which ended in Palestinian exhaustion.

In the first months of the uprising, Israeli Prime Minister Barak adopted tough security measures, but displayed openness on "final status" issues. To Palestinians he appeared brutal, whereas to Israelis he appeared weak. His December 2000 concessions on Palestinian sovereignty in East Jerusalem showed that Palestinian concern about the *haram al-sharif* could get a response. In the heat of the *intifada*, however, the Palestinians demanded total Israeli evacuation of the West Bank and East Jerusalem, with removal of all Jewish settlements.

Barak summoned early prime ministerial elections in February 2001 to salvage his sagging authority, but went down to defeat by Sharon. The Israeli public was desperate; Barak's initiatives had reaped only rejection.

Sharon had a checkered past. In 1983, an Israeli commission of inquiry found him unfit to retain his post as defense minister because of "indirect responsibility" for the September 1982 massacre of about 800 Palestinians by Lebanese Forces militiamen, Israel's Christian allies, in West Beirut. Sharon was also the architect of the Likud-led drive through the 1980s to establish Jewish settlements in the heart of the Palestinian population on the West Bank highlands. He was thus an unlikely source for a peace formula. For the Israeli majority, however, his ferocious reputation made him the man of the hour for reestablishing security.

In the intensified Israeli-Palestinian confrontation after Sharon took office, the two sides adopted untenable postures. On the Israeli side, Sharon dumped Barak's peace ideas, emphasized that Israel would keep East Jerusalem and the Jewish settlements, and proposed a Palestinian state on bits of the West Bank. To suppress the uprising, he favored sieges of Palestinian towns and villages, assassination of Palestinian militants (a tactic of proven futility against Hizballah in Lebanon), and destruction of the PA's security facilities. Israeli perceptions of Arafat's involvement in the violence made it easy for Sharon to form a "national unity" government including the Labor party, with Shimon Peres as foreign minister and Benyamin Ben-Eliezer, the new Labor leader, taking the defense ministry.

As for the Palestinians, activists from the Islamic movements, the Tanzim militia, Arafat's Fatah (al-Aqsa Martyrs Brigade), and the Popular Front for the Liberation of Palestine (PFLP) set the pace. They conducted armed operations against Israeli soldiers and settlers, and mortar strikes into Israel from the Gaza Strip. After June 2001, Hamas and al-Aqsa Brigade members carried out an unprecedented wave of suicide attacks against civilians in Israeli cities. Arafat made little effort to restrain the militants; the PA leader hoped that attrition would bring Israeli concessions or an international observer force.

Through 2001, the two sides drifted into a bloody cul-de-sac, from which the only exit was a return to the political process. Sharon's drive against Arafat and the PA could not ensure "security." Sharon's own West Bank settlement schemes had created such an interpenetration of Israeli and Palestinian populations that no amount of Israeli power could secure Israelis from assaults except through expulsion of the Palestinians or Israeli withdrawal.

There was no certain military remedy to the problem of suicide bombings inside Israel. Tens of thousands of Palestinians in East Jerusalem and the West Bank inhabited areas Israel wanted on its side of a security barrier. Within Israel, the 18% Palestinian Arab minority was increasingly alienated, a powder keg behind any line Israel cared to draw vis-à-vis their West Bank and Gaza brethren. As for Arafat, Palestinian requirements would not change with his demise.

For their part, the Palestinians pursued a ruinous struggle against a stronger opponent backed by the world's greatest power. A fraction of Israel's military might was sufficient to wreck the Palestinian economy and eliminate freedom of movement for Palestinian civilians. Israel could invade PA territory as it pleased. Criticism of Israel in the West blinded Palestinians to their isolation. Major Arab regimes valued their relations with the US above the Palestinians. Anger on the Arab street only expressed Arab impotence.

US withdrawal from the Arab-Israeli arena after Clinton's failure allowed events to assume their own momentum. In 2001, the new administration of President George W. Bush took the view that the violence was simply a local problem in the Levant. Efforts to get the two sides to return to negotiation, such as the "Mitchell Plan," were futile without presidential engagement. The Bush Administration's reluctance to tackle a difficult problem while backing Israel as a strategic ally gave Sharon a free hand against the Palestinians.

The 11 September 2001 terrorist attacks on New York and Washington D.C. changed the global environment. The US now needed to contain Israeli-Palestinian violence, thereby removing a distraction from its new campaign against "terror." On the Palestinian side, Arafat and the militants hesitated between a cease-fire and raising the stakes. Israeli military actions in December 2001 and January 2002 propelled the Palestinian factions toward escalation. However, far from bringing international pressure on Israel to relieve the Israeli army's constriction of the West Bank and Gaza, such escalation enabled Israel to enroll the US in a massive blow against the PA.

First, Israel's January 2002 interception of a large arms shipment acquired by Arafat's aides from Iranian sources exposed Palestinian connections with Iran and Lebanon's Hizballah, both considered enemies by the Bush Administration. At the same time, Jordan accused Iran of cooperating with Palestinian and Lebanese Islamic activists to smuggle weapons from Syria into Jordan for attacks against Israel from Jordanian territory.[243] The hard-line camp within the Iranian regime plainly looked to expand its influence in Gaza and the West Bank, thereby gaining a new foothold in the Levant.

Second, a procession of suicide bombings in March 2002 serviced Israel's argument that it was in the same trench as the US against global terror—even as the Bush Administration welcomed a Saudi initiative for normalized Arab relations with Israel in exchange for Israeli withdrawal from the occupied territories. The Saudi plan foundered in the crosscurrents of the Levant at the very moment of its endorsement at an Arab summit meeting in Beirut on 28 March. Syrian President Bashar al-Asad used his summit speech to justify assaults on civilians inside Israel,[244] the Jordanian and Egyptian leaders declined to attend a summit in Syrian-dominated Lebanon, and a particularly nasty suicide bombing near Tel Aviv precipitated an Israeli onslaught on the West Bank.

Through April 2002, Israel implemented a prolonged military operation to dismantle radical Palestinian organizations in the PA-controlled areas of the West Bank. This involved the invasion and reoccupation of the West Bank cities, with Arafat imprisoned in his headquarters in Ramallah. The Bush Administration viewed the operation as an adjunct to its "war against terror." Israel and the US calculated that large-scale use of force would enable new realities to be created in the southern Levant. It would also refurbish Israel's deterrent capability, battered by Israel's retreat from southern Lebanon and eighteen months of indecisive confrontation with the Palestinians.

In the months after the operation Israel plainly had the upper hand, despite deepening economic difficulties. The Israeli army greatly damaged the West Bank networks of Hamas, Islamic Jihad, the Tanzim, and al-Aqsa' Brigade, even if these organizations retained their Gaza Strip structures and their mobilization potential among a furious population. With the Palestinians reduced to penury and the PA infrastructure shattered, Arafat and his associates faced US and Israeli demands for cooperation as well as new Palestinian anger at PA incapacity.

Further suicide attacks merely cemented US identification with the Israeli position that there could be no discussion of Israeli-Palestinian issues before cessation of violence—anything else would be "a reward for terrorism." The insistence of Palestinian Islamic militants that Israel could be made to crack stiffened the determination of Israeli generals to continue the use of force to crack the Palestinians.

In early 2003, the Israeli-Palestinian conflict was in limbo, contained by Israeli power underwritten by Washington, and awaiting an outcome to the US confrontation with Saddam Husayn of Iraq. Plainly, both sides could sustain the prevailing level of violence for a long time. The death toll of 1,800 Palestinians and 700 Israelis in 28 months was modest compared with late-twentieth-century episodes in the northern Levant—bouts of fighting during Lebanon's war regularly caused equivalent losses in shorter periods, and in February 1982 at least 10,000 died in the Syrian regime's three-week showdown with the Muslim Brotherhood in Hama.

The Outlook

Looking ahead, there are two futures for Israeli-Palestinian affairs. On the one hand, there is practical compromise, perhaps building on the Clinton-Barak proposals and the Taba discussions. A compromise must address the interests of the three million Palestinians in the Arab Levant states, but Israel will not concede their "right of return." Compromise will therefore only partially answer Palestinian grievances while the Israelis must surrender virtually all their 1967 conquests, with limited adjustment of the 4 June 1967 lines in Jerusalem.

This sounds unpalatable to both sides, but it could facilitate a decent life for coming generations. It might be a basis for Israel and the new Palestinian state to establish a confederation, reflecting realities of economic interdependence and the need for freedom of movement in such a small space.

The Israeli-Palestinian conflict centers on territorial issues—East

Jerusalem, a West Bank-Gaza Palestinian state, Jewish settlements in these areas, and security arrangements to compensate Israel for loss of high ground and strategic depth in the West Bank and the Jordan Rift.

Although a water deficit developed in geographical Palestine by the late twentieth century, and Israel draws on West Bank aquifers for its metropolitan centers and new settlements, water sharing will not be an insuperable problem after agreements on territory and security. Desalinization technologies are improving, with lowering costs, and water consumption can be directed away from agricultural uses if Israel and Palestine import more food.

Of course, this requires stabilization of the population of geographical Palestine, perhaps at about 14 million. It also assumes that the worst scenarios for global warming and climate change will not materialize.

There should be no illusions about the second path into the future for Israelis and Palestinians. The alternative to compromise is a continued war of attrition, with peaks and interludes but no exit. There is even the possibility of descent into a medieval-style religious war. Already religious-nationalist extremism grips significant portions of the two populations, and it will not be easy for a pragmatic compromise to surpass the short life span of, for example, Frederick II's 1229 agreement with the Sultan al-Kamil for sharing Jerusalem, buried by 1244.

Israel might note the limited longevity of political orders in the Levant through the last two thousand years. Small states within the Levant have had a high casualty rate—the Jewish Hasmonean kingdom, the medieval Islamic emirates, the four Crusader principalities, and the Cilician Armenians. Israel's strength depends on its ties with the West. Readiness for compromise with the Palestinians will help to sustain these ties.

For their part, Arabs would be unwise to anticipate emulating Salah al-Din or the Mamluks. Israel's power is buttressed by nuclear weapons and the US. Use of weapons of mass destruction, for example between Israel and a Syrian-Iranian alliance, would be as devastating for the Arab Levant as for Israel, because the same environmental precariousness applies in both cases. Also, a future nuclear exchange between Israel and Iran would be deadly for the Palestinians, given the juxtaposition of Israeli and Palestinian populations.

Finally, a warning needs to be sounded about demographic competition. Palestinian Arab natural increase and Jewish immigration have already made the population density of non-desert parts of geographical Palestine equivalent to the most heavily populated regions of Western Europe. The notion in some Arab circles that Palestinians should not compromise because they can overwhelm Israel by numbers promises a miserable future, especially for the Palestinians. If Israel retreats to a territory in which the Jewish majority is sustainable, the Palestinians will simply find themselves crippled by their numbers.

In any case, it seems certain that the Jewish and Palestinian Arab populations of former Mandatory Palestine will each reach seven million before 2015, from 2003 figures of 5.4 million and 4.5 million respectively. Further, the three million Palestinians in neighboring Arab states can be expected to exceed five million by 2015. This assumes a moderate decline of growth rates from their late-twentieth-century peak, and takes into account the youthful Palestinian age structure.

Even assuming an Israeli-Palestinian "final status" agreement on territory, security, and water by 2010, the demographic outlook poses awkward questions for the subsequent phase of Israeli-Palestinian coexistence.

The Arab Levant States

Although Syria, Jordan, and Lebanon comprise the bulk of the territory and people of the Levant, the three countries have been disadvantaged in relation to Israel and Turkey since the end of the Cold War. Israel has absorbed the talents of more than one million Jews from ex-Soviet lands, and established its own high-tech electronic industries. Turkey has assumed a new significance for the West as the hinge state of Europe, Asia, and the Middle East—a vital prop for US influence in Iraq and former Soviet republics.

I updated my firsthand knowledge of Lebanon's sectarian splintering in December 2001. On this occasion, my experience was mainly with the Shi'ites. For most Shi'ites, social and physical circulation is overwhelmingly within the community, between Beirut's southern suburbs and villages in southern Lebanon and the Biqa'. Daily circulation includes jobs in West Beirut, where workplaces provide multisectarian interaction, but such mixing hardly exists beyond work.

Lebanon's sectarian compartments are well marked. In Beirut, Christmas decorations ended abruptly as one crossed from Christian 'Ayn al-Rumanah into Shi'ite Shiyah, where streets featured posters of Hizballah martyrs and Iranian Ayatollahs. Moving on to largely Sunni areas north of Corniche Mazra'a, the martyrs gave way to portraits of Sunni Prime Minister Rafiq al-Hariri. Toward the Syrian border, in Ba'albak, pro-Syrian decoration joined the Hizballah paraphernalia, including a prominent new statue of Hafiz al-Asad erected by the municipality.

The *'id al-fitr* holiday in mid-December provided an opportunity to hear Shi'ite "street" perspectives. Conspiracy theories abounded regarding the September 2001 attacks in the US, with ordinary people convinced that Usama bin Laden was an American creation. There was uniform hostility to the American interpretation of "terror." Conversations in a southern Lebanon village indicated that Hizballah remained highly popular, bolstered by a mix of religion and Shi'ite-oriented Lebanese nationalism fed out by its relentless publicity machine. Villagers unanimously condemned Israel in terms that made peace between Israel and Lebanon seem beyond possibility, at least for the Shi'ite "street."

This, however, did not mean that people viewed Syria, Lebanon's leaders, or other Arabs more positively. On the way through the dismal slum of Hay al-Sulam, a maze of potholed tracks between incredibly ugly apartment blocks that makes other parts of the generally dilapidated southern suburbs seem like the Champs Élysée, the sight of a huddle of Syrian laborers provoked a Shi'ite minibus driver to mutter: "Kharrabu Lubnan" [they have destroyed Lebanon]. I also heard repeated angry accusations that Syrian army officers had bankrupted the well-known Summerland hotel by demanding free facilities and parties. At the end of 2001, Lebanon's Shi'ite community was in a cynical and truculent mood.

In economic terms, the Arab Levant states fell further behind Israel through the late twentieth century. Steady population inflation in Syria and Jordan negated income gains and created a growing burden of young people whom the labor market could not absorb. In 2000, the combined GDP of Syria, Jordan, and Lebanon was only $42 billion—less than half of Israel's $112 billion.[245] This was for more than four times Israel's population.

Syria: Anchor of the Arab Levant

The economic gap is worst for Syria, the regional power of the Arab Levant. Syria is the sump of the Levant as regards per capita income. Syria's income per head in 2000, adjusted for purchasing power parity, was $3,340, compared with $3,950 for Jordan, $4,550 for Lebanon, and $19,330 for Israel.[246] The Palestinian uprising has not been good for Israel's economy, but it has not even dented Israel's advantage over its neighbors.

From the military perspective, Syria received no significant supplies of new weaponry after the early 1990s and had no hope of replenishing equipment in the event of war with Israel. The demise of its Soviet patron and of superpower bipolarity was disastrous for Damascus. In contrast, Israel continued to receive substantial aid from the US to update and reorganize its armed forces in line with the so-called Revolution in Military Affairs. In these conditions, Syria's only deterrence option was the acquisition of ballistic missiles capable of delivering chemical and biological agents—an admission of failure in the conventional arms race.

Syria's frenetic investment in Eastern European–style industrialization in the 1970s and single-minded concentration on military parity with Israel in the 1980s turned to dust in the 1990s. Syria needs to reduce the bloated public sector of its economy, which cannot produce goods at competitive prices or cope with increments to the labor force, and to adopt advanced information technology.

The problem is that the required changes go against the basic interests of the ruling elite. Downsizing the public sector, which includes the state bureaucracy, most industries, and the inflated security agencies, means eroding the fiefdoms of top officials and penalizing the regime's most loyal constituency. Liberalizing access to the global electronic network means allowing the Syrian people to interact on a larger scale with the wider world. Syria's security chiefs fear the political effects of such interaction. At the outset of the twenty-first century, only a small fraction of the Syrian bourgeoisie had even passing acquaintance with the US-led electronic revolution.

Despite the rhetoric of Syria's new president, the regime continued to restrict Internet access—in 2002 the proportion of Syria's population using the World Wide Web was less than 0.2%, compared with about 2% in Jordan, 12% in Lebanon, and 20% in Israel.[247] Further, after the Ba'thist nationalization drive in the 1960s, Syria had no private banks up to 2003, and its financial regulations and bureaucratic processes remained incompatible with serious foreign investment. Syria may well be unable to function effectively even as a cheap subcontracting partner for Turkey or the EU.

Syria's people have been in a time warp for a third of a century. The semi-socialist Ba'thist regime that took power in the mid-1960s provided for numbers that increased from five million to 17 million through the late twentieth century at the cost of rigorous regimentation, frugal living standards, rationing of basic commodities, and seclusion from the outside world. In the early twenty-first century the Syrian people are poorly prepared for economic and political decompression, and the Ba'thist elite, terrified of foundering, would like to keep them in a "Rip van Winkle" stasis for a few more years.

Syria's predicament is particularly sad when one recalls the proud role of Damascus and Aleppo through much of the history of the Levant. In the early twentieth century these venerable cities incubated Arab nationalist politics, and in 1954 Syria conducted the freest parliamentary elections ever seen in the modern Arab world, to which the new Arab nationalist Ba'th party contributed honorably.

Thereafter, political rivalries and the interventions of Iraq, Egypt, the West, and the Soviet Union fractured the Syrian state and army, with cohesion forcibly restored in 1966 by a Ba'th party transformed into the instrument of Alawite military officers. The Ba'thist takeover was a revolution—the Sunni Muslim merchant, landholding, and religious families that had dominated Syrian society since late Ottoman times gave way to lower-middle-class personnel from the rural and sectarian fringes.

Syria's economic failure in the late twentieth century was a consequence of the drive to be a regional power. It was the destiny of Ba'thist Syria to project itself as the leading confrontation state against Israel when Egypt retired from the arena in the mid-1970s. For the Ba'th, this followed naturally from the role of Damascus as the citadel of Salah al-Din and original capital of the Arab Islamic Caliphate. In addition, a secular regime commanded by Alawites, members of a minority sect, had to flaunt Arab nationalist and Sunni Islamic credentials.

The personal background of Hafiz al-Asad, who took control of Syria in 1970, ensured top-level promotion of Arab causes. Asad came from a locally prominent Alawite peasant family in the village of Qardaha, in the Mediterranean coastal hills. He became a Ba'thist activist in high school in the first years of Syria's independence and a middle-ranking air force officer in the 1950s. He exemplified the sort of person who was both empowered and radicalized by French mandatory rule. French patronage of the Alawite community, humiliation of urban Sunni politicians, and extension of education opened opportunities that might not otherwise have arisen for people from the margins of Syrian society.

Asad was committed to social reform and restoration of Arab dignity after the 1949 Palestine defeat. The trauma of losing the Golan Heights to Israel while he was defense minister in 1967 stiffened his insistence on the return of every square inch of occupied Syrian land. The mixture of clan and military elements in Asad's make-up encouraged a tight leadership style, reliance on a limited circle of associates, strategic realism, and patient persistence in converting Syria from a victim into a player.

Two ironies characterized Syria's ascent under Hafiz al-Asad. First, Syria became a regional power on the basis of autocratic regulation of a fractious population, economic autarky, diversion of resources into the military, and an alliance with Soviet Russia. These all became liabilities after the early 1980s. Syria lost its superpower backer, its armed forces faced obsolescence, and autocracy and autarky mired Syria in stagnation.

Second, the regime worked to enhance its legitimacy by land reforms and public sector expansion, benefiting poorer Sunni Muslims, alongside steadfastness against Israel. Asad's staffing of power centers in the security apparatus, however, principally involved trusted friends and relatives, mainly Alawites from his home region. The state's formal façade of parliament, ministers, and party officials did not betray such a sectarian coloration, but this fooled nobody. Syria therefore became more cohesive and monolithic, but the regime's legitimacy remained tentative, particularly among the Sunni majority.

In some respects, Syria has been poorly placed for confrontation with Israel. After June 1967, Syria's front line with Israel was the crest of the Golan Heights, only about fifty miles in length and well fortified on both sides. The Golan front is uncomfortably close to Damascus but relatively distant from Israel's main cities.

Unlike the Crusaders, the Israelis established secure positions on Mount Hermon and the Golan plateau, thereby holding the topographic advantage vis-à-vis Syria. The Syrians temporarily penetrated Israeli lines in their October 1973 surprise attack, coordinated with the Egyptian offensive across the Suez Canal, but the Israelis now have a technological edge that they lacked in the early 1970s.

Lebanon and Jordan represented flanks that Syria had an obvious interest in commanding. Lebanon's Biqa' Valley provided pathways for Israeli invasion of central and northern Syria, and Beirut's openness to external influences, whether Arab or Western, challenged Damascus. Jordan obstructed Syrian access to the West Bank Palestinians, separating Syria from the Israeli-Palestinian arena. As a state friendly to the West, Jordan was also a potential base for US and Israeli pressure on Syria, in the event of an Israeli-Palestinian accord.

Syria's internal affairs did not change under Bashar al-Asad after the death of his father in June 2000. A collective leadership has run the country, with an inner circle of security personnel from several Alawite clans plus Sunni associates of the Asads, including business sector advisors. Political relaxation, at first favored by the new president, was soon throttled. In late 2001, the security services clamped down on "human rights clubs" and arrested two parliamentary deputies, one of whom showed overmuch interest in a cell phone contract financially beneficial to regime personalities. Economic reform proceeded at a snail's pace, avoiding fundamental restructuring.

In such conditions, does Syria have a serious interest in peace in the Levant? Peace would force the opening up of Syria to external influences, and might therefore destabilize the position of the ruling elite. Turmoil between Israel and the Palestinians has had the attraction of reinforcing the Syrian regime's mastery of the northern Levant. Syrian officials have been able to deflect public attention to the necessities of confronting "the enemy," lecture other Arabs about their deficiencies in facing Israel, and present Lebanese criticism as treason.

Nonetheless, a peace arrangement would restore the Golan to Syria and ease Syria's access to funds and technology, especially from the EU. Syria could deploy its alliance with Iran and its patronage of radical groups as cards for a bargain with the US and Israel. Refusal would deprive Syria of the means to salvage its economy and take care of its still rising population. Bashar has played to all the galleries, with an outburst against Jews during the May 2001 papal visit to Damascus[248] and peace signals to Israel when Syria's circumstances became tighter after the March 2003 US invasion of Iraq.

Lebanon and Jordan

Lebanon and Jordan are the westernized wings of the Arab Levant. These two states are also the last strongholds of the late Ottoman bourgeoisie—overthrown in Syria, displaced from Israel, and marginalized in the West Bank and Gaza. Only in Jordan and Lebanon do prominent families of the "old order" still play a central role in politics. They have been joined by "new rich" elements, especially Palestinians in Jordan and Shi'ites in Lebanon. Nonetheless, the older leading families give a flavor of conservatism and historical continuity that distinguishes Lebanon and Jordan from Ba'thist Syria as well as from Israel and the Turkish republic.

For Lebanon, cultural dualism has been a consequence of its gateway function for the West on the Mediterranean coast. Mount Lebanon's Christians and central location in the Levant made it the main European entry point into the region after 1800.

Jordan's orientation toward the west reflects the conjunction of

British and Hashemite interests after the First World War. The Transjordan plateau was a critical strategic link between British imperial investments in Egypt and the Persian Gulf from the 1920s to the 1950s. When King Husayn terminated Britain's involvement with his Bedouin army, after the Anglo-French confrontation with Nasir in 1956, British influence was firmly embedded in the Jordanian bureaucracy and emerging middle class. This provided a platform for Jordan's close relations with the US at the end of the twentieth century.

There is nothing new about the detachment of Mount Lebanon and Transjordan from Damascus. The Romans made these areas into the separate provinces of Phoenice and Arabia (map 4). The Umayyads and 'Abbasids created the provinces of Urdun (Jordan) and Filastin (Palestine), continuing the Roman division of Transjordan from Damascus. Under the Fatimids, Tripoli, on the Lebanese coast, rivalled Damascus as a political center. Later, Mount Lebanon was part of the Latin Levant, with a military frontier facing Damascus, while an Ayyubid prince in Karak carved out a domain in Transjordan and the modern West Bank in the early thirteenth century (map 8).

These distinctions continued under the Mamluks, with Tripoli and Karak as provincial capitals. Only the Ottomans made Transjordan administratively subordinate to Damascus, while Mount Lebanon became the informal principality of Fakhr al-Din and the Shihabs, the basis for the autonomous province after 1861. Syrian Arab nationalists could justifiably resent the 1920 extension of Lebanon to include the Biqa', but in historical terms they were on weak ground in opposing the political autonomy of Mount Lebanon and its coast.

Lebanon and Jordan have an advantage over Syria in their openness to globalized financial and electronic networks, but this cannot be compared to Israel's position as an integrated outlier of the capitalist West. Also, the instability of the Levant has largely negated the Lebanese and Jordanian advantage.

Failure to resolve the Arab-Israeli conflict has left Lebanon exposed to hostilities as a front-line territory and Jordan exposed to the frustration of the Palestinian majority of its population. In both cases, this discouraged external investment. Through the 1990s, Lebanon reconstructed its war-damaged infrastructure by expanding public debt, leaving the country vulnerable to financial crises.[249]

Jordan implemented unpopular reforms, reducing its bureaucracy and cutting subsidies, to satisfy the IMF and the World Bank. These reforms hurt the indigenous people of Transjordan, the support base of the monarchy, but did not bring adequate financial inflows. Deterioration between Israel and the Palestinians after 1996 dashed Jordanian hopes for economic dividends from the 1994 treaty with Israel. Expectations that the country might be an economic hinge between Israel and the Arab world proved illusory.

Internal cohesion has been a more immediate problem for Lebanon and Jordan than for Syria. The isolation and regulation of the Syrian people still postpones the potential crisis arising from domination of the country's two-thirds Sunni Muslim majority by members of the one-eighth Alawite minority. Syria has also had more capacity for independent initiative as a regional power, and less exposure on the Arab-Israeli front line than Lebanon and Jordan.

Lebanon, the state of the mountain communities, had no majority group after France extended its boundaries in 1920. It could only function on the basis of a power-sharing compromise encompassing its Christians, led by the Maronites, its Sunni and Shi'ite Muslims, and the Druze. The Maronites, whose will for political autonomy created Lebanon, held the advantage through the mid-twentieth century, accepted by the others in exchange for their political shares.

The arrangement involved a competitive political system that became a casualty of Palestinian, Israeli, and Syrian intrusions after the 1967 Arab-Israeli war.[250] In the 1990s, after fifteen years of decomposition into militia fiefdoms, with a demographic shift in favor of the Shi'ite Muslims, the US and Saudi Arabia backed a new political dispensation dominated by Syria. This confirmed Lebanon's sectarian compartmentalization, but without any leading group, which facilitated divide-and-rule by Syria.

After 1990, Lebanon only had cohesion courtesy of Damascus, the broker among the sectarian political leaders, who all declared themselves Syria's allies. The individual communities were more than ever distinct political domains, with few cross-sectarian political parties.[251]

The Shi'ite 35% of the population became most influenced by the

Islamic activists of Hizballah, inflated beyond their natural popularity by Israeli occupation and bombardments in southern Lebanon. Buttressed by Iran and Syria through the 1980s and 90s, Hizballah acquired a regional significance in challenging Israel that it was loath to abandon after Israel's May 2000 departure from Lebanon. This led to a dangerous situation in which Shi'ite southern Lebanon served as a base for revisionism against Israel, with Hizballah receiving lavish Iranian supplies of Katyusha rockets capable of reaching Haifa, and seeking a role in the new Palestinian uprising. Hizballah leader Hasan Nasrallah boasted that "the party has outgrown the country and the [Shi'ite] community."[252]

Circumstances also elevated religious leadership among the Christian 35% of the population. After 1990, secular political leaders were either in exile in Paris or subordinated to Syria. Most Christians opposed Syria's hegemony and rallied to Maronite Patriarch Nasrallah Sufayr, who repeatedly demanded that Syria respect Lebanon's sovereignty. Though in political recession in the late twentieth century, the Maronite community remains pivotal in Lebanon as the majority and dynamo of the Christians, who continue to dominate Mount Lebanon. Christians still command much of Beirut's banking sector, vital to Syria's economic survival.

In 1998, Syria tried to pacify the Christians by selecting army chief Emile Lahhud as a "strong" occupant of Lebanon's presidency, a Maronite preserve. The presidency was downgraded in the 1989 constitution in favor of the Council of Ministers, headed by the Sunni Muslim prime minister. Maronites, however, spurned Lahhud because of his loyalty to Damascus and his moves to create a Syrian-style regime centered on security agencies.

In 2000, after the Israeli withdrawal from Lebanon, open hostility to Syria's role in the country spread beyond the Christians when Druze leader Walid Junblat resuscitated the Ottoman Druze-Maronite mountain partnership. Junblat condemned Syrian interference in the details of Lebanese political life.[253] The Syrian regime briefly declared Junblat persona non grata in Damascus in November 2000. This sparked protests in the Jabal al-Druze in southern Syria, a reminder of potential spillover from Lebanon into Syria's own sectarian mosaic.

The legendary solidarity of the Druze and their concentration in mountain territories near Beirut and on the Syrian-Lebanese and Syrian-Jordanian borders gives them a significance beyond their 5% and 3% shares of the Lebanese and Syrian populations.

As for the Sunni Muslim one-quarter of Lebanon, Syria monitored both billionaire Prime Minister Rafiq al-Hariri and the Islamic militants of Tripoli and Sidon. After the early 1990s, Damascus needed Hariri's Western and Saudi connections to keep the Lebanese and Syrian economies afloat, but was suspicious of his autonomy. The Sunni militants were forcibly weaned from their links with the anti-Ba'thist Muslim Brotherhood of Syria, which itself was smashed when it challenged Asad's regime in northern Syria in 1979–82. Nonetheless, they could still be an embarrassment. The bloody Afghan-Arab-led rebellion in the Tripoli hills in December 1999, involving ties with Usama bin-Laden's al-Qaeda and evocation of apocalyptic Christian millennial prophecies, showed that nothing is too weird for the Levant.

Syria has been adept at maneuvering among the Lebanese, but without Israel's errors in alienating the Shi'ites during its occupation of southern Lebanon after 1982, Lebanon's complexities would have been too much for Damascus. Syria profited from the fractiousness of the Shi'ites and Maronites, and from US willingness to back Damascus to stabilize Lebanon.

In the early twenty-first century, the Syrians aimed to reconcile Maronites and Shi'ites under Syrian Alawite patronage, by playing on Maronite-Shi'ite hostility to the permanent settlement of 350,000 Sunni Palestinians living in Lebanon. Syria, however, also had to juggle Lebanese Sunnis and Shi'ites, and to contain Maronite, Sunni, and Druze anger regarding the ascent of Hizballah under Syrian cover.[254]

In contrast to Lebanon, Jordan maintained its internal integrity and avoided external domination through the late twentieth century. The Hashemite monarchy passed its severest test in 1970, when it confronted the Palestinian guerillas using its territory to attack Israel in the Jordan Rift after 1967. Unlike Lebanon, Jordan had a decisive leader backed by loyal armed forces. King Husayn steered clear of Israel and Syria, and balanced between the Transjordanian and Palestinian components of his people. He aligned himself with Egypt, Iraq, and the smaller Gulf states through the 1980s to offset deteriorating relations with Damascus and Saudi coolness, a legacy of the Saudi expulsion of the Hashemites from Mecca and Medina in the 1920s.

In 1988, King Husayn finally withdrew Jordan's claim to the West Bank in favor of a future Palestinian state. He thus consolidated relations with his Palestinian subjects and Arafat's PLO at a time when Jordan had to attend to Iraq and Syria. King Husayn supported Iraq in its 1980–88 war with Iran, giving Saddam Husayn a valuable outlet. Acting as Ba'thist Iraq's strategic depth earned the enmity of Ba'thist Syria, compounded by Jordan's opposition to Syrian domination of Lebanon. Jordan thus took sides in the personal feud between Asad and Saddam, and against the Syrian-Iranian alliance.

The alignment with Iraq led Jordan into its worst crisis since 1970 when Saddam seized Kuwait in August 1990. The kingdom had to absorb 300,000 Palestinians expelled by the Kuwaitis after Saddam's defeat in 1991, and its economy reeled from the loss of cheap oil supplies and trade revenues from Iraq. Jordan's neutrality in the war between Iraq and the US-led coalition meant a temporary freeze in relations with the West. King Husayn also had to swallow Syria's triumph in Lebanon and its new respectability after joining the anti-Saddam alignment. Jordan's predicament in 1990–91 illustrated the vulnerability of Levant states to changes in the broader neighborhood.

Jordan survived intact because the issue did not divide its indigenous and Palestinian citizens, because the country had a cohesive elite, and because the US needed Jordan after its promises to its Arab allies to push for an Arab-Israeli settlement. King Husayn also made shrewd moves after 1988 to contain internal critics, especially the Muslim Brotherhood, in a new multi-party system. Limited democracy strengthened the monarchy by providing a safety valve without compromising royal power.

The Sunni Islamic credentials of the Hashemites, direct descendants of the Prophet Muhammad, meant that King Husayn could outflank the Islamists even while promoting a treaty with Israel. In sectarian terms, the king was at one with 95% of his people, and the Christian minority was super-loyal. Here Jordan differed from Syria and Lebanon, and

King Husayn could make experiments with political liberalization that the Alawites in Damascus did not dare to emulate.

After the relaxation in the southern Levant in the mid-1990s, Jordan again faced stress when the Israeli-Palestinian rapprochement faltered in the late 1990s. Conditions on the Transjordan plateau at the end of the twentieth century were not propitious. Five million people inhabit a narrow belt of semi-arid land between the Syrian border and Karak in the south, with the worst water deficit in the Levant. This population almost equals the Levant's total for its pre-twentieth century peak in Roman times, on the poorest margins of its non-desert territory. The natural increase rate remains near 2.5% per annum. After the influx from Kuwait, nobody pretends that Palestinians, of less than absolute loyalty to the Hashemites, are not the local majority. Native Transjordanians in Ma'an and Karak have rioted because of economic hardship.

In February 1999, King Husayn died after a 47-year reign, and the regime had to manage a transition to his son 'Abdullah. After September 2000, the Palestinian uprising required Jordan to juggle support for Arafat with an unpopular treaty with Israel.

In such a context, the solidity of the monarchy inherited by 'Abdullah II stands out, even if it can never be more than a secondary actor in the Levant. The velvet glove of pluralism that softens the steel fist of the most sophisticated security apparatus in the Arab Levant has enabled normal political life to persist while the security forces monitor the Islamic parties and the Palestinian refugee camps around 'Amman. The elite—royal advisors, leading families, security chiefs, and wealthy Palestinians—has closed ranks around the new king to defend their common interests.

More than a decade of disengagement from the West Bank has given Jordan a little insulation from events across the river. King 'Abdullah also has the advantage in relations with the Syrians, who are on the defensive under uncertain leadership.

For the US, the current "war against terror" has emphasized the usefulness of Jordan's intelligence services, especially given the presence of groups regarded by Washington as "terrorist" in Syria, Lebanon, the West Bank, and Gaza—in other words, everywhere else in the Arab Levant. The conjunction of a stable regime, a precarious economic base, and a cockpit location amid four important countries—Israel, Syria, Iraq, and Saudi Arabia—gives Jordan salience for the US in the early twenty-first century.

Turkey in the Levant: The New Byzantium?

The northern arc of the Levant—Cilicia, Hatay, and much of the Jazira—is part of the Turkish republic. At the end of the First World War, the British and French ordered Ottoman forces out of Cilicia, despite an attempt by Mustafa Kemal's army to stay after retreating from Syria. This repeated the situation of the Emperor Heraclius in 640. Like the Byzantines, the Turks were determined to regain these territories. By 1921, they had succeeded in removing the French from Cilicia. In 1939, like Nicephorus Phocas in 965, Atatürk recovered Antakya (Antioch), with the extraction of Hatay from French mandatory Syria.

In general, the strategic situation of modern Turkey resembles that of the Byzantine state between the seventh and eleventh centuries. In both cases, Anatolia became the base of a major regional power after the collapse of a larger empire: East Rome in the 630s and the Ottomans in 1917–18. A glance at political maps shows the geographical coincidence between Byzantium in the eighth century and modern Turkey. The former held a little more of the Balkans beyond Thrace, and the latter holds rather more of eastern Anatolia.

Modern Turkey faces similar requirements for geopolitical juggling as did medieval Byzantium. In both cases, there have been multiple preoccupations—to the north (Russia), the west (the Balkans), and the southeast (the Arabs). Moreover, modern Turkey has shared medieval Byzantium's ambivalent relations with Western Europe.

On the fringes of the Levant, the Kurdish population of southeastern Anatolia has presented problems for Turkey similar to those faced by Byzantium with the Armenians. Syrian encouragement of the Kurdish Workers Party (PKK) rebellion against the Turkish state in the 1990s had a forerunner in Umayyad attempts to manipulate eastern Anatolian Armenians against Byzantium. The Turkish-Kurdish relationship also resembles its Byzantine-Armenian predecessor in its duality of friction

165

and integration. Turkish President Turgut Özal had Kurdish blood and Armenians became Byzantine emperors.

To the south, the Armenians of late medieval times had uncertain relations with the Muslim rulers of the Levant. In the end, they lost Cilicia to the Mamluks. The same has applied to the Kurds in the contemporary Levant. Their Syrian ally deprived many Syrian Kurds of their citizenship and suppressed the Kurdish language[255] while it allowed PKK training camps in northern Syria and Lebanon's Biqa' Valley and hosted PKK leader Abdullah Öcalan in Damascus. Armenians like Heraclius and John Tzimisces and Kurds like Salah al-Din and Ali Janbalad have played significant roles in the history of the Levant, but neither people has fared well in regional politics.

The Turkish-Syrian border since the Turkish incorporation of Hatay (Alexandretta) roughly corresponds to the Byzantine frontier in the Levant between 969 and 1071, after the conquests of Nicephorus Phocas. The major exception is the coast, where the Byzantines controlled the Alawite hills. The border also marks the cultural divide between Turks and Arabs. The linguistic separation, Turkey's ties with the West, and the distinctive evolution of Anatolian Islam differentiate the Turkish Levant, with its predominantly Turkish and Kurdish inhabitants, from the rest of the region.

Turkey played little part in the affairs of the Levant beyond its own territory from the Second World War to the 1980s. It was preoccupied with its role in NATO vis-à-vis Soviet Russia, and preferred to turn its back on the Ottoman Arab provinces. Many Turks bitterly resented the prompt Arab repudiation of the Ottomans after the British victory in Palestine in 1918. Many Arabs came to view secularized Turkey as a "fifth column" for the West.

The Turks briefly threatened Syria in 1957 when the US sought to overthrow Soviet influence in Damascus, but from the 1960s to the 1980s the Syrian Ba'thists had Soviet cover. Turkey also temporarily developed lucrative commercial links with Iraq and the Persian Gulf states after the oil price boom in the 1970s. This required stable relations with Syria as an important Arab state and transit route to the Gulf.

From the 1980s on, however, Turkey had increasing prominence as a regional power, while the commercial significance of the Arabs to Turkey shrank and relations with Syria deteriorated. Turkey's new situation resulted from the demise of the Soviet Union, the 1991 US defeat of Iraq, the recession of oil prices, and Turkey's strategic significance between Europe and Asia after the Cold War.

It is the combination of Turkish capability in the northern Levant with Turkey's status as a territorially satisfied state that makes the post-1990 similarity to the Byzantium of Basil II particularly striking. These days, Turkey asserts its friendship with its Arab neighbors, but the wretched circumstances of Syria and Iraq make the friendship similar to Basil II's patronizing attitude toward Byzantium's Muslim protectorates in Aleppo (the Hamdanids) and the upper Jazira (the Marwanids).

Syria's recent relationship with Turkey resembles the Hamdanid interaction with Byzantium in the tenth century—hostility to a superior power followed by pragmatic accommodation. In Syria's case, the challenge was Turkey's Southeast Anatolia Project (GAP) for Turkish use of Euphrates waters. The Syrians watched Turkish dam construction in the early 1990s with apprehension. Turkey's dismissal of Syria's claim to equal rights to the resource prompted the Syrians to sponsor the PKK, thereby undermining Turkey's territorial integrity.

In late 1998, after repeated Turkish warnings and the discovery that Syrian army officers were operating inside Turkey,[256] Turkey threatened an air assault on Syria and the Lebanese Biqa'. Egyptian President Husni Mubarak informed Asad that the threat was serious and that Syria would not have "Arab" backing in a conflict arising from Syrian involvement with the PKK.[257] Syria bowed to Turkey's military supremacy. It signed a security agreement with Turkey at Adana in November 1998, abandoning its Kurdish ally. The Syrians asked PKK leader Öcalan to leave Damascus and closed PKK facilities.

In April 2002, my family and I visited a Turkish-Syrian border crossing south of Şanlıurfa. Relaxation between the two countries had limits. A triple barbed-wire fence marching across the flat plain marks the boundary. The boundary gates were shut, with a Syrian driver and his car caught in the few yards of no-man's land. My wife, who is Lebanese, opened a conversation in Arabic with the Syrians on the other side of the gates. The Syrians seemed surprised and asked where she was from. "I am from your neighbor," said my wife. A Syrian responded: "What neighbor?" My wife shot back: "Where is your army now?" There was a brief pause. "You mean *Lubnan* (Lebanon)," someone shouted across the fences. My wife turned away, terminating the exchange. She said to a Turkish official: "We don't love them." "We too," he replied.

Thereafter, both countries favored relaxation. Syria's main preoccupation was to the south—managing Lebanon, confronting Israel, and influencing the Palestinians and Jordan. Difficulties with Turkey compromised Syria's position in the Levant. Nonetheless, despite Bashar al-Asad's promotion of commercial and military cooperation after 2000,[258] Syria's economic backwardness and unclear geopolitical agenda still constrained relations. Turkey's diversion of Euphrates water will also exacerbate the water dispute whenever there is a drought, as in 2000–2001, even while the normal river flow remains adequate for the two countries.

Turkey enhanced its profile in the Levant in the mid-1990s by fostering a strategic partnership with Israel. There were advantages for both countries—friendship with Israel assisted Turkey's access to military technology and its relations with the US, while alignment with Turkey buttressed Israel vis-à-vis the Arabs. Israel's rapprochement with the Palestinians in 1993 and Turkey's anger with Syria after PKK infiltration across the border into Hatay in 1995 opened the door to this partnership, overcoming Turkish reservations.

Through the late 1990s, Israel and Turkey intensified their military collaboration with strong US approval. When combined with Jordanian involvement and Turkey's military thrusts into Iraqi Kurdistan, this alignment squeezed Syria from the north, south, and east.

At the outset of the twenty-first century, Turkey's consolidation of

168

its power, its significance to the US after the September 2001 terrorist attacks, and Syria's adjustment to Turkish requirements made the Israeli relationship less pivotal for Turkey. This, however, does not necessarily mean that the Arab Levant will become more important to Turkey relative to its other priorities in the early twenty-first century. Like Basil II's Byzantium, Turkey is aloof from its southern neighbors, except when they impinge on its own interests within its own boundaries—in Turkey's case meaning water, Hatay, and the Kurds. Turkey's ascent as a regional power makes it less in need of special relationships with the Levant states—whether Israel or the Arabs. Turkey's attention is more toward northern Iraq, because of oil and the problematic future of the Kurdish autonomous zone.

Problems of mutual comprehension are, if anything, worse between Turkey and the Arab Levant than between Israel and the Arabs. Arabs, for example, believe that Turkish Islamic revivalism is more like its Arab counterparts than is in fact the case. In 1996–97, Syria's promotion of the Kurdish PKK through the term of Turkish Islamist Prime Minister Necmettin Erbakan left a bitter taste for Turkish Islamist politicians.[259] Turkey is a terra incognita in the Arab Levant. When Ahmet Necdet Sezer became Turkish president in 2000, the Beirut- and London-based Arabic daily *al-Hayat* initially misrepresented his name as "Qaysar" (Caesar).[260]

Turkey's relationship with the US is one area in which Turkey diverges from the Byzantine model. Unlike medieval Byzantium, which was an isolated power, Turkey is part of a wider alliance (NATO) headed by a greater power. Washington's linkage with Ankara buttresses US supremacy in the Levant and the Middle East.

In the post-September 2001 "war against terror," Turkey sought to balance its US connection with relaxed interactions with Syria and Iraq. This was viable as long as the main attention was on al-Qaeda, and Syria cooperated with the US. It became less so when the Bush administration turned to regime change in Iraq, while Syria's Bashar al-Asad continued a post-2000 rapprochement with Saddam Husayn and trafficked in Iraqi oil. Removal of Saddam threatened the existing order in the northern Levant, especially when the Syrian regime confronted the US project to transform Iraq.

Modern Turkey's similarities to Basil II's Byzantium implied aversion to adventurous US behavior. As a state in a comfortable strategic position vis-à-vis the Levant and Iraq after 2000, Turkey was not enthusiastic about geopolitical revisionism with unpredictable consequences. In the regional order of 2000–2003, Turkey had solid influence over the Kurds in northern Iraq, lucrative cross-border trade relations with Iraq, and a newly cooperative Syria. Turkey, like Byzantium in its détente with the Fatimids, looked for peace and profitable commerce in the eastern Mediterranean.

In the run-up to the March/April 2003 Anglo-American occupation of Iraq, the new Justice and Development Party government of Turkey and the Bush administration miscalculated one another.[261] Turkish politicians thought they could stop a war by stalling US access to Iraq through Turkey. US officials thought that Turkey's economic vulnerability compelled it to allow passage of American troops in exchange for financial inducements. In the event, the US took Baghdad and disposed of Saddam without access through Turkey. Nonetheless, the US and Turkey needed a solid partnership after as much as before the war. Turkish public opinion trended against Washington and Turkey's economy strengthened, but unlike Basil II's Byzantium, Turkey could not operate alone. On the one hand, US sensitivities circumscribed Turkish openings to Syria and options in northern Iraq. On the other hand, Turkey could help to limit Syrian interference against the US in post-Saddam Iraq, especially because Damascus looked to Ankara for relief from US pressure.

Overall, the Levant's predicaments—the Iraq crisis, the Israeli-Palestinian deadlock, and severe economic and demographic stress—have heightened regional interest in Turkey's future relations with Europe. If Turkey enters the EU, the Turkish-Syrian boundary will become Europe's boundary, with profound implications for both the Aleppo/Antakya/Gaziantep border zone and the whole Levant. This will not be the "Europe beyond Europe" of the Mandatory and Crusader incursions. Nothing like it has loomed since the East Roman reassertion in northern Syria in the tenth century. Around 2015 Europe may extend uninterrupted to the Jazira, through the enthusiastic agency of the Turks, Byzantium's Muslim heirs.

What's Next in the Levant?

In the early twenty-first century, the survival of the post-1920 order in the Levant is dubious. The holds of Israel on most of former British Mandatory Palestine and of Turkey on the far north are set in stone in foreseeable scenarios, but prevailing arrangements in the Arab countries can only be termed shaky. Social, demographic, and legitimacy challenges facing Syria and Jordan represent major concerns.

As in the past, the Levant's topographic and social fragmentation will feature prominently in its future. Will ethnic, religious, and sectarian diversity remain the invitation for bigotry that it became in the twentieth century, or will dynamic interaction overshadow compartmentalization? The Israeli-Palestinian impasse, stubborn sectarian instincts in Lebanon, and the arrogant self-righteousness of Islamic militants and Israeli religious nationalists are still antidotes to optimism. The intolerance evident after the mid-twentieth century equaled the worst in the Levant's long history. When King Amalric of Jerusalem died in 1174, Salah al-Din wrote in sympathy to his son, Baldwin IV. Hafiz al-Asad of Syria could not bring himself to do anything similar after an Israeli right-wing fanatic killed Yitzhak Rabin in 1995, despite Ba'thist Damascus claiming Salah al-Din as its model.

One byproduct of turbulence is the hemorrhaging of the region's professional middle class by emigration. Palestinian Arab Christians, for example, have felt squeezed between Israeli pressure and Islamic militancy and have sought refuge in the West, but middle-class Palestinians and Lebanese of all sects have looked for opportunities to depart. The same may apply to secularized Jews in Israel in the event of another security collapse. Bourgeois emigration will not much affect demographic trends, except for further shrinking some Christian communities. It would, however, weaken the more moderate and innovative portion of the Levant's population.

For the immediate future, meaning 2005–2007, three arenas of change are worth watching: Iraq, Israel-Palestine, and Syria-Lebanon.

Iraq and the Levant

The March/April 2003 US invasion of Iraq and overthrow of Saddam Husayn transformed the strategic environment of the Levant. The implications were as far-reaching as those of the Seljuk Turkish capture of Baghdad in 1055 and the Mongol advance through the region in the 1250s.

Despite the incompetence of the US-led Coalition Provisional Authority in 2003–2004, and the global hyperpower's difficulties with Iraqi insurgencies, the US army became the dominant strategic factor in the "fertile crescent," a situation set to persist into 2006 and beyond. The US army separates the Syrian regime from Iran, and restricts Syria's interactions with Iraq, a radical change from the increasingly cozy relationship between Bashar al-Asad's Syria and Saddam's Iraq up to March 2003. Under the US umbrella, an interim Iraqi government, endorsed by the UN, became "sovereign" in Baghdad in June 2004 and organized elections for a provisional national assembly on 30 January 2005. Iraq's transformed political landscape derives from the US intervention.

Shi'ite Arab political prominence is the primary feature. Saddam and his predecessors back to the 1920s ruled through the Sunni Arabs of central Iraq, perhaps 20% of the population. His overthrow released the repressed Shi'ites of the south, more than 55% of the country's people. The political center of gravity has therefore shifted decisively. For the first time in modern Arab history, Twelver Shi'ites look to dominate the central government of an Arab state—not just any Arab state, but the key country for the future of the eastern Arab world. The prospective Shi'ite ascent, principally involving Shi'ite religious personalities and parties, is a seismic shock for Sunni Arabs and an impetus for Sunni insurgency within Iraq.

Two main scenarios for the evolution of Iraq in the next three years can be elaborated, each with fundamental repercussions for the Levant. First, the US project for a pluralist Iraq, with a federal regime reflecting the diversity of the population, received a boost from the January 2005 elections, despite the abstention of most Sunni Arabs. Under appalling security conditions, 58% of the electorate participated, with commendable mobilization in Shi'ite and Kurdish areas. Political pluralism is the only basis on which Iraq can exist, because the Kurdish north, with 20% of Iraq's people, will secede if a new Iraqi Arab dictatorship, religious or secular, looms on the horizon. The days of Arab strongmen bullying Iraqi Kurds are over—and if not, a pragmatic association between Iraqi Kurdistan and Turkey, especially a Turkey entering the EU, becomes conceivable.[262]

Credible elections within credible federalism are the pillars of a new Iraq. A central government in which the Shi'ite Arab majority predominates will be more tolerable to others if regional governments guard social and legal affairs, and have security and financial capability. Many Shi'ite and Sunni Arabs may vote for Islamic movements, but in a federal Iraq these will be able to implement their programs only at the provincial level. In any case, the fragmentation of Iraqi political Islam renders an Islamic state unviable. Like the Levant, Iraq largely lives in its compartments.

Crystallization of a pluralist Iraq, with improved security and an expanding economy, must be positive for the Levant. A dynamic Iraq, with its oil wealth, market possibilities, and potential financial power, could be the "motor" that will help pull Syria, Jordan, and the Palestinians through the coming years of population pressure and environmental stress. Even by 2008, Iraq may overshadow Syria and Jordan, with Baghdad setting political standards for Damascus and beginning to challenge Amman as a business center. For the Lebanese, with their skills and global networks, the new Iraq would be a land of opportunity, as well as a counterweight to Syria. US alignment with a rising Iraq could also assist progress toward peace in Israeli-Palestinian affairs.

The second scenario is indefinite turbulence. In mid-2005, the US army remains the main factor limiting chaos. The contest encompasses the opponents of the new Iraq, notably among Sunni Arabs, and foreign fighters infiltrating across the Syrian, Iranian, and Saudi borders to cause mayhem. In particular, religious fundamentalists,

Ba'thists, and criminal gangs manipulated by Syria's intelligence agencies have intimidated western Iraq.[263] Failure to deflate them risks de facto separation between the Sunni Arab center of Iraq and the rest of the country.

Iraq getting stuck in a version of Lebanon's fifteen years of chaos after 1975, with prolonged economic devastation, an Arab-Kurdish split, and separate Shi'ite and Sunni domains, would be catastrophic for the Levant. There would be no economic engine to the east to raise hopes and incomes in the Arab Levant, and Sunni Islamist extremism in Iraq would interact balefully with its counterparts in Jordan and the Palestinian territories. There would be no impetus to take risks for an Israeli-Palestinian peace, meaning perpetuation of the poisonous confrontation on the West Bank. Israel would remain in a state of siege, and more than ever be seen by the US as its anchor in the Middle East.

Israeli-Palestinian Affairs

US preoccupation with Iraq after March 2003 gave Israel more of a free hand than usual in its dealings with the Palestinians. The only exception was Washington's half-hearted attempt in May 2003 to activate the "road map" to Israeli-Palestinian relaxation and a Palestinian state drawn up by the international "quartet" of the US, the UN, the EU, and Russia. The US compelled PA chairman Yasir Arafat to appoint a prime minister who would restrict the chairman's role and work with Israel for an end to the Palestinian uprising in exchange for Israeli army withdrawals and a freeze on Jewish settlement construction. The "road map," however, led only to roadblocks. Each side demanded that the other move first; Arafat made sure that his prime minister had no authority with Palestinian security agencies; and suicide bombings, Israeli raids, and settlement expansion all continued unaffected. In September 2003, Mahmud Abbas (Abu Mazen) gave up as Palestinian prime minister, and the objective of a 2005 Israeli-Palestinian final status agreement became a dead letter.

Israeli Prime Minister Ariel Sharon took advantage of the Israeli-Palestinian deadlock and American diversion to unveil a unilateral scheme for the West Bank and Gaza that attracted US support on the basis of it being the first step toward a "two state" outcome. Sharon knew that the massive US investment in Iraq indicated potential pressure on Israel. Also, three years of violence after he took office in 2001 propelled him toward "painful sacrifices" to ensure Israel's long-term viability.[264] Sharon's plan involves Israeli withdrawal (*hitnatkut*) from the Gaza Strip and much of the West Bank interior, with evacuation of Jewish settlements in those areas. The expensive West Bank "security barrier" intended to separate Israelis from Palestinians and stop suicide bombers, on which work began in 2002 and which Sharon opposed before he embraced territorial contraction, marks potential Israeli borders carving into the West Bank.

Sharon's problem in 2005 is that much of the Israeli right, including a substantial segment of his own party, has not accompanied him on his new path. The Likud, triumphant in Israel's January 2003 elections, albeit on Sharon's coattails, holds the key to stable Israeli public acceptance of any peace arrangement. The party, ideologically founded on the "whole land" of Revisionist Zionism, has a solid constituency among the disproportionately lower-income 35–40% Oriental Jewish fraction of Israel's population. This vote has fluctuated between the Likud and the religiously oriented Shas movement, but heavily returned to the Likud in 2003. Oriental Jews, or Sephardim, distrust the Arab states many fled after 1948, and most remain alienated from Labor, seen as a European Jewish (Ashkenazi) party and as responsible for dumping Sephardi immigrants in poor development towns in the 1950s. Likud also benefits from the security fears of many Jews of European background (40–45% of Israel's population, including most of the 15% who came in the migration waves of the 1990s).

Persuading the mass of the Likud constituency to accept not merely Sharon's *hitnatkut*, but overall compromise with the Palestinians, means sidelining the party's ideology and will require exceptional leadership. On the one hand, an Israeli popular majority endorses the first stage of Sharon's plan—evacuation of twenty-one Gaza settlements, involving 8,000 Israelis in 15% of the Gaza Strip, and withdrawal from four settlements in the northern West Bank. On the other hand, a formidable minority of settler and hard-right elements threatens disruption. This is a foretaste of the hostility certain to meet more sweeping

West Bank evacuations, opposed by a larger section of the Israeli public.

Arafat's death on 11 November 2004, followed by confirmation of the moderate Mahmud Abbas as PA leader in West Bank/Gaza elections on 9 January 2005, pointed to peace possibilities. These events came together with Sharon's reestablishment of the Likud-Labor partnership broken in late 2002, and a re-elected US President George W. Bush committed to democratization of the Middle East. In February 2005, pressed by the US after the Iraqi elections, the PA and Israel agreed to a cease-fire. Mahmud Abbas, who regards the armed *intifada* as a Palestinian mistake, began rebuilding Palestinian institutions, obtained consent of Hamas and other militants to an Israeli-Palestinian truce, and looked ahead to new final status negotiations.

Nonetheless, the future should be viewed cautiously. First, Sharon's final West Bank outcome, under which Israel keeps East Jerusalem, generously buffered, and slices of the better-watered western side of the territory, all with expanding Israeli settlements, falls short of Ehud Barak's position in 2000. There may have to be some detailed redrawing of the 4 June 1967 line, but Israel foreclosing East Jerusalem and 7–8.5% of the rest of the West Bank makes deadlock certain.[265]

Second, Palestinian legitimization of compromises with Israel is not assured. Abbas is an elderly PLO functionary who lacks charisma and whose elevation depends on the acquiescence of younger personalities in Fatah and Hamas. Hamas scored well in December 2004/January 2005 municipal voting in the West Bank and Gaza Strip. It has confidence it can do the same in the July 2005 poll for the Palestinian legislature. Palestinian public opinion has recently moved against violence, but not against the militant organizations.[266]

Third, Israel's own parliamentary fragmentation, within as well as beyond the Likud, and the steady electoral decline of the center-left, the primary Israeli "peace partner" of 1992–2001, do not bode well. There is no guarantee that new Israeli elections will bring decisive change, or that conservative Laborites will be more amenable than Likudniks to far-reaching concessions.

Given the size of the main Jewish settlement clusters—more than 200,000 Israelis in and around East Jerusalem, 40,000 in Gush Etzion, and about 60,000 in western Samaria—plus American endorsement of

Israel retaining some clusters, the 2001 Taba proposals and the similar 2003 Geneva (Beilin/Abd-Rabbo) document represent the limit of Israeli thinking. Such flexibility assumes reconfigured Palestinian politics, with militants adapting or declining, and a parallel Israeli softening. Will Sharon's August 2005 settlement evacuations presage a broader Israeli pullback in the West Bank, including East Jerusalem? Quiet won't last long if there is no further change on the ground and no economic recovery for Palestinians. Another round of violence would involve great embitterment. It could prejudice democratization in the Arab Levant, where perceived US partiality toward Israeli outlooks handicaps promotion of political freedoms against authoritarianism and religious militancy.

Apart from Egypt and Jordan, which exert moderating influences in Gaza and the West Bank, existing Arab regimes are unlikely to affect events positively, and they cannot dent Israel's military supremacy. The US has promised close mediatory involvement in the new Israeli-Palestinian scene, but the impact depends on a clear turn toward a successful new pluralist Iraq. Syria's enforced retreat in Lebanon in 2005 may reshuffle regional cards. It could deflate Syria as a sponsor of militants, improving prospects for Israeli-Palestinian relaxation and for stabilization in Iraq. As for the Golan Heights, Sharon dismissed November 2003 and September 2004 Syrian overtures as intended "only to soften or remove US pressure on Syria."[267] Syria's interference in Iraq and recklessness in Lebanon have helped Israel to shelve the Golan issue.

Damascus Takes Chances

Caught between the US army to the east and Israel to the south, the Syrian regime pursued risky policies after the overthrow of Saddam's Iraq. Although Bashar al-Asad cooperated with the US against al-Qaeda, Syrian "volunteers" fought American troops in Iraq during and after March/April 2003. The Syrian president talked of peace with Israel while backing Palestinian Islamic militants and treating Lebanese Hizballah leader Hasan Nasrallah, enthusiastic for Israel's destruction, as a mentor. Bashar's father, who viewed Hizballah purely as an instrument, would never have approved such elevation. In July 2003, Syrian Foreign Minister Faruq al-Shar'a termed the Bush Administration "the most violent and stupid" US government ever, noting pressure on Syria unprecedented since the Ottoman conquest in the sixteenth century.[268] The Syrian regime condemned the new reality in Iraq, also declaring itself unable to supervise its eastern border, thus disclaiming responsibility for whatever crossed into Iraq.

In 2003–2004, Washington, usually tolerant of Syrian double gaming, lost patience and issued severe warnings. Secretary of State Colin Powell took the message directly to Bashar, and referred for the first time to "Syrian occupation" of Lebanon. The US Congress passed the "Syria Accountability and Lebanese Sovereignty Restoration Act," which mandated sanctions against Damascus and was signed into law by a hitherto reluctant President Bush in December 2003.

At home, the Syrian regime faced spillover from affirmation of Kurdish rights in Iraq. In mid-March 2004, Syrian Kurds rioted in Qamishli and Damascus after a football match dispute, raising political slogans inspired by the new Iraqi interim constitution. Kurds clashed with Arabs in Aleppo. The security forces responded with a violent crackdown, causing dozens of deaths.[269] Kurds are about 10% of Syria's population, comprising a majority in parts of the northeast. Ba'thist Syria had not seen such an upheaval since the smashing of the Muslim Brotherhood in 1982.

By mid-2004, the Syrians concluded that they had best appear to appease the US in Iraq while preserving other options. They indicated more amenability regarding the Syrian/Iraqi border. The August 2004 Najaf conflict, pitting US and Iraqi forces against the militia of the young Iraqi Shi'ite firebrand Muqtada al-Sadr, opened a mediation possibility. Bashar asked Nasrallah, as Lebanon's preeminent Shi'ite militant, to help pacify Sadr.[270] This was a sideshow alongside the intervention of Grand Ayatollah Ali al-Sistani, no friend of Nasrallah, and the US had no reason to view it as other than Syrian opportunism.

The real significance lay in the northern Levant. Syria's leaders believed that adjustment in Iraq freed them to dictate Lebanon's late 2004 presidential election.[271] On 27 August, brushing aside American and French calls for a normal vote for a new head of state in the

Lebanese parliament, the Syrian president summoned Lebanese Prime Minister Rafiq al-Hariri to Damascus. Bashar ordered Hariri to have parliament change the constitution to extend the term of President Emile Lahhud: "You will go and make the extension because I am Lahhud."[272]

The 128-member parliament, well padded with Syria's allies after fourteen years of Syrian management of Lebanese politics, produced the requisite two-thirds majority. Death threats lowered the number of opposing deputies from 50 to 29.[273] Druze leader Walid Junblat and Maronite patriarch Nasrallah Sufayr defied the Syrian imposition, which aroused widespread "bitterness" in Beirut.[274]

Syria's coup affronted the US and France, who co-sponsored the first-ever UN Security Council resolution against Damascus, calling for removal of the 18,000 Syrian troops still in Lebanon, termination of external interference in Lebanese politics, and disarming of militias, meaning Syria's Lebanese Shi'ite ally Hizballah. A senior Jordanian official noted that resolution 1559, passed on 2 September, gave Syria an opportunity "to review the results of the long years of its policy toward Lebanon, and to understand the reality of international changes."[275]

Bashar al-Asad had no intention of reviewing Syria's domination of Lebanon. Faced with invigorated local opposition, the Lebanese regime responded thuggishly. Security forces made dawn raids on Druze villages in the Shuf hills. On 1 October, a bomb badly injured Junblat's colleague Marwan Hamade, who had resigned from the government to protest Lahhud's extension. Junblat denounced the Syrian and Lebanese authorities. He identified "a dangerous Syrian-Lebanese mafia," and demanded that Syrian intelligence operatives leave Lebanon, taking Lahhud with them "in their last truck."[276]

Hariri, who resigned as prime minister after his humiliation by Bashar, committed his capability as Lebanon's top Sunni Muslim politician to an opposition campaign to overturn the Syrian-backed regime in scheduled May 2005 parliamentary elections.[277] In early February 2005, a new opposition front, with strong Christian, Sunni, and Druze representation, publicly endorsed the Security Council resolution 1559 demand for full Syrian withdrawal from Lebanon. Hariri was the prime mover of this defiance,[278] and on 14 February he was murdered, with nineteen others, in a massive explosion on the Beirut seafront.

Hariri's death intensified the crisis. Competitive demonstrations showed that hostility to the Syrian regime, widely regarded in Lebanon as having ordered the assassination, had the advantage. Hizballah mobilized Shi'ites for a show of strength more to emphasize its existence than to support Damascus. Christian/Sunni/Druze coalescence proved able to produce double Hizballah's crowd. In mid-March, under intense US and European pressure, Syria bowed with bad grace to resolution 1559 and pulled troops and intelligence agents out of coastal Lebanon into the Biqa' Valley, then made a general military withdrawal from Lebanon in late April.

Syria's penetration of Lebanon's institutions and the joint interests of Syrian and Lebanese elites, however, complicate disentanglement of the two countries. Lebanon's multi-sectarian opposition depends on coordination among Junblat, General Michel Aoun, Patriarch Sufayr, and Hariri's son Sa'ad, its principal surviving "poles," together with a variety of Sunni and Christian politicians. It can almost certainly win elections, but Maronite fracturing and weakness among Shi'ites are concerns. Bashar has proclaimed that "the power and role of Syria in Lebanon are not dependent on the presence of Syrian forces there," and the Syrian information minister has described the Syrian/Lebanese border as "phony."[279]

In May 2005, Lebanon, Syria, and Syrian/Lebanese relations stand at a crossroads. The hubris of the 39-year-old Syrian president, who provoked the US, France, and most Lebanese, has propelled the two countries to this crossroads. Lebanon, unexpectedly, finds the way opening to restored independence. The discrediting of security agencies in the March 2005 UN report on the Hariri murder may even help Lebanon tackle the corruption and political abuse that debilitate the Lebanese state. For its part, Hizballah, knowing that at most it represents one-quarter of Lebanese from one community, grudgingly prepares to adapt. Its Iranian patron is distant, its Syrian ally is in trouble, and its environment is becoming less favorable to its military dimension. The Iranians themselves see benefits in relations with Lebanon and Hizballah without Syrian intrusion, and recently signaled that Iran doesn't support "Syria's presence in Lebanon" because "Lebanon's sovereignty is [more] important."[280]

Syria, its prestige in tatters, heads into the unknown. Might Bashar try to reinvent himself as a reformer and unload responsibility for his disaster in Beirut on venal colleagues and relatives, who have plundered Syria and Lebanon under his oversight for half a decade?[281] For "stability," other Arab leaders would like the Syrian regime to stay afloat and see off investigation of the Hariri murder.

The Asads have made Syria a political wasteland devoid of serious opposition. Even Saddam's Iraq never achieved this flattening. In such a landscape, a regime makeover could degenerate into violent jostling among Alawite and security force mafias, opening fissures for Sunni, Druze, and Kurdish assertions. Lightweight Syrian bourgeois dissent aside, do building blocks for pluralism exist in Syria? The answer has to be that Syria operated semi-democratic politics in the 1950s, and that real regime change, however difficult, will bring forth new political players. Almost anything is better for the future of the long-suffering Syrian people than the present bankrupt and parasitic autocracy.

The Longer View

Beyond the immediate future, the Arab interior will face a protracted social crisis, whatever the political evolution. Population growth in Syria is slowing, and the same can be expected in Jordan, the West Bank, and the Gaza Strip. The youthful bulge in the age structure, however, means that it will take thirty years for the numbers to stabilize, with populations nearly doubling in the meantime. A new Syrian regime and an Arab-Israeli compromise would probably enable the existing geopolitical order, adjusted to accommodate a Palestinian state, to survive the next few decades, although this would require buttressing from the US and the EU.

Can Syria and Jordan manage the increasing strain? Neither country has any hope of meeting future popular expectations and employment demands out of its local resources. An Arab-Israeli settlement would facilitate aid and investment, easing the passage. The outlook would improve if the ruling clique in Damascus, disgraced by its behavior in Lebanon, gives way to genuine political accountability.

In contrast to the Syrian Ba'thists, the Jordanian monarchy has implemented tentative political liberalization, and its cooperation with the West implies external support, assuming reform advances decisively. Much depends on the monarchy's credibility with a growing population, and its ability to contain the emotive local "street." Without the popular touch of his father, King 'Abdallah II has a difficult task ahead.

If there is no Arab-Israeli settlement and no fundamental change in Damascus, a combination of West Bank–Gaza turmoil with limited regime legitimacy in Syria and Jordan will guarantee convulsions. These may be both within the Arab Levant and between Israel and the Palestinians. Scenarios include the demise of Mahmud Abbas and the West Bank moderates, and regime breakdown in Syria and/or Jordan. A future West Bank eruption could spill onto the Transjordan plateau, where demographic and social conditions are problematic despite Jordan's recent positive economic performance.

EU investments and a strengthened Turkish economy—if Turkey proceeds on track toward EU entry around 2015—may provide relief for the Arab Levant, though at the cost of dependence. On the other hand, if Iraq fragments and Syria destabilizes, Turkey and the EU will view the Jazira as a security frontier, perhaps with Iraqi Kurdistan and even Aleppo as a de facto buffer belt, repeating the Marwanid and Hamdanid functions for Basil II's Byzantium. If the EU rejects Turkey, the latter would likely become a less economically dynamic, pricklier, and more self-absorbed neighbor for the Arab Levant. It is worth noting that Turkish media interest in Turkey's 2004 trade agreement with Syria focused on Syrian recognition of the Hatay (Alexandretta) border after sixty-six years of rejection.[282]

Challenges for Syria and Jordan will increase as population pressures reach their peak toward 2030, and as climate change begins seriously to bite. In the 2020s, Syria will probably face increased frequency of drought, somewhat lowered annual rainfall, and a three degrees Fahrenheit (two degrees Celsius) temperature rise, all while trying to cope with ten million more people. Turkey, under whatever government and whether in or out of the EU, will look to its own interests, meaning less Euphrates water for Syria. Jordan will struggle against environmental difficulties with an extra four million people. Syria and Jordan will be better placed if they have open, liberalized, and accountable political systems. It would therefore be to Syria's longer-term benefit if its regime crisis comes early.

Islamic fundamentalists have little time for addressing demographic and environmental problems, and their ascent to power, for example in Jordan, would terminate Western support and bring calamity. Lebanon, with its access to global financial networks and its sophisticated emigrant communities, could be a safety valve for the Arab Levant, but only if it has new relations of dignity and equality with Syria. As for Israel, the path of wisdom will be to establish an axis of cooperation with the Palestinians and Jordanians across the southern Levant. This has a price, but the notion that there is security behind fences encompassing not just Israel itself, but also confiscated lands on the West Bank, is a delusion.

The course of events in the Levant has depended and will depend on a shifting combination of power relations, chance, and the quality of leading personalities. In the past, accidents and personal factors have had critical ramifications. If Baldwin IV of Jerusalem had not contracted leprosy in the 1170s he would probably have continued to frustrate Salah al-Din until the latter faced a breakdown of warlord allegiances in Syria by 1190. The demise of the Latin Levant was not inevitable, despite unpromising aspects of the Frankish situation. Similarly, if Hülegü Khan had not been diverted by surprise events in Central Asia in 1259, the Levant and Egypt would undoubtedly have fallen to the Mongols, with momentous implications.

On other occasions, imbalances of power have determined historical outcomes in a foreseeable manner—the Mamluk reduction of Cilician Armenia, the Ottoman conquest of the Mamluk Levant, and the British breakthrough in Palestine in 1918. This is not to belittle the roles of Baybars, Selim the Grim (*Yavuz Selim*), or General Edmund Allenby, or to deny that incompetent political or military leadership of the stronger power might have brought different developments.

Recent history has also indicated the significance of unpredictable events and salient personalities alongside power and economics. First, the 1995 assassination of Yitzhak Rabin tipped the balance toward years of deterioration in the southern Levant. Second, Bashar al-Asad's gambling in Lebanon in 2004–2005 may have shifted the trajectory of the northern Levant into a new track. It certainly illustrates the chanciness of dynastic succession in Syria's "republican monarchy."

In the early twenty-first century Levant, three issues require resolution to enable the region to manage its deepening social, demographic, and environmental crises. First, there should be a fair two-state solution for the Israeli-Palestinian conflict, which requires Israel to cease to be an occupying power and for the two sides to come to terms on a basis of unequivocal mutual respect. Second, there should be full disengagement of Syria from Lebanon, so that Lebanese Christians, Muslims, and Druze can properly reconstruct their polity and economy by agreement among themselves. Syria's military withdrawal only begins the disengagement. Third, there should be rapid political empowerment of the populations of the Arab interior, toward full democracy in Syria and Jordan. Jordan has taken steps along the road; Syria has done nothing.

The three issues are intertwined and need to advance simultaneously. This would address, for example, the concerns of southern Lebanese Shi'ites, who are at once in Lebanon and on the Arab-Israeli front. Democratization in Damascus parallel to Israeli-Palestinian progress will facilitate an Israeli-Syrian settlement, and return of the Golan to Syria. The Levant is at once a mosaic and a unity.

Given that the various parties are unlikely to proceed toward solutions without assistance, unified political will is needed from the international community. Real removal of Syria from Lebanon, free Lebanese elections, and identifying those responsible for Hariri's murder through the investigation established under UN Security Council Resolution 1595, together represent a crucial test. Success would raise the profile of international intervention, and thereby aid engagement with the Israeli-Palestinian arena. Failure would mean that the international community might as well pack up and leave the Levant to its undoubtedly dismal future.

May 2005

NOTES

1. Room, 1997, p. 349.
2. Kennedy, 1986, pp. 280–81. Also see Bosworth, 1992, section 14, pp. 278–79 and Haldon, 1999, p. 41.
3. For an excellent analysis of the physical constraints on maritime operations in the Crusader period, see Pryor, 1988, pp. 112–34.
4. Kennedy, 1986, pp. 338–39.
5. Douwes, 2000, pp. 26–27.
6. Bull, 1999, pp. 27 and 33, interprets the First Crusade as "a devotional act of pilgrimage" and "a 'satisfactory' penance capable of undoing all the sins which intending Crusaders confessed."
7. Richard, 1999, pp. 107–9; Phillips, 1999, pp. 113–14.
8. Phillips, 1999, p. 114.
9. Hillenbrand, 1999, p. 364, cites the Spanish traveller Ibn Jubayr on this matter: "Our way lay through continuous farms and ordered settlements, whose inhabitants were all Muslims, living comfortably with the Franks. God protect us from such temptation."
10. Amitai-Preiss, 1995, p. 55.
11. Fawaz, 1983, pp. 50–51.
12. Perthes, 1995, p. 183.
13. Halawi, 1992, pp. 68–70.
14. Hamilton, 2000, p. 47. Holt, 1986, p. 33, refers to an estimate of "at most 250,000" for the Frankish population of all the Crusader states in the mid-twelfth century, "about half of whom were in the Kingdom of Jerusalem." Also see Prawer, 1972, p. 396.
15. Issawi, 1988, p. 16.
16. Ibid., p. 28, for Damascus, Aleppo, and Beirut.
17. Metropolitan areas defined as "central city and neighboring communities linked to it by continuous built-up areas or many commuters" (projections for December 2000 by Thomas Brinkhoff: City Population, <http://www.citypopulations.de>).
18. Timothy D. Mitchell and Mike Hulme, "A Country-by-Country Analysis of Past and Future Warming Rates," Tyndall Centre Working Paper no. 1 (November 2000), University of East Anglia, Norwich, UK, <http://www.tyndall.ac.uk/publications/working_papers/wp1.pdf>.
19. Hadley Centre for Climatic Prediction and Research, the UK Meteorological Office, <http://www.met-office.gov.uk/research/hadleycentre/

models/modeldata.html>: higher estimate, <http://www.metoffice.gov.uk/ research/hadleycentre/models/modeldata/HadCM2_IS92a_map_P_DJF_ 19601990_20702100.gif> (Change in December–January–February average precipitation from 1960–1990 to 2070–2100 from HadCM2 IS92a); lower estimate, <http://www.metoffice.gov.uk/research/hadleycentre/ models/modeldata/HadCM3_IS92a_map_P_DJF_19601990_20702100 .gif> (Change in December–January–February average precipitation from 1960–1990 to 2070–2100 from HadCM3 IS92a).

20. Plutarch, trans. Warner, 1972, p. 186.
21. Ibid., p. 197.
22. Ibid., p. 198.
23. Ibid., p. 193.
24. Millar, 1993, p. 18.
25. Isaac, 1990, p. 61.
26. Ibid., p. 318.
27. Avi-Yonah, 1976, p. 19, estimates the Jewish population of Palestine (including Transjordan) in the early second century at about 1.3 million.
28. Tacitus, trans. Wellesley, 1964, p. 279.
29. Ibid.
30. Josephus, trans. Williamson, 1959, p. 166.
31. Ibid., p. 223.
32. Ibid., pp. 274 and 265.
33. Ibid., p. 355.
34. Millar, 1993, pp. 118–19.
35. Ibid., p. 124.
36. Talbert, 1985, p. 171. Also see Jones, 1964, vol. 1, p. 57.
37. For elaboration, see Avi-Yonah, 1976, pp. 89–110.
38. Ibid., pp. 92–93, 118.
39. For detailed discussion of the episode, see Millar, 1994, pp. 165–73 and Isaac, 1990, pp. 220–28.
40. Under Diocletian, 26–28 legions were available for the eastern frontier. This was about 40% of the Roman army. See Jones, 1964, vol. 1, pp. 57–58; vol. 2, pp. 682–85.
41. Isaac, 1990, p. 254.
42. Treadgold, 1997, p. 62; Jones, 1964, vol. 1, pp. 123–24.
43. Millar, 1992, pp. 181–85.
44. In the first and second centuries C.E., the legion appears to have been a unit of 3,500–6,000 men. According to Jones, new legions raised by Diocletian in the late third century were also of this size. Through the fourth century, however, the average legion gradually declined to 1,000–3,000 men. (Goldsworthy, 1996, pp. 22, 33; Jones, 1964, vol. 2, pp. 679–81.)
45. Stemberger, 2000, pp. 10–11.

46. Isaac, 1990, p. 171.
47. Jones, 1964, vol. 2, pp. 944–50.
48. Shahid, 1995, p. 3.
49. Jones, 1964, vol. 1, p. 297; vol. 2, p. 968.
50. Shahid, 1995, p. 435.
51. Ibid., p. 469.
52. Kaegi, 1992, p. 45.
53. Ibid., p. 27.
54. Jones, 1964, vol. 2, p. 823 ("East of Antioch, in what is now desert, there are ruins of scores of well-built . . . villages. They were all built in the fifth and sixth centuries").
55. Kaegi, 1992, p. 27.
56. Ibid., pp. 83–84. Kaegi is the best guide for the Islamic conquest.
57. Avi-Yonah, 1976, p. 241.
58. Kaegi, 1992, p. 108.
59. For elaboration, see Haldon, 1990.
60. Kaegi, 1992, pp. 147–80 on Mesopotamia and "territory for time."
61. Haldon, 1990, p. 220.
62. Treadgold, 1997, pp. 315–17, argues strongly for the late 650s as the timing of the main defensive reorganization in Anatolia. Kaegi, 1992, p. 283, is less committal, but views the role of Constans II as "critical." Also see Haldon, 1999, p. 77.
63. Treadgold, 1997, pp. 332–33. According to Treadgold, 12,000 Mardaites moved in 686–87, with their families, and another 6,500 in 689. The Byzantines recognized that the long-term position of the Mardaites in the Levant was untenable and took the opportunity to supplement their military manpower while they could. Also see Bosworth, 1996, section 13, pp. 6–7 (citing the Byzantine historian Theophanes), and Kaegi, 1992, pp. 255–56.
64. Kennedy, 1986, p. 92. Kennedy comments that the competition became more intense in Syria than it had been in Arabia.
65. Ibid., p. 99.
66. Ibid., p. 144.
67. Bosworth, 1996, section 12, p. 57, and section 14, p. 270.
68. Haldon, 1999, pp. 79, 176–80; Bosworth, 1996, section 15, p. 183.
69. Bosworth, 1996, section 14, pp. 281–82 (citing the Arab geographer Tarsusi).
70. Hitti, 1951, pp. 543–44, suggests that Homs still had a Christian majority in the mid-ninth century, when local Christians rebelled against discriminatory edicts by the Caliph al-Mutawakkil (for example, that Christians and Jews attach "images of devils to their houses" and wear yellow cloaks). The rebellion was ruthlessly suppressed, and Christians were

expelled from Homs.

71. Moosa, 1986, pp. 36–37, and Salibi, 1988, p. 88 (both citing the Arab historian al-Mas'udi).
72. Hitti, 1951, pp. 542–43, comments that the uprising coincided with the presence of a Byzantine fleet off the coast near Tripoli.
73. Salibi, 1977, pp. 47–48.
74. Kennedy, 1986, p. 183.
75. Salibi, 1977, p. 50 (citing the Muslim historian al-Mas'udi).
76. Ibid., p. 53.
77. Ibid., p. 60.
78. Ibn Khaldun, trans. Rosenthal and abridged Dawood, 1978, p. 124.
79. Ibn Khaldun gives a fine description of the roles of the "sword" and the "pen," but without relating regime failure to institutional weakness—ibid., pp. 193 and 213.
80. See, for example, Salamé, 1987.
81. Hitti, 1968, p. 460 (citing the Muslim historian Ibn Hawqal). Also see Kennedy, 1986, p. 270.
82. Haldon, 1999, p. 185.
83. Whittow, 1996, pp. 374–90.
84. Ibid., p. 336. In 1941, Turkey raised the same difficulty when declining a British offer of Aleppo in exchange for a joint intervention in Vichy-ruled Syria (according to Foreign Minister Şükrü Saraçoğlu, Turkey "did not wish to include non-homogeneous peoples within her frontiers")— Olmert, 1987, p. 443.
85. Edwards, 1987, pp. 4–5.
86. Sharf, 1971, pp. 107–12.
87. Hitti, 1968, p. 639. Dajani-Shakeel, 1990, pp. 162–63, stresses economic revival in Fatimid times, before new disruptions by the Turks and Crusaders after 1060.
88. Kennedy, 1986, p. 335.
89. Salibi, 1977, p. 103.
90. Psellus, trans Sewter, 1966, p. 67.
91. Salibi, 1977, p. 110.
92. Halm, 1991, p. 159.
93. For elaboration, see Khuri, 1991, pp. 49–61; Halm, 1991, pp. 156–58.
94. Halm, 1991, p. 159, refers to conversion of "the rural population," though the Byzantines presumably would have acted if al-Tabarani had targeted Orthodox Christians. Communities of Orthodox and Maronite Christians remain in these hills and on their coastal fringe to the present day.
95. Stephenson, 2000, p. 92, makes this point. He notes the success of Constantine IX against Pecheneg nomads in the Balkans when the emperor divided the field army into small units for guerrilla strikes. Apparently

the Byzantines did not try such experiments on the eastern border. Also see Cahen, 1968, pp. 65–66.

96. Treadgold, 1997, pp. 595–96, citing the Byzantine historian John Skylitzes. Also see Ostrogorsky, 1968, pp. 342–43.
97. Edwards, 1987, p. 4.
98. Cahen, 1968, p. 78; Salibi, 1977, pp. 144–46.
99. Lilie, 1993, pp. 19, 23–24.
100. Ibid., p. 161.
101. Prawer, 1988, p. 8.
102. Prawer, 1972, pp. 331–32.
103. Rogers, 1992, p. 68, points to the Venetian victory over the Fatimid fleet near Ascalon in 1123 as "facilitating" the Crusader conquest of Tyre.
104. Asbridge, 2000, pp. 70–72.
105. Smail, 1995, p. 208.
106. On occasion, however, such separation could be convenient to Muslim leaders. Holt, 1986, p. 51 suggests that Salah al-Din may have found Crusader Transjordan a useful buffer between himself in Cairo and Nur al-Din in Damascus in the early 1170s.
107. Richard, 1999, p. 148.
108. Ibid., p. 107.
109. Lewis, 1967, pp. 108–9.
110. Smail, 1995, pp. 55–56.
111. Asbridge, 2000, pp. 44, 54, 58, 68, 78.
112. Ibid., pp. 60–61, 65–66.
113. William of Tyre, 15:1 (Huygens edition, 1986, p. 675).
114. Richard, 1999, pp. 189–90; Rogers, 1992, pp. 85–86.
115. Hamilton, 2000, p. 131.
116. William of Tyre, 21:6–8 (Huygens edition, 1986, pp. 967–74).
117. Lyons and Jackson, 1982, p. 253.
118. Prawer, 1972, p. 359 ("The great granaries of the Crusader Kingdom and of Moslem Damascus were the lands east of the Jordan and north-east of Lake Tiberias.").
119. Hamilton, 2000, pp. 184–85.
120. Richard, 1999, p. 196; Hamilton, 2000, p. 226.
121. Richard, 1999, p. 197.
122. Ibid., pp. 208, 212–13; Smail, 1995, p. 73.
123. Rogers, 1992, pp. 224–36, notes the increased naval capability of the Western monarchies relative to the Italians, and the importance of Richard's capture of Byzantine Cyprus in providing "a central base for subsequent Latin operations in Palestine and Egypt."
124. Lyons and Jackson, 1982, p. 324.
125. Edwards, 1987, pp. 7–9.

126. Boase, 1978, p. 15.
127. Ibid., p. 19.
128. Ibid., p. 21.
129. Richard, 1999, p. 315.
130. Hallam, 1997, pp. 260–61.
131. Richard, 1999, p. 319.
132. Humphreys, 1977, pp. 266–67, notes the hostility of Islamic scholars in Damascus to Al-Salih Ismail's concessions.
133. Richard, 1999, p. 328.
134. Marshall, 1992, pp. 46 and 182; Richard, 1999, p. 330.
135. Humphreys, 1977, pp. 276–77.
136. Richard, 1999, p. 355.
137. Amitai-Preiss, 1995, pp. 28–29; Grousset, 1970, p. 363.
138. Grousset, 1970, p. 364, refers to an attack from Crusader Sidon against a Mongol patrol, provoking a Mongol reprisal raid. Grousset comments that the split between the Mongols and the Franks of Acre made Ketbugha's strategic position in the Levant precarious, given his limited forces.
139. Amitai-Preiss, 1995, pp. 74–75. These communications included horse relays, pigeon post, and watch-post bonfire lines (see map 10). According to Amitai-Preiss, warning of a Mongol attack on the Euphrates front-line could be in Cairo within one day. The Mamluk watch-post system was similar to the line of bonfires maintained by the Byzantines in Anatolia in the tenth century, giving similarly rapid warning to Constantinople from the Taurus front (Haldon, 1999, p. 150).
140. Amitai-Preiss, 1995, p. 54.
141. Ayalon, 1994, section 13, pp. 251–53; Ayalon, 1977, section 6, pp. 7–12.
142. Irwin, 1986, p. 48; Amitai-Preiss, 1995, p. 114.
143. Marshall, 1992, pp. 247–48.
144. Amitai-Preiss, 1995, pp. 98–99.
145. Richard, 1999, p. 462; Irwin, 1986, p. 75.
146. Marshall, 1992, p. 224.
147. Lewis, 1967, pp. 122–23.
148. Tritton, 1948, p. 569; Irwin, 1986, pp. 49 and 66. The Fadl sometimes played off the two powers.
149. Amitai-Preiss, 1995, p. 66.
150. Boase, 1978, p. 26.
151. Edwards, 1987, pp. 46–47, contrasts the urban, coastal concentration of Crusader settlement with the rural, mountain focus of the Cilician Armenians, who left the Cilician coastal plain largely deserted apart from the trade outlets of Ayas and Korykos.
152. Irwin, 1986, p. 100.

153. Ayalon, 1977, section 7, p. 329.
154. Ayalon, 1977, section 6, p. 9.
155. Ibid.
156. Irwin, 1986, p. 118.
157. Ibid., p. 145.
158. Ayalon, 1977, section 6, pp. 11–12; Amitai-Preiss, 1995, p. 76.
159. Amitai-Preiss, 1995, pp. 70, 76–77.
160. Holt, 1986, p. 153. Salibi, 1957, pp. 297–300, reviews the mountain uprisings.
161. Amitai-Preiss, 1995, p. 70; Ayalon, 1977, section 6, p. 10.
162. Irwin, 1986, p. 111.
163. Ayalon, 1977, section 1, pp. 72–73, citing the historian Khalil bin Shahin al-Zahiri.
164. Venzke, 2000, p. 407, notes the significance of Elbistan (Dulgadir) as a Mamluk buffer and manpower source against the Mongols and Armenians. The Turcoman chiefs (*begs*) of Elbistan were subject to the Mamluk governor of Aleppo after 1298. Following the Mongol collapse in Anatolia, they established a principality under Mamluk patronage in 1337. They were troublesome clients, regularly involved in Syrian revolts, and playing among the Mamluks, Ottomans, and Iranian Safavids after 1450.
165. Irwin, 1986, pp. 68–69.
166. Qalawun imposed a monetary tribute of half a million Armenian silver dirhams in 1285, doubled by al-Nasir Muhammad in 1315. According to Holt, these sums were a "substantial contribution" to general Mamluk resources—Holt, 1986, p. 159; Irwin, 1986, p. 120.
167. Boase, 1978, p. 31; Irwin, 1986, p. 120.
168. Boase, 1978, p. 31.
169. Ibid.
170. Dols, 1977, pp. 219 and 162, suggests a loss of 38% of the population of Damascus in 1348–49 (about 30,000 deaths), and catastrophic death rates in Palestinian villages (for example, only one survivor in Jenin).
171. Ibid., pp. 185–93.
172. According to Dols, many people from Antioch fled into Anatolia, infecting Karaman and Kayseri but probably not getting any further ("a number attempted to escape to Rum [Anatolia] but most died en route"—Dols, 1977, p. 174).
173. For more on Tankiz, see Irwin, 1986, p. 107, and Holt, 1986, pp. 114–15.
174. Manz, 1989, p. 73, observes that Timurlane had scores to settle with both sultanates, which had sheltered his opponents and refused to surrender them.
175. Venzke, 2000, p. 410.

176. Holt, 1986, p. 185.
177. Dols, 1977, p. 188. There is nothing in the literature to indicate that Otto-man janissaries or other units were affected by plague to anything like the same extent.
178. Venzke, 2000, p. 429.
179. Dols, 1977, p. 203, cites A. N. Poliak, "The Demographic Evolution of the Middle East: Population Trends Since 1348," *Palestine and the Middle East* 10, no. 5 (1938): 201, as estimating this figure from the levy of Mamluk soldiers in Sidon, Beirut, and the Biqa'. The regime required one soldier for every 250 people. Poliak extrapolates from Lebanon to the Levant as a whole on the basis of Lebanon being one-sixth of the region's population in 1800, adjusted to one-eighth to allow for faster growth in Lebanon from the seventeenth century on.
180. Barbir, 1980, pp. 101–2.
181. Raymond, 1984, p. 458, cites an estimate of 60,000 for Aleppo's popu-lation in 1516, with an increase to about 80,000 in 1537 (based on a count of housing units).
182. Inalcik in Inalcik and Quataert, 1994, p. 338.
183. Abu-Husayn, 1992, p. 669.
184. Inalcik in Inalcik and Quataert, 1994, p. 347.
185. Ibid., p. 244.
186. Abu-Husayn, 1992, pp. 671–72.
187. Inalcik in Inalcik and Quataert, 1994, p. 248.
188. Ibid., p. 330.
189. Suraiya Faroqhi in Inalcik and Quataert, 1994, p. 611.
190. Barbir, 1980, pp. 104–5.
191. Faroqhi in Inalcik and Quataert, pp. 499–502.
192. Raymond, 1984, p. 455 (1683 census of housing units, indicating rapid suburban development).
193. Faroqhi in Inalcik and Quataert, p. 506.
194. Barbir, 1980, p. 45.
195. Ibid., pp. 67–97.
196. Bruce McGowan in Inalcik and Quataert, 1994, p. 647.
197. Barbir, 1980, p. 140.
198. Harik, 1968, pp. 31–32.
199. McGowan in Inalcik and Quataert, 1994, p. 673.
200. Barbir, 1980, p. 106.
201. Marcus, 1989, p. 339.
202. Halawi, 1992, p. 45.
203. Douwes, 2000, p. 87.
204. Barbir, 1980, p. 179.
205. Douwes, 2000, pp. 90, 207.

206. Ibid., pp. 70, 115–16.
207. Kushner, 1997, pp. 600–603, describes the isolation and clan struggles of Hebron and Nablus, until firmer exertion of Ottoman authority in the late nineteenth century.
208. Thompson, 1993, p. 458.
209. Ibid., p. 466. Thompson notes an incident in 1846 in which Damascus weavers attacked an Orthodox Christian business importing cheap British thread.
210. Harel, 1998, pp. 87, 88. Harel refers, for example, to the "imposing entry" of the Greek Catholic patriarch into Aleppo in August 1850.
211. Ibid., p. 87.
212. Ibid., p. 89.
213. Fawaz, 1994, pp. 164, 226. Also see Masters, 2001, p. 164.
214. Quataert in Inalcik and Quataert, 1994, p. 817.
215. Shorrock, 1970, pp. 133–35, 140–42.
216. Issawi, 1988, p. 28.
217. Ibid.
218. Abu Manneh, 1992, pp. 17–22.
219. Khalidi, 1997, pp. 28–34.
220. Issawi, 1988, p. 16.
221. Buzpinar, 2000, p. 84, notes, however, that such calm could be easily disturbed. The 1882 British occupation of Egypt reignited Muslim hostility toward Christians in the Levant, particularly in secondary centers (Ladhiqiyya, Hama, Homs, Tripoli, Nazareth, Acre, and elsewhere).
222. Kayali, 1997, pp. 26 and 86.
223. Prawer, 1986, p. 3.
224. The Jews of Aleppo <www.jewishgen.org/sefardsig/AleppoJews.htm>.
225. Prawer, 1986, p. 4.
226. *The Jewish Encyclopedia*, vol. 4, 1903, p. 417.
227. *The Jewish Encyclopedia*, vol. 1, 1901, p. 338.
228. Cohen and Lewis, 1978, p. 161.
229. Issawi, 1988, p. 21.
230. Ibid.
231. Harel, 1998, p. 80.
232. Issawi, 1988, p. 73.
233. The Maronites wanted this detachment. As for the Alawites, Philip Khoury notes that Shaykh Salih al-'Ali's 1921 resistance to French penetration "was not motivated by Arab nationalist sentiments emanating from Damascus; on the contrary, he was interested only in protecting the Alawite districts from all external interference"—Khoury, 1988, p. 100.
234. Shambrook, 1998, p. 182, refers to a 4 October 1935 memorandum from the French Minister of War to the Quai d'Orsay on the strategic impor-

tance of the mountains: "Two upland regions overlook Tripoli and the Homs valley: Lebanon in the south and the Alawite State in the north. To re-attach the Alawite region to an independent Syrian state would deprive our forces in Tripoli of all security on their northern flank . . . It should not be forgotten that the Alawites and Druzes are the only war-like races in the territories under Mandate. They are excellent soldiers and from whom we recruit our best local troops."

235. Hale, 2000, pp. 124–27.
236. Text of the September 1994 Orontes water agreement in *al-Diyar*, 22 September 1994. For comparison, a Lebanese proposal in the 1950s, when political power relations were different, had stipulated that Lebanon should have 40% of the resource.
237. Barak plainly envisaged the withdrawal commitment as pressure on Lebanon and Syria to become more amenable to general peace and security arrangements. In a 12 February 2000 interview with Israel's Channel Two television, he noted: "If there is not an agreement [with Lebanon and Syria] by April or May, and we don't see an agreement on the horizon—we know what to do. Everyone can understand what will happen if there is not an agreement." —*Ha'aretz*, 13 February 2000.
238. Israel would have sub-surface sovereignty.
239. The Palestinians would initially receive about 73% of the West Bank, with a 10–25 year timetable for transfer of additional territory in the Jordan Rift —<http://www.mideastweb.org/CampDavid2.htm> (Camp David II Proposals by Israel).
240. Camp David II Proposals by Israel, and Israeli Private Response to the Palestinian Refugee Proposal of 22 January 2001 (Non-Paper-Draft 2, 23 January 2001) —<http://www.mideastweb.org/Taba.htm> (The Taba Proposals and the Refugee Problem).
241. R. Hammami and S. Tamari, "Anatomy of Another Rebellion" —*Middle East Report* 217, Winter 2000; <http://www.mideastweb.org/lastmaps.htm> (Projections of the Israeli offer in December 2000, and the Bridging Proposal of US President Clinton).
242. Iran and Hizballah repeatedly urged the Palestinians to rebel after Israel's May 2000 retreat from Lebanon. In a July 2000 meeting in Tehran with Hizballah Secretary-General Hasan Nasrallah, Iran's supreme religious guide Ali Khamene'i expressed the hope that Hizballah's example would "push the new Palestinian generation to confrontation and jihad against the Zionist regime" —*al-Hayat*, 6 July 2000.
243. *The Times,* 7 February 2002.
244. For Arabic text, see *al-Hayat*, 28 March 2002.
245. Economist Intelligence Unit Country Reports—Syria (August 2001),

Jordan (September 2001), Lebanon (October 2001), and Israel (October 2001).

246. World Development Indicators database, World Bank, April 2002: <http://www.worldbank.org/data/databytopic/GNPPC.pdf>.

247. Internet usage estimates for Syria, Lebanon, and Israel from <http://cyberatlas.internet.com/big_picture/geographics/article/ 0,1323,5911_151151,00.html> (The World's Online Populations, March 21, 2002). Data for Jordan from <http://www.weforum.org/pdf/ DigitalDivide/Jordan_Country_Report_100902.pdf> (World Economic Forum, Global Digital Divide Initiative, Educational ICT Pilot Initiative: Jordan).

248. Bashar al-Asad as quoted in *al-Hayat*, 6 May 2001: "They try to kill all the principles of the Semitic religions with the same mentality involved in the betrayal and torture of Christ and in the same way they tried to deceive the Prophet Muhammad."

249. See, for example, *al-Nahar* (Beirut), 6 March 2002, on Standard and Poor's pessimistic outlook regarding Lebanon's ability to pay off its debt, and *al-Wasat,* 25 February 2002, on a decision by the Lebanese central bank to cease publishing debt figures. According to *al-Wasat,* the public debt stood at $29.8 billion in early 2002 (160% of GDP).

250. For full elaboration, see el-Khazen, 2000.

251. In December 1998, the prominent Lebanese Shi'ite scholar Muhammad Husayn Fadlallah lamented his country's persistent sectarianism at a Ramadan *Iftar*: "We . . . are several sects but we feel that we are several states . . . Is it believable that the country is occupied by an enemy [Israel] . . . and we [spend our time] debating whether the Shi'ite sect or the Sunni sect or the Maronite sect has the biggest numbers." *Al-Hayat,* 1 January 1999.

252. Report by Ibrahim Bayram, *al-Wasat*, 23 October 2000.

253. In April 2000, Junblat compared Lebanese emigration with the inflow of Syrian workers into Lebanon "as if what is wanted is the replacement of one people by another, and the pauperization and humiliation of what remains of the Lebanese" —*al-Hayat,* 17 April 2000. In August, he accused the Syrians of interfering in the Lebanese parliamentary elections: "I want to know why some Syrian authorities ask [village headmen] for the election of the opposing candidate list" —*al-Hayat,* 26 August 2000.

254. The author heard expressions of such anger from Druze while in Beirut in December 2001, particularly after a Hizballah military parade with open displays of weaponry. Shi'ite responses were dismissive.

255. Human Rights Watch (HRW) Report on the Kurdish minority in Syria,

vol. 8, no. 4(E) (October 1996). HRW notes "a comprehensive plan to Arabize the resources-rich northeast of Syria, an area with the largest concentration of non-Arabs in the country." <http://www.hrw.org/summaries/s.syria9610.html> (Summary, paragraph 2).

256. Zeynep Gurcanli in *Hürriyet,* 15 May 1998 (FBIS Daily Report) —information from Turkish interrogation of Semdin Sakik, second-in-command of the PKK.

257. Author's interview with senior Turkish Foreign Ministry official, May 1999.

258. See, for example, Avni Özgürel in *Radikal,* 20 May 2002 —"Suriye ile yeni bir sayfa" (A new page with Syria).

259. Islamist Refah Party deputy leader Abdullah Gül to *al-Hayat* —"The Syrians 'lost a precious opportunity' [while Refah was in government] when they didn't stop PKK activities or those of Öcalan on Syrian territory." *Al-Hayat,* 15 February 1998.

260. See *al-Hayat*, 6 and 17 May 2000.

261. "Missteps with Turkey Prove Costly." Glenn Kessler and Philip Pan in the *Washington Post*, 28 March 2003.

262. Hilal Köylü in *Radikal*, 9 September 2004, notes Turkish "lack of confidence toward the [Iraqi] Kurds (Kürtlere güvensizlik)," but also that both major Iraqi Kurdish parties maintain representatives in Ankara and "have striven to develop relations with Turkey."

263. Salim Arif in *Al-Zaman* (London), 24 February 2005, gives an extraordinary account of Syrian intelligence activities in Mosul.

264. Ariel Sharon to *Ha'aretz* (Hebrew edition), 14 April 2003.

265. Even according to the February 2005 reduced routing of the "security barrier," 7% of the West Bank outside East Jerusalem (8.5% with extension to Ariel) would be on the "Israeli" side—*Ha'aretz* (Hebrew edition), 18 February 2005. Of 250,000 West Bank settlers, 144,000 live in this 7% of the territory (163,000 with Ariel), intended "as part of the state of Israel in the future"—*Ha'aretz* (Hebrew edition), 7 April 2005. This involved about one-eighth of fertile land on the West Bank.

266. Polls taken by the Palestinian "Jerusalem Media and Communication Center" among West Bank/Gaza Palestinians indicate support for Islamic factions fluctuating 24–30%, 2002–2004, and a fall in support for military operations from 65% to 41% between June and December 2004 <http://www.jmcc.org/publicpoll/opinion.html>.

267. Ariel Sharon to *Ha'aretz* (Hebrew edition), 14 September 2004.

268. As reported by Ibrahim Hamidi in *al-Hayat*, 28 July 2003.

269. *Al-Zaman* (London), 15 and 17 March 2004. Also see *al-Hayat*, 13 and 14, 17 and 18 March 2004.

270. Walid Shuqayr in *al-Hayat*, 9 September 2004.

271. Ibid.

272. As recounted by Hariri to Walid Junblat—*Al-Ra'y al-'Aam*, 18 February 2005.

273. See *Al-Nahar*, 1 and 3 September 2004.

274. Hazim al-Amin in *al-Hayat*, 29 August 2004. *Al-Nahar*, 30 September 2004, cites a poll indicating that 74% of the Lebanese electorate favored throwing the deputies who voted for the constitutional amendment out of parliament.

275. *Al-Hayat*, 8 September 2004.

276. *Al-Nahar*, 27 January and 15 March 2005.

277. See Randa Taqi al-Din in *al-Hayat*, 18 February 2005.

278. In early February 2005, Hariri told the Iranian ambassador in Paris that his "strategic goal" was "the exit of Syrian forces and the recovery of Lebanon's independence"—*Al-Hayat*, 21 February 2005.

279. Text of Bashar al-Asad's speech to the Syrian parliament in *al-Hayat*, 6 March 2005. Syrian information minister quoted in *al-Nahar*, 7 March 2005.

280. Iranian sources to *al-Hayat*, 21 February 2005.

281. See, for example, *al-Hayat*, 19 May 2005, on charges levelled by the Beirut "Medina Bank" director "against the brothers of Rustum Ghazaleh for embezzling millions of dollars." Rustum Ghazaleh was the head of Syrian military intelligence in Lebanon (effectively, Syria's high commissioner for commanding its neighbor) from 2002 until the April 2005 Syrian withdrawal, and in May 2005 remained Bashar al-Asad's chief deputy for dealing with Lebanese affairs.

282. See, for example, *Hürriyet*, 10 January 2005 ("Sixty-six year Hatay problem ended").

GLOSSARY

Religious and Ethnic Groups

Alawites: Offshoot sect from Twelver Shi'ite Islam. Believe in the divinity of the Caliph 'Ali. Emerged in al-Nusayriya hills of coastal Syria in the eleventh century. The community encompasses four major clan groups—the Kalbiyah, Khayyatun, Haddadun, and Matawirah. Alawites number about two million in Syria and 100,000 in northern Lebanon.

'Alid Muslims: Muslims loyal to the Caliph 'Ali, cousin and son-in-law of the Prophet Muhammad (also see **Shi'ites**). These Muslims were hostile to 'Ali's Umayyad opponents, and to the Umayyad Caliphate. Separated into various Shi'ite groups between the seventh and tenth centuries.

Armenians: Clans in eastern Anatolia and the Caucasus who converted to Christianity in the fourth century. Armenians, who speak an Indo-European language that has no close relatives, regard themselves as the first Christian "nation." The Armenian Gregorian church adopted the Monophysite doctrinal position (see **Monophysites**) in the sixth century, challenging Byzantine Orthodoxy. There are at least 400,000 Armenians in the Levant.

Assassins: Isma'ili Shi'ites who maintained small mountain principalities in Iran and the Nusayriya hills of Syria in the twelfth century. Trained Assassin agents undertook political killings, chiefly of Sunni Muslim leaders. Termed "Hashishiyun" because they reputedly smoked hashish.

Druze: Sect derived from Isma'ili Shi'ite Islam in the eleventh century. Believe in the divinity of the Fatimid Caliph al-Hakim. Druzes number about 700,000 in the Levant (200,000 in Lebanon, 400,000 in Syria, and 80,000 in Israel).

Greek Catholics: In the 1720s, after decades of French-supported Catholic infiltration of the Orthodox patriarchate of Antioch, Catholics (formerly Orthodox) in Aleppo asserted a separate church in communion with Rome. Through the eighteenth century, many migrated to Lebanon (e.g. Zahle) and Palestine, following commercial openings. Like the Maronites, they have their own patriarch and liturgy. There are about 500,000 Greek Catholics in the Levant, mainly in Syria and Lebanon. Third largest church in the region after the Orthodox and Maronites.

Hospitallers: Staff of a hospital founded in Jerusalem in 1070 for poor pilgrims. Became a religious order under the Pope after the Crusader conquest, then a military order to defend pilgrim routes in the 1130s. Later held fortresses such as Margat and Crac des Chevaliers.

Isma'ili Shi'ites: Isma'ilis recognize a line of seven Imams, diverging from Twelvers after the sixth Imam, Ja'afar al-Sadiq (founder of the Shi'ite Ja'fari school of religious law). There are about 150,000 Isma'ilis in Syria, mainly in the surrounds of Hama.

Jacobites: Syrian Monophysite Christians. Church founded by Jacob Baradaeus in the late sixth century. Minority went into communion with Rome in seventeenth century as Syrian Catholics. The two churches together have about 200,000 adherents in the Levant.

Kurds: Tribal groups in eastern Turkey, northern Syria, and northern Iraq who speak an Indo-European language distantly related to Persian. Kurds are mainly Sunni Muslims, but are ethnically distinct from Turks and Arabs and regard themselves as descendants of the ancient Medes.

Mardaites: Christian tribespeople in the Amanus mountains (Nur Dağları) who resisted Islamic rule in the early Umayyad period.

Maronites: Christians in northern Syria who adopted a doctrinal compromise between Orthodox and Monophysite Christianity suggested by the Emperor Heraclius in the seventh century. Became the predominant Christian community of Mount Lebanon. Went into communion with Rome in the sixteenth century. Maronites number about 800,000 in Lebanon, and are probably the majority of the global Lebanese diaspora.

Monophysites: Adherents of the Christian doctrinal position that Christ has only a single nature, with the human element subsumed in the divine. The single-nature doctrine emerged in the fifth century in reaction to the Nestorian concept (see **Nestorians**). The Church Council of Chalcedon declared it a heresy in 451. This eventually led to the separation of Syrian Jacobites and Egyptian Copts from Byzantine Orthodoxy.

Nestorians: Adherents of the Christian doctrinal position that Christ is two separate persons (divine and human) in one body. Thus Mary mother of Christ, but not mother of God. Nestorius, Bishop of Constantinople, proposed this position in the early fifth century. The Church Council of Ephesus declared it a heresy in 431. Followers of Nestorius moved to Persian territory. Nestorian missionaries traveled across Central Asia to China in the seventh century.

Orthodox Christians: Members of the Byzantine "orthodox" church. Like Roman Catholics, adhere to doctrines established by the Church Council of Chalcedon in 451. Believe that Christ has two distinct natures (divine and human) united in one person. Split from the Roman church in eleventh century over dogma (Roman adoption of double procession of Holy Spirit from Father and Son—for Constantinople, only from the Father), Byzantine use of leavened bread in communion, jurisdictional disputes between the papacy and the patriarchate of Constantinople, and general estrangement between "Latin" West and "Greek" East. There are about 1.3 million Orthodox Christians in the Levant, under the patriarchates of Antioch and Jerusalem.

Qaramita: Isma'ili Shi'ites who gained command of much of northern Arabia and the Syrian steppe in the early tenth century. The Qaramita, hostile to all other Islamic authorities, organized Bedouin tribes for assaults on the Levant and Iraq. Also known as the Karmathians.

Samaritans: Originally the Jewish population of the Biblical northern kingdom of Israel, mixed with colonists imported by the Assyrians. They split from the Jews of Judea over the succession to the high priesthood, and did not acknowledge additions to the Pentateuch (first five books of the Bible) as holy scripture. In the Roman period, Samaritans were separate from the Jews and became the majority in the Samarian highlands. Persecuted by the Christian Roman authorities from the fourth century on, and dwindled in numbers.

Shi'ites: Muslims who assert that the Caliph 'Ali was the sole legitimate heir of the Prophet Muhammad as leader of the Islamic community, and reject the first three caliphs (also see **'Alid Muslims**). Believe in a line of divinely guided personalities (Imams) as successors to 'Ali. Shi'ites are members of the "faction" (*Shi'ah*) of 'Ali.

Sunnis: Muslims who follow the "tradition" (*Sunna*) of the Prophet Muhammad and the four "rightly-guided" caliphs. Sunnis do not accept the Shi'ite elevation of 'Ali, and do not acknowledge any special status for Shi'ite Imams. Sunnis are frequently termed "orthodox" Muslims, and represent about 60% of the population of the Levant south of the Syrian-Turkish boundary.

Templars: Order of Knights installed in the Temple area of Jerusalem in 1118. Like the Hospitallers, the Templars were directly under the Pope. They held Safed and fortresses in the Amanus range in the thirteenth century.

Turcomans: Turkish nomadic tribes that moved southwest from central Asia into Iran, eastern Anatolia, and the Levant from the early eleventh century on.

Twelver Shi'ites: The main Shi'ite community. Twelvers recognize a line of twelve Imams. They believe the last Imam went into hiding, and will return to reorder the world before the final judgment. Twelver Shi'ism is the state religion of Iran. There are about 1.2 million Twelvers in Lebanon.

Wahhabis: Puritanical Sunni Islamic movement in the Arabian Peninsula. Founded by Muhammad 'Abd al-Wahhab in the late eighteenth century. 'Abd al-Wahhab aligned with the influential al-Sa'ud clan. Aim to restore the original Islamic community of Muhammad, with all embellishments eliminated (Sufi mysticism, Shi'ism, veneration of holy personalities).

Tribal Groups

'Anaza Bedouin: Confederation of tribes that moved north from the Arabian Peninsula into the steppe margins of the Levant in the late seventeenth century.

Ghassanids: Christian Arab tribal group in the Syrian steppe that became allied with Rome in the early sixth century.

Isaurians: Cilician hill tribes in the Roman period.

Ituraeans: Arab tribes in Mount Lebanon in the early Roman period. Proved difficult for Rome to subdue. Later served in Roman armies as horsemen and archers.

Kalb Bedouin: Tribal confederation in Damascus region in the 'Abbasid period.

Kilab Bedouin: Tribal confederation that moved from northern Arabia into the Homs and Aleppo areas in the late ninth century. Took leadership of Qaysi Arab faction and became entrenched north and east of Aleppo.

Lakhmids: Tribal allies of the Persians in the desert between Iraq and Syria in the sixth century.

Mawali Bedouin: Tribal allies of the Mamluks and Ottomans in the Syrian steppe between the thirteenth and eighteenth centuries. The Mawali disintegrated under pressure from the 'Anaza Bedouin in the eighteenth and nineteenth centuries.

Qaysis: Northern tribal faction in the Arabian Peninsula in pre-Islamic times. Opposed to southern "Yamani" faction. Division imported into the Levant with the Islamic conquest. Tribes moving into northern Syria tended to be "Qaysi." The dispute soon lost its original Arabian meaning; "Qaysi" and "Yamani" simply became labels for new tribal factions in the Levant and Iraq (also see **Yamanis**).

Taghlib: Muslim Arab tribe in the Jazira in the 'Abbasid period. The Hamdanid dynasty in Aleppo had Taghlib origins. Taghlib tribesmen opposed to the Hamdanids joined the Byzantines.

Tayy Bedouin: Tribal confederation that entered Transjordan and Palestine from Arabia in the late ninth century. Came under Qarmati Shi'ite influence and challenged Tulunid, Ikhshidid, and Fatimid authority in the southern Levant.

Yamanis: Southern tribal faction in the Arabian Peninsula in pre-Islamic times. Opposed to northern "Qaysi" faction. With the Islamic conquest, tribes moving into Palestine tended to be "Yamani" (also see **Qaysi**). The modern name "Yemen" refers to the "right side" or south of Arabia.

Rulers, Dynasties, States

'Abbasids: Succession of Muslim caliphs from the 'Abbasid branch of the Prophet Muhammad's family who ruled most of the Islamic world from Iraq after displacing the Umayyads in 749. Lost control of areas beyond Iraq by the early tenth century and then generally lost temporal authority even within Iraq. Survived as Islamic spiritual leaders until the Mongols sacked Baghdad in 1258.

Ayyubids: Family of the Kurdish warlord Salah al-Din Yusuf ibn Ayyub. Ruled Egypt and the Muslim Levant after Salah al-Din's death in 1193 until displaced by the Mamluks in 1250.

Buhturids: Family of Buhtur, a mid-twelfth-century leader of the Tanukh clan in the Suq al-Gharb hills southeast of Beirut. The Tanukh clan converted to Druzism in the 1020s, but the Buhturids publicly professed Sunni Islam and gave allegiance to the Muslim rulers of Damascus in the late twelfth century. Despite some recalcitrance, they were careful in relations with the Franks.

Buyids: Shi'ites from the Caspian mountains of Iran who gained control of much of the Iranian plateau in the early tenth century and ruled Baghdad, 945–1055, subordinating the 'Abbasid caliphate. Removed by the Seljuk Turks.

Caliphs and sultans: It is useful to understand the distinction between these two words. Caliph (*khalifa*) originally meant "successor" of the Prophet Muhammad as spiritual and temporal leader of the Islamic community. Late 'Abbasid caliphs lost temporal authority to warlords, and eventually recognized political reality when they granted Seljuk Turkish leaders the title sultan, or "ruler." The office of caliph, however, continued to imply Sunni Islamic moral authority. Mamluk sultans maintained a puppet caliph in Cairo, supposedly of 'Abbasid descent.

Fatimids: Isma'ili Shi'ite rulers of Tunisia who seized Egypt in 969 and founded an Isma'ili caliphate in Cairo that lasted until abolished by Salah al-Din in 1171. Controlled much of the southern Levant from 978 until pushed back by the Crusader Kingdom of Jerusalem in the early twelfth century.

Hamdanids: Twelver Shi'ite Arab dynasty that ruled Aleppo from 945 to 1005.

Ilkhanate: Mongol state established by Hülegü in Iran, Iraq, and the Jazira in the 1250s. "Il-khan" meant provincial khan (leader), technically subordinate to the supreme khan in China. The Ilkhanate began to disintegrate in the 1320s.

Ikhshidids: Military rulers of Egypt and parts of the Levant from the 930s until the Fatimid invasion in 969. Acknowledged 'Abbasid suzerainty. Given the Persian title of Ikhshid by the 'Abbasid caliph.

Karamanids: Turkish principality in southeast Anatolia after the collapse of Ilkhanate supremacy in the 1320s. Capital at Konya. Annexed by the Ottomans in 1397, restored by Timurlane in 1403, and permanently extinguished by the Ottomans in 1475.

Khawarizmians: Turks from the region south of the Aral Sea (Khwarizm or Khiva). Their Shah controlled Iran and Transoxiana from 1194 to 1220, when Genghis Khan overran his "empire." Brief Khawarizmian restoration in western Iran and the Caucasus, 1224–1230. Defeated in eastern Anatolia in 1230 by a Syrian Ayyubid– Seljuk Turk alliance and then by the Mongols. In 1244, Khawarizmian bands joined the Egyptian Ayyubids against the Syrian Ayyubids and the Franks.

Mamluks: Slave soldiers of mainly Turkic and Circassian origin who ruled Egypt, 1250–1517. From 1250 to 1382, rulers were Kipchak Turks, in hereditary succession after Qalawun. From 1383 to 1517, rulers were Circassian Mamluk commanders. Mamluk ranks were continually replenished by new recruits from southern Russia and the Caucasus. The Arabic term means "owned."

Marwanids: Kurdish dynasty that controlled the Diyarbakir area of the upper Jazira, 990–1096. Capital at Mayyarfariqin (Silvan). Created a tolerant and prosperous small eleventh-century state.

Mirdasids: Arab dynasty of Kilabi Bedouin origin that controlled Aleppo, 1023–1079.

Ottomans: Turkish clan that migrated from Khurasan in eastern Iran to Anatolia after 1220. Given lands by the Seljuks on the Byzantine frontier, a position the Ottomans used to carve out an expanding state that eventually took the place of both the Seljuks and the Byzantines. Name from Osman, the first Ottoman ruler in northwest Anatolia, 1280–1326.

Parthians: Leaders of the Parthian tribes east and south of the Caspian Sea before the time of Alexander the Great. The Parthians ended Seleucid Greek control of Persia after 250 B.C.E. Ruling dynasty of the resurgent Persian Empire, 250 B.C.E.–225 C.E.

Safavids: A family of Twelver Shi'ite Sufi mystics that took over Iran in 1502. The Safavids converted most of the Iranian population to Twelver Shi'ism and resurrected Iran as an imperial state. Imported religious specialists from the Lebanese Twelver Shi'ite community.

Sassanids: Rulers of the Persian Empire, 226–636. Descendants of a Persian priest, Sassan, whose son seized Persia and whose grandson dethroned the Parthians. The Sassanids made Zoroastrianism the state religion (Ahura Mazda as deity in permanent struggle against balancing force of evil). This gave the political conflict with the Christian Roman Empire a strong religious dimension.

Seleucids: Dynasty of Seleucus, one of Alexander's generals. Kings of

Syria and varying other territories, 312–63 B.C.E.

Seljuks: Turkish clan that moved south of the Aral Sea and became Muslim in the early eleventh century. Invaded Iran in 1040 and captured Baghdad in 1055, inaugurating the Great Seljuk Sultanate (sultan means "ruler"—the 'Abbasid caliph remained as a spiritual leader). Seljuk states also established in Anatolia after the defeat of the Byzantines in 1071.

Tulunids: Turkish warlord dynasty that took control of Egypt and much of the Levant under nominal 'Abbasid suzerainty, 860s–905.

Umayyads: Prominent merchants in Mecca at the time of the Prophet Muhammad. The Umayyads were the family of the Caliph Uthman and his governor in Syria, Mu'awiya. They ruled the Islamic caliphate, 661–750, after Mu'awiya's displacement of the sons of the Caliph 'Ali.

'Uqaylids: Bedouin Arab dynasty from the Banu 'Uqayl tribe of the Jazira. Controlled Mosul and much of the Jazira between 996 and the late eleventh century.

Zengids: Family of Zangi, Turkish commander *(atabek)* of Mosul in the 1120s, who took charge of Aleppo in 1126. His son Nur al-Din united Aleppo and Damascus in 1154, and promoted the "holy war" against the Franks. From 1174 to 1183, the Aleppo Zengids resisted Salah al-Din's takeover of Syria, aligning with the Crusader Kingdom of Jerusalem.

Modern Political Factions and Movements

Al-Aqsa Brigade: Clandestine militant cells formed out of Fatah and the Tanzim after the September 2000 launching of the Palestinian 'Al-Aqsa' *intifada*. Implemented suicide bombings inside Israel in 2001–2002.

Ba'th: Secular Arab nationalist party founded in Damascus in 1943 by Michel Aflaq (Orthodox Christian) and Salah al-Din Bitar (Sunni Muslim). The Ba'th called for Arab unity, socialist reforms in Arab states, and freedom from Western influences. In 1953 merged with the Syrian Socialist Party of Akram Hawrani to form the Arab Socialist Ba'th. In the 1960s, the Ba'th became the ruling party in both Syria and Iraq, as the political framework for authoritarian regimes.

Fatah: Palestinian Arab resistance movement against Israel founded by Yasir Arafat in 1958. Joined the PLO in 1968 and became its principal component. Largest armed Palestinian organization in Jordan, 1967–70, and Lebanon, 1967 on. Fatah has been the major element in the Palestinian Authority in the West Bank and Gaza, 1993 on.

Hamas: Militant Palestinian Sunni Islamic faction founded in 1987 in the Gaza Strip as an offshoot of the Muslim Brotherhood. Initially encouraged by the Israelis because of its hostility to the secular PLO. In the 1990s, Hamas (the Islamic Resistance Movement) expanded as a social and political organization with a military wing, the 'Iz al-Din al-Qasim brigade, that promoted armed actions, including suicide bombings, against Israel. Hamas became the main political rival of the Palestinian Authority, gaining up to 20% support from the Palestinian public.

Hizballah: Militant Lebanese Shi'ite Islamic organization founded after the 1982 Israeli invasion of Lebanon. Hizballah (the Party of God) called for armed resistance against Israel and an Iranian-style Islamic state in Lebanon. Promoted suicide bombings against the US embassy and marines in Beirut in 1983–84, during the ill-conceived US intervention in Lebanon after the Israeli invasion. Splinter groups associated with the party kidnapped Westerners in Beirut through the 1980s. In the 1990s, Hizballah tried to reconcile with non-Shi'ite Lebanese by shelving its "Islamic state" program while attacking the Israeli-occupied security zone in southern Lebanon.

Islamic Jihad: Militant Palestinian Sunni Islamic faction. Emerged in the Gaza Strip in the 1970s as a small group favoring an Islamic state. In the 1990s, promoted violence against Israelis from its headquarters in Damascus. Unlike Hamas, Islamic Jihad has remained simply an armed organization. In 1995, the Israelis killed the faction's leader, Fathi Shaqaqi, in Malta.

Israeli Labor Party: Main center-left Israeli political party. Formed in 1968 as the union of three left-leaning parties with Mapai, the principal force in Zionist and Israeli politics after its founding in 1930, as the primary element. Mapai and Labor led Israeli coalition governments from 1948 to 1977. Labor's representation in the Knesset (parliament) declined from 44 in 1992 to 34 in 1996 and 26 in 1999, but it remained the largest party in the post-1999 Knesset.

Knesset: Israeli parliament, with 120 seats. Elected on a proportional voting system, so contains a multiplicity of parties. Elections every four years unless there is an early dissolution.

Lebanese Forces: Formed in 1980 by Lebanese Maronite militia chief Bashir Jumayyil by combining several Christian militias, principally those of the Kata'ib (Phalange) and National Liberal Parties. The Lebanese Forces represented the largest militia in Lebanon through the 1980s, with about 20,000 members. Suppressed by the Syrian-dominated Lebanese government in the 1990s.

Likud: Main center-right Israeli political party. Formed in 1973 as the union of four conservative parties. Led by Menachem Begin's Herut, the principal opposition to Mapai in Israeli politics after 1948. The Likud represents Revisionist Zionism, which from the 1930s demanded Jewish and Israeli rule over the whole of geographical Palestine (Eretz Yisrael—The Land of Israel), as opposed to the more pragmatic Labor Zionist policy on territory. The Likud became the ruling party in Israel after the 1977 elections, and retained the political advantage until 1992. Its representation in the Knesset declined from 41 in 1984 to 32 in 1992 to 19 in 1999. The Likud is the party of Ariel Sharon, who displaced Ehud Barak in the 2001 prime ministerial elections.

Muslim Brotherhood: Sunni Islamic revivalist movement founded by Hasan al-Banna in Egypt in 1928. The Brotherhood has generally espoused a gradualist strategy of persuasion and infiltration to Islamize society and eventually capture the state. Branches founded in Jordan and Syria in the 1950s. Officially banned in Egypt since 1954, but operates through front organizations as the main opposition to the regime. Rebelled against the Syrian regime, 1979–82, and smashed by the Syrian army and security agencies.

Palestinian Authority (PA): Palestinian governing authority set up in parts of the West Bank and the Gaza Strip as a result of accords between Israel and the PLO in 1993–95. Comprises an executive headed by Yasir Arafat from 1994 to 2004, an elected assembly, civil bureaucracy, and security agencies. The P.A. is principally under Fatah influence.

PFLP: Popular Front for the Liberation of Palestine. George Habash established the PFLP in 1967 as a Palestinian Arab nationalist organization with a Marxist orientation. The PFLP joined the PLO in 1968. It suspended its participation in the PLO in 1993 in protest against the Oslo accord with Israel. Entered reconciliation talks with Arafat in 1999. Headquarters in Damascus.

PKK: The Kurdish Workers Party. Founded as a small Marxist-Leninist group among Turkish Kurds in 1974. In 1984, launched a violent campaign in southeast Anatolia against the Turkish state. Sought an independent Kurdish state. Viewed by Turkey as a separatist terrorist organization. Rebellion peaked in the mid-1990s. Broken by the Turkish army in 1998.

PLO: Palestine Liberation Organization. Founded in 1964 as the umbrella organization of Palestinian Arab nationalism. Headed by Yasir Arafat after Fatah became its largest component in 1968. Evolved a range of institutions, including the Palestine National Council, the Palestinian Arab "parliament in exile."

Revisionist Zionism: See Likud.

Tanzim: Armed wing of Fatah in the West Bank and the Gaza Strip. Established by Arafat in 1995 to counter Islamic groups and balance the PA Preventive Security Service. Became a strong grassroots organization in the West Bank under Marwan Barghouti.

Zionism: Modern Jewish nationalist movement that emerged among European Jewry in the late nineteenth century to recreate a Jewish national state in Palestine. Zionism was a response to nineteenth-century European nationalism and anti-Semitism. Established as a political movement led by Theodor Herzl, who called the first Zionist Congress in Basel in 1897.

REFERENCES

Abu Husayn, Abdul-Rahim. "Problems in the Ottoman Administration of Syria during the Sixteenth and Seventeenth Centuries: The Case of the Sanjak of Sidon-Beirut." *International Journal of Middle East Studies* 24 (1992): 665–75.

Abu Manneh, Butrus. "The Establishment and Dismantling of the Province of Syria." In *Problems of the Modern Middle East in Historical Perspective: Essays in Honour of Albert Hourani,* edited by J. Spagnolo, pp. 7–26. Reading: Ithaca, 1992.

Akarli, Engin. *The Long Peace: Ottoman Lebanon, 1861–1920.* London: I.B. Tauris, 1993.

Amitai-Preiss, Reuven. *Mongols and Mamluks: The Mongol-Ilkhanid War, 1260–1281.* Cambridge: Cambridge University Press, 1995.

Asbridge, Thomas. *The Creation of the Principality of Antioch, 1098–1130.* Woodbridge, Suffolk: Boydell Press, 2000.

An Atlas of Palestine (The West Bank and Gaza). Jerusalem: Applied Research Institute (ARIJ), 2000.

Avi-Yonah, M. *The Jews of Palestine: A Political History from the Bar Kokhba War to the Arab Conquest.* Oxford: Blackwell, 1976.

Ayalon, David. *Studies on the Mamluks of Egypt, 1250–1517.* London: Variorum, 1977.

———. *Islam and the Abode of War.* Aldershot: Variorum, 1994.

Barbir, Karl. *Ottoman Rule in Damascus, 1708–1758.* Princeton: Princeton University Press, 1980.

Boase, T. S. R., ed. *The Cilician Kingdom of Armenia.* Edinburgh & London: Scottish Academic Press, 1978.

Bosworth, Clifford. *The Arabs, Byzantium, and Iran: Studies in Early Islamic History and Culture.* Aldershot: Variorum, 1996.

Bull, Marcus. "Origins." In *The Oxford History of the Crusades,* edited by J. Riley-Smith, pp. 15–34. Oxford: Oxford University Press, 1999.

Buzpinar, S. Tufan. "The Repercussions of the British Occupation of Egypt on Syria, 1882–83." *Middle Eastern Studies* 36, no. 1 (2000): 82–91.

Cahen, Claude. *Pre-Ottoman Turkey.* London: Sidgwick & Jackson, 1968.

Cohen, Amnon, and Bernard Lewis. *Population and Revenue in the Towns of Palestine in the Sixteenth Century.* Princeton: Princeton University Press, 1978.

Dajani-Shakeel, Hadia. "Natives and Franks in Palestine: Perceptions and

Interaction." In *Conversion and Continuity: Indigenous Christian Communities in Islamic Lands, Eighth to Eighteenth Centuries*, edited by Michael Gervers and Ramzi Jibran Bikhazi, pp. 161–84. Toronto: Pontifical Institute of Mediaeval Studies, 1990.

Dols, Michael. *The Black Death in the Middle East*. Princeton: Princeton University Press, 1977.

Douwes, Dick. *The Ottomans in Syria: A History of Justice and Oppression*. London: I.B. Tauris, 2000.

Edwards, Robert. *The Fortifications of Armenian Cilicia*. Washington, D.C.: Dumbarton Oaks, 1987.

El-Khazen, Farid. *The Breakdown of the State in Lebanon, 1967–1976*. London: I.B. Tauris, 2000.

Fawaz, Leila. *Merchants and Migrants in Nineteenth-Century Beirut*. Cambridge, Mass.: Harvard University Press, 1983.

Goldsworthy, Adrian. *The Roman Army at War, 100 BC–AD 200*. Oxford: Oxford University Press, 1996.

Grousset, René. *Empire of the Steppes: A History of Central Asia*. New Brunswick: Rutgers University Press, 1970.

Halawi, Majid. *A Lebanon Defied: Musa al-Sadr and the Shi'a Community*. Boulder, Colo.: Westview, 1992.

Haldon, John. *Byzantium in the Seventh Century: The Transformation of a Culture*. Cambridge: Cambridge University Press, 1990.

———. *Warfare, State and Society in the Byzantine World, 565–1204*. London: UCL Press, 1999.

Hale, William. *Turkish Foreign Policy, 1774–2000*. London: Cass, 2000.

Hallam, Elizabeth, ed. *Chronicles of the Crusades: Eye-Witness Accounts of the Wars between Christianity and Islam*. Godalming, Surrey: CLB International, 1997.

Halm, Heinz. *Shiism*. Edinburgh: Edinburgh University Press, 1991.

Hamilton, Bernard. *The Leper King and His Heirs: Baldwin IV and the Crusader Kingdom of Jerusalem*. Cambridge: Cambridge University Press, 2000.

Harel, Yaron. "Jewish-Christian Relations in Aleppo as Background for the Jewish Response to the Events of October 1850." *International Journal of Middle East Studies* 30 (1998): 77–96.

Harik, Iliya. *Politics and Change in a Traditional Society: Lebanon, 1711–1845*. Princeton: Princeton University Press, 1968.

Harris, William. *Taking Root: Israeli Settlement in the West Bank, the Golan, and Gaza-Sinai, 1967–80*. New York: John Wiley, 1981.

———. *Faces of Lebanon: Sects, Wars, and Global Extensions*. Princeton: Markus Wiener, 1997.

Hillenbrand, Carole. *The Crusades: Islamic Perspectives*. Edinburgh:

Edinburgh University Press, 1999.

Hitti, Philip. *History of Syria, including Lebanon and Palestine.* London: MacMillan, 1951.

———. *Syria: A Short History.* New York: MacMillan, 1959.

———. *History of the Arabs.* New York: St. Martin's Press, 1968.

Holt, P.M. *The Age of the Crusades: The Near East from the Eleventh Century to 1517.* London: Longman, 1986.

Hooper, Nicholas, and Matthew Bennett. *Cambridge Illustrated Atlas of Warfare: The Middle Ages, 768–1487.* Cambridge: Cambridge University Press, 1996.

Humphreys, R. Stephen. *From Saladin to the Mongols.* Albany: SUNY Press, 1977.

Ibn Khaldun. *The Muqaddimah: An Introduction to History.* Translated by F. Rosenthal, abridged by N. Dawood. London: Routledge & Kegan Paul, 1978.

Inalcik, Halil, and Donald Quataert, eds. *An Economic and Social History of the Ottoman Empire, 1300–1914.* New York: Cambridge University Press, 1994.

Irwin, Robert. *The Middle East in the Middle Ages: The Early Mamluk Sultanate, 1250–1382.* Carbondale and Edwardsville: Southern Illinois University Press, 1986.

Isaac, Benjamin. *The Limits of Empire: The Roman Army in the East.* Oxford: Clarendon, 1992.

Issawi, Charles. *The Fertile Crescent, 1800–1914: A Documentary Economic History.* New York: Oxford University Press, 1988.

The Jewish Encyclopedia, vols. 1 and 4. London: Funk and Wagnalls, 1901 and 1903.

Jones, A.H.M. *The Later Roman Empire, 284–602: A Social, Economic, and Administrative Survey.* 3 vols. Oxford: Blackwell, 1964.

Josephus, Flavius. *The Jewish War.* Translated by G. Williamson. Harmondsworth: Penguin, 1959.

Kaegi, Walter. *Byzantium and the Early Islamic Conquests.* Cambridge: Cambridge University Press, 1992.

Kayali, Hasan. *Arabs and Young Turks: Ottomanism, Arabism, and Islamism in the Ottoman Empire, 1908–1918.* Berkeley: University of California Press, 1997.

Kennedy, Hugh. *The Prophet and the Age of the Caliphates: The Islamic Near East from the Sixth to the Eleventh Century.* London: Longman, 1986.

Khalidi, Rashid. *Palestinian Identity: The Construction of Modern National Consciousness.* New York: Columbia University Press, 1997.

Khoury, Philip. *Syria and the French Mandate: The Politics of Arab Nationalism, 1920–45.* London: I.B. Tauris, 1987.

Khuri, Fuad. "The Alawis of Syria." In R. Antoun and D. Quataert, eds., *Syria: Society, Culture, and Polity.* Albany: State University of New York Press, 1991.

Kushner, David. "Zealous Towns in Nineteenth Century Palestine." *Middle Eastern Studies* 33, no. 3 (1997): 597–612.

Lewis, Bernard. *The Assassins: A Radical Sect in Islam.* London: Weidenfeld and Nicolson, 1967.

Lilie, Ralph-Johannes. *Byzantium and the Crusader States, 1096–1204.* Oxford: Clarendon, 1993.

Lyons, Malcom, and D.E.P. Jackson. *Saladin: The Politics of the Holy War.* Cambridge: Cambridge University Press, 1982.

Manz, Beatrice. *The Rise and Rule of Tamerlane.* Cambridge: Cambridge University Press, 1989.

Marcus, Abraham. *The Middle East on the Eve of Modernity: Aleppo in the Eighteenth Century.* New York: Columbia University Press, 1989.

Marshall, Christopher. *Warfare in the Latin East, 1192–1291.* Cambridge: Cambridge University Press, 1992.

Masters, Bruce. *Christians and Jews in the Ottoman Arab World: The Roots of Sectarianism.* Cambridge: Cambridge University Press, 2001.

Millar, Fergus. *The Roman Near East, 31 BC–AD 337.* Cambridge, Mass.: Harvard University Press, 1993.

Moore, R.I., ed. *Hamlyn Historical Atlas.* Middlesex: Hamlyn, 1981.

Moosa, Matti. *The Maronites in History.* Syracuse: Syracuse University Press, 1986.

Olmert, Yossi. "Britain, Turkey and the Levant Question during the Second World War." *Middle Eastern Studies* 23, no. 4 (1987): 437–52.

Ostrogorsky, George. *History of the Byzantine State.* Oxford: Blackwell, 1968.

Parker, Geoffrey, ed. *Times Atlas of World History.* 4th ed. Maplewood, N.J.: Hammond, 1993.

Perthes, Volker. *The Political Economy of Syria under Asad.* New York: I. B. Tauris, 1995.

Phillips, Jonathan. "The Latin East, 1098–1291." In *The Oxford History of the Crusades,* edited by J. Riley-Smith, pp. 111–38. Oxford: Oxford University Press, 1999.

Plutarch. *Fall of the Roman Republic.* Translated by R. Warner. London: Penguin, 1972.

Prawer, Joshua. *The Latin Kingdom of Jerusalem: European Colonialism in the Middle Ages.* London: Weidenfeld & Nicolson, 1972.

———. *The History of the Jews in the Latin Kingdom of Jerusalem.* Oxford: Clarendon Press, 1988.

Pryor, John. *Geography, Technology, and War: Studies in the Maritime*

History of the Mediterranean 649–1571. Cambridge: Cambridge University Press, 1988.

Psellus, Michael. *Fourteen Byzantine Rulers.* Translated by E. Sewter. London: Penguin, 1966.

Raymond, André. "The Population of Aleppo in the Sixteenth and Seventeenth Centuries According to Ottoman Census Documents." *International Journal of Middle East Studies* 16 (1984): 447–60.

Richard, Jean. *The Crusades, c.1071–c.1291.* Cambridge: Cambridge University Press, 1999.

Rogers, Randall. *Latin Siege Warfare in the Twelfth Century.* Oxford: Clarendon Press, 1992.

Room, Adrian. *Place Names of the World.* Jefferson, N.C.: McFarland, 1997.

Salamé, Ghassan. "'Strong' and 'Weak' States, a Qualified Return to the *Muqaddimah.*" In *The Foundations of the Arab State,* edited by G. Salamé, pp. 205–40. London: Croom Helm, 1987.

Salibi, Kamal. "The Maronites of Lebanon under Frankish and Mamluk Rule." *Arabica* 4 (1957): 288–303.

———. *Syria Under Islam: Empire on Trial, 634–1097.* New York: Caravan, 1977.

———. *A House of Many Mansions: The History of Lebanon Reconsidered.* London: I.B. Tauris, 1988.

Shahid, Irfan. *Byzantium and the Arabs in the Sixth Century.* Washington, D.C.: Dumbarton Oaks, 1995.

Shambrook, Peter. *French Imperialism in Syria, 1927–36.* Reading: Ithaca, 1998.

Sharf, Andrew. *Byzantine Jewry: From Justinian to the Fourth Crusade.* London: Routledge & Kegan Paul, 1971.

Shorrock, William. "The Origins of the French Mandate in Syria and Lebanon: The Railroad Question, 1901–1914." *International Journal of Middle East Studies* 1 (1970): 133–53.

Smail, R.C. *Crusading Warfare, 1097–1193.* Cambridge: Cambridge University Press, 1995.

Stemberger, Günter. *Jews and Christians in the Holy Land: Palestine in the Fourth Century.* Edinburgh: T & T Clark, 2000.

Stephenson, Paul. *Byzantium's Balkan Frontier: A Political Study of the Northern Balkans, 900–1204.* Cambridge: Cambridge University Press, 2000.

Tacitus, Cornelius. *The Histories.* Translated by K. Wellesley. London: Penguin, 1995.

Talbert, Richard, ed. *Atlas of Classical History.* Beckenham, Kent: Croom Helm, 1985.

———, ed. *Barrington Atlas of the Greek and Roman World.* Princeton:

Princeton University Press, 2000.

Thompson, Elizabeth. "Ottoman Political Reform in the Provinces: The Damascus Advisory Council in 1844–45." *International Journal of Middle East Studies* 25 (1993): 457–75.

Tibawi, A.L. *A Modern History of Syria.* London: Macmillan, 1969.

Treadgold, Warren. *A History of the Byzantine State and Society.* Stanford: Stanford University Press, 1997.

Tritton, A.S. "The Tribes of Syria in the Fourteenth and Fifteenth Centuries." *Bulletin of the School of Oriental and African Studies* 12 (1948): 567–74.

Tübinger Atlas des Vorderen Orients (TAVO), Sheet B IX 23. "Osmanisches Reich: Die Provinzverwaltung am Ende des 19. Jahrhunderts." Wiesbaden: Dr. Ludwig Reichert Verlag, 1974.

Venzke, Margaret. "The Case of a Dulgadir-Mamluk Iqta': A Re-Assessment of the Dulgadir Principality and its Position Within the Ottoman-Mamluk Rivalry." *Journal of the Economic and Social History of the Orient* 43, no. 3 (2000): 349–475.

Vilnay, Zev. *The New Israel Atlas.* London: Humphrey, 1968.

Westermann's Grosser Atlas zur Weltgeschichte. Braunschweig: Georg Westermann Verlag, 1966.

Whittow, Mark. *The Making of Orthodox Byzantium. 600–1025.* London: MacMillan, 1996.

William of Tyre. *Willelmi Tyrensis Archiepiscopi Chronicon.* R.B.C. Huygens, ed., Corpus Christianorum Continuatio Mediaevalis, 63–63A. Turnhout: Brepols, 1986.

Newspaper Sources

Arabic: *Al-Diyar* daily newspaper (Beirut)
Al-Hayat daily newspaper (London and Beirut)
Al-Nahar daily newspaper (Beirut)
Al-Ra'y al-'Aam daily newspaper (Kuwait)
Al-Wasat weekly newsmagazine (London)
Al-Zaman daily newspaper (London and Baghdad)

Hebrew: *Ha'aretz* daily newspaper (Tel Aviv)

Turkish: *Hürriyet* daily newspaper (Istanbul)
Radikal daily newspaper (Istanbul)

English: *The Times* (London)
The Washington Post

INDEX OF NAMES

ABOUT THE AUTHOR

WILLIAM HARRIS, University of Otago, New Zealand, lived in the Middle East for several years and visits the region regularly. He has had close personal contacts with leading officials, journalists, and scholars from a variety of backgrounds in Lebanon, Syria, Israel, Palestine, Jordan, and Turkey. He taught at Haigazian University College in Lebanon for two years and contributed the annual chapter on Lebanon to the Middle East Contemporary Survey, a project of Tel Aviv University's Dayan Center, for fourteen years. He has been a visiting professor at the Middle East Technical University, Ankara, Turkey, a Rockefeller Foundation International Relations Fellow at the Johns Hopkins University, and a lecturer at Exeter University in England and the University of New South Wales, Australia. He was a visiting professor at Princeton University in 1995–96.

WILLIAM HARRIS is the author of *Taking Root: Israeli Settlement in the West Bank, Golan and Gaza-Sinai* (1980) and of *Faces of Lebanon: Sects, Wars, and Global Extensions* (1997), which has been heatedly debated in Western and Middle Eastern scholarly journals and popular newspapers and magazines. He has also published numerous book chapters and journal articles on the affairs of the Levant and the Persian Gulf.